ROMANCING
MARY JANE

ROMANCING MARY JANE

A YEAR IN THE LIFE OF A FAILED MARIJUANA GROWER

MICHAEL POOLE

GREYSTONE BOOKS
Douglas & McIntyre
Vancouver/Toronto

98 99 00 01 02   5 4 3 2 1

Greystone Books
A division of Douglas & McIntyre Ltd.
1615 Venables Street
Vancouver, British Columbia
V5L 2H1

CANADIAN CATALOGUING IN PUBLICATION DATA

Poole, Michael, 1936-
 Romancing Mary Jane

 ISBN 1-55054-583-3

 1. Poole, Michael, 1936- 2. Cannabis. 3. Marijuana.
4. Sunshine Coast (B.C.)—Biography. I. Title.
SB295.C35P66 1998   633.7'9   C98-910792-2

Editing by Barbara Pulling
Jacket design by Barbara Hodgson
Jacket photograph by Trevor Bonderud / First Light
Text design by Val Speidel
Typesetting by Brenda and Neil West, BN Typographics West, and Val Speidel
Printed and bound in Canada by Friesens
Printed on acid-free paper ∞

The publisher gratefully acknowledges the support of the Canada Council for the Arts and of the British Columbia Ministry of Tourism, Small Business and Culture. The publisher also acknowledges the financial support of the Government of Canada through the Book Publishing Industry Development Program.

Permission to quote from the following books is gratefully acknowledged: *Peaceful Measures: Canada's Way Out of the "War on Drugs"* by Bruce Alexander. Copyright © 1990 by Bruce Alexander. Published by University of Toronto Press. *The Natural Mind: An Investigation of Drugs and the Higher Consciousness* by Andrew Weil. Copyright © 1986 by Andrew Weil. Published by Houghton Miffin Company.

For Carole

friend, lover, partner in crime

CONTENTS

The names of some of the people in this book have been changed to disguise their identity. Except for a few composite characters, they are real people nonetheless, whose words and deeds are theirs alone.

On a beautiful spring day in the early 1990s, I hit bottom at the end of a forty-year slide into depression and despair. With my mind racing uncontrollably and the dogs of suicide nipping at my heels, I thought I was finished, washed up, kaput. But my gloomy prognosis, I am pleased to say, turned out to be premature. Given some expert help and a miracle drug that plugged a chemical "hole" in my brain, I was soon on the mend. But mending was not enough. A full recovery required a change in occupation.

I came to this conclusion reluctantly, painfully. My trade and obsession for nearly thirty years had been documentary film-making. I'd had a great run—travel to distant corners of the world, contact with fascinating people and subjects, awards, even an income of sorts—but filmmaking had changed, and so had I. There was less money around and a lot more interference from network bosses and investors. At the same time, I was within hailing distance of sixty and losing my drive. I had long been unhealthily addicted to my work, and in the classic pattern of addictions I needed a bigger fix every year to get the same high. Now, with the fire in my belly burning out, I was no longer able to give myself the narcotic I needed. So down I went, into the vortex.

My new occupation was to be wholesome physical toil—specifically, the cultivation of marijuana. Why marijuana? First, because it's a healthy, outdoor trade, one I believed would be conducive to peace of mind. Second, having paid two hundred dollars an ounce for pot, it was obvious to me that with a modicum of effort I could become fabulously rich. Third, I had already cultivated marijuana for one season and imagined I knew just about all there was to know about it. Such was the foundation on which my mental health was to be rebuilt. As time would tell, it had not the slightest connection to reality.

My wife, Carole, and I prefer marijuana to alcohol or other drugs. We use it as an enhancer for sensual pleasures, for food, music and sex, and we like the up mood it gives us—long on laughs without the penalty of a hangover or creeping addiction. Sure, it's against the law, but like two or three million other toking Canadians we blow smoke rings at any attempt to control our private lives. And yet for years the law had forced us to buy grass of unknown quality from shady characters on the street. Too often, it gave us headaches and depressing side-effects, and we wondered if we were smoking pesticides or other additives. The solution was to grow our own.

I was well positioned for such an undertaking. Carole and I have a waterfront cabin on British Columbia's Sechelt Peninsula, less than two hours upcoast by ferry and car from our home in North Vancouver. I grew up on the Peninsula, had a little farm there for twenty years and once knew the bush and backroads pretty well. Although retirees, urban refugees and even commuters were flooding in, there was still plenty of wild land where a marijuana patch could be tucked away from prying eyes.

That first season my intention was only to grow a little pot for our own use. Casting about for some quality seeds, I planted a modest garden in a sunny glade not far from our cabin. Five months later, blessed with beginner's luck, I harvested more than four pounds of prime buds. Even with the most dedicated application to the task, I knew we could never smoke that much marijuana in a year, and yet I had no idea how to go about selling the surplus. Then, almost immediately—more beginner's luck—a buyer turned up, waving $3,200 in crisp new bills, the going price for a pound.

And so began my life in crime. My little exercise in amateur gardening had blossomed into cultivating and trafficking in marijuana, a serious offence punishable by hefty fines and several years in jail. On the other hand, I had discovered the pleasure and profit of growing one of nature's loveliest plants. And when I did the golden calculus of pounds and dollars that beguiles every aspiring marijuana grower, the prospect of turning this into my livelihood was irresistible. I'd make a bundle, live like a lord and while away the winters on tropical beaches.

The next year I put in a commercial crop and ... well, things didn't go exactly as planned. While I had my share of little triumphs, I did not spend the following winter in Costa Rica. But there were compensations—unforgettable sun-shot days in my mountain gardens, glimpses into the mysterious lifeways of birds and animals, wonderfully restored health in mind and body. There were encounters with resourceful and principled people in the cannabis culture and discoveries about the science, history and folklore of marijuana. Closer to home, marijuana launched me on forays into the human psyche, beginning with my own. In short, my season as a marijuana grower became a trip of sorts, an omnibus ride with unexpected passengers to an unknown destination. This book is the story of that journey.

CHAPTER 1

BREAKING GROUND

I'm lost, clueless, bamboozled in my own home country. Setting out on this early March morning in search of places to grow marijuana, I discover that this part of the Sunshine Coast has changed beyond recognition. I've been away too long. Old, familiar roads have vanished beneath an invading army of alders, and new roads have been punched miles back into the hills. The virgin stands of fir, cedar and hemlock that I hiked through in my youth have been replaced by jungles of second growth or yawning expanses of recently logged land, the slash charred black under the spring rain. And so, without plan or direction, I simply drive, dead-ending in mud and windfalls or wandering so high on the Caren Range I am surrounded by rotting snow.

Up here, at least, I can get my bearings. Hunched against a wind that flattens the stunted trees, I slog to the edge of a cliff whose granite dome is split by frost. Spread below me, from southeast to northwest, the grey expanse of the Strait of Georgia is flecked with whitecaps. Farther off on the horizon, Vancouver Island rises ridge upon ridge to peaks lost in cloud. The gale is driving rain squalls against the bluff face of Texada Island, upcoast to my right, and rolling breakers over the reefs off Sabine Channel. Away in the distant south, Valdes, Salt Spring and other high islands loom through the mist like a pod of ghostly whales. And hidden by ridges to the east, the faint scribble of Vancouver's skyline is only thirty miles away.

This juxtaposition of wilderness and throbbing metropolis has always been the great appeal of the Sunshine Coast. Elbow room, with the amenities of the city barely an hour away. Recently, with Vancouver's population exploding by nearly a million people in the past decade, the isolation is breaking down. There's still no road to Vancouver around precipitous Howe Sound and probably never will be, but as the car ferries get bigger and faster the city is spilling in. Gibsons, a village only a skip and a hop from the ferry landing at Langdale, and Sechelt, a dozen miles up the coast, are growing. But here, between Sechelt and Pender Harbour, the country below me is an unbroken expanse of forest. Hidden by trees and tumbling bluffs, there are roads and houses down there, including our own cabin, but the human presence is still no more than a tenuous string along the shore.

My home turf as a kid was the other end of the Sunshine Coast, a steamship dock and post office called Granthams Landing, now sandwiched between Gibsons and Langdale. Then, all of the Sunshine Coast was known simply as "the Peninsula," although properly the peninsula is only the thirty-odd miles of land west of Sechelt, which sits on the half-mile-wide isthmus between Porpoise Bay and Georgia Strait. The Sunshine Coast applies to everything between Port Mellon, the pulp mill at the Langdale end of the road, and Egmont, a pub and straggle of houses ninety minutes' drive to the northwest. Accurate or not, the name Sunshine Coast should have been left to the soaps. For me, the Peninsula it was and the Peninsula it remains.

With the wind rocking Henry the Ford, my long-suffering

truck, I turn up the heater and eat my lunch, watching ravens doing barrel rolls like stunt pilots over the slash. Then, more driving. The afternoon is a repeat of the morning: dead-ends, mudholes and fruitless tramps through the rat's-ass tangle of old logging slash. It's dark by the time I get back to the cabin, soaked and frustrated. The fire is out, and the woodbox, of course, is empty. Grumbling over wet kindling and my lack of foresight, I manage a sulky blaze and contemplate supper, which is even now lurking in the fridge. Carole, a great cook, regularly sends me up here with a few meals prepared in advance. But when those run out, I lapse into slovenly ways and something called goop, a mishmash of beans, corn, tomatoes and any other canned goods that come to hand, all dumped into a pot large enough to last at least four days. With meal number four coming up, the goop has rather overstayed its welcome.

Now come the restoratives. First, open a homebrewed Bass ale, black as roofing tar and 6.5 per cent alcohol. Second, shed my clothes in a heap of mud and water and make the dash through the rain to the outside shower at the back of the cabin. And here I stand, ten, fifteen, twenty minutes in steamy defiance of the storm raging in the trees overhead. Another sprint back to the fireside, bollocks flinging water like the dewlaps on a bloodhound, a change into dry clothes and I'm reborn. Though stimulating, the conditions here are admittedly primitive. The cabin is, after all, really only a workshop in waiting, tarted up until we build a proper house. Of which I'm reminded when I switch on the radio and can barely hear it over the deafening roar of rain on the uninsulated tin roof.

Later, feet toasting on the heater rail, I go back over the day. Why should it be so difficult to find a place to grow marijuana? The requirements are simple enough: sunlight, soil, water and security. In my case, the list is even shorter because I plan to haul in both soil and water. Security, though, will be more of a concern, as my gardens will have to be fairly close to a road for the hoses to reach.

Most of what I saw today was forest, logging slash or rock bluff. Forest is too shady for marijuana, and the bluffs I checked out were either too far from the road or too exposed to hide pot plants from police helicopters. That leaves the slash, and not just any slash. After walking miles of it, I realize that logging slash has to be about ten years old to be suitable for dope growing. Younger, and there's nôt enough cover to hide the plants; older, and there is too much.

Juggling all these requirements, I am coming to appreciate how incredibly lucky I was with my beginner's garden last year. With no precise idea what I was looking for, I stumbled upon a natural opening within the dense regrowth on an old forest fire burn, accessible only by a tunnel I cut through the bush. And my luck held through every stage of the growing cycle, from planting to harvest. A week of unseasonably warm weather in early May germinated nearly 100 per cent of my seeds. Then, for no apparent reason, the slugs, though present in their usual multitudes, ate only a few of my seedlings. And in July, when the plants showed their sex, lady luck determined that nearly three-quarters of them would be females, rather than useless males. Even the local bear co-operated, eating only one small plant while leaving all the others undisturbed.

My luck continued through August and into a hot, dry September, perfect for ripening marijuana, and peaked with the incident of the bulldozer. It happened just before harvest. Hiking up an abandoned logging road towards my garden, I found myself following fresh bulldozer tracks and was appalled when they turned aside onto an old skid road that passed within a few yards of my plants. Saplings were crushed flat, including the screen of brush I had erected to hide my patch. Riding as he was, high off the ground, the 'dozer operator could not have missed seeing the dark purple plants. And yet, when Carole and I returned the next day to harvest them, nothing had been touched.

There may be bigger and better harvests ahead, but none more satisfying than that first payoff. We came back to the cabin with three big cardboard boxes packed full with prime marijuana. We made tea and just sat there looking at it, inhaling its powerful essence and marvelling at our good fortune. After years of grubbing for grams and ounces of mediocre pot, we had more top-quality grass than we could smoke in ten years. Chopping a bud up fine and quick-drying it on the heater, we toked up and pronounced it dynamite dope, easy on the throat yet strong enough to lift your scalp. Even then, we were luckier than we knew.

A few days later, I met the man on the bulldozer. He was hostile and suspicious at first but relaxed when I waved my binoculars and said I went there often to bird-watch. He volunteered the information that he had almost run over a marijuana patch. "I don't know anything about that stuff," he said, "so I told my partner about it and he came tearing right up here to get it, but it was already gone. He told me it would have been worth $100,000. Hell, if I'd known that, I'd have grabbed it myself." Although such a price tag for the crop was pure fantasy, my luck in salvaging it was real enough. The would-be marijuana thief, it turned out, had come later on the same day that we harvested, only hours behind us.

Lying abed in the dark, listening to the wind and the crash of waves, I think back to this morning on the mountain. It occurs to me now that something was missing from the expanse of green I looked down on from the cliff top. Within the past century, virtually every square foot of that land has been logged, and the aboriginal forest has been pushed back almost to timberline. Walking today in the dense regrowth at lower elevations, what I missed was the mystical power of those original solemn giants. Among them, you feel the life force of things that have withstood the storms and fires, the droughts and crushing snows of five, seven, even ten centuries. That's gone, and with it, the spiritual heart of the country.

After two more days of driving and miles of walking, I hit pay dirt almost within hollering distance of the Sechelt village limits. Travelling a vaguely remembered logging road—I swear I recognize its pond-sized potholes from twenty years ago—I turn onto a goat track heading straight up the mountainside through second-growth timber. A few hundred yards of clawing in bull-low over boulders and washouts and I break suddenly onto a slash that is made-to-order for marijuana. For about half a mile on either side of the road, the logged-over land is sporadically covered with six- to ten-foot firs and thickets of salmonberry and young alder. It's rough country, broken by ravines and rock outcrops that afford many good places to hide plants. Best of all, tilting as it does steeply to the south, the place is a sun trap, a furnace just waiting for summer to turn up the heat. It's perfect.

But there's more. Back on the goat track, another half mile of jolting uphill brings me to a second slash of similar age. It's a bowl, ringed on three sides by timbered ridges and rock bluffs, sloping at the center into a marsh two or three acres in size. Between the boggy ground and the timber, there are good sites for dope gardens among the young firs.

From there, the road climbs more steeply than ever to dead-end on a third slash, draped like a green blanket over the top of a ridge. Stepping out of the truck, I feel as if I'm on the roof of the world. The land falls away on all sides, and way off to the west, I can see Georgia Strait, a sparkling slit of blue and gold. With growing excitement, I start scouting for garden sites, imagining the sun pounding in here from dawn to dusk, supercharging marijuana buds with psychedelic energy. But my daydreams are cut short. As if from nowhere, a Beaver floatplane thunders overhead so low my fillings rattle. This will never do. From that height, the pilot would have to be blind or drunk to miss seeing marijuana plants. Apparently, the ridge is on the flight path to and from the seaplane base in Porpoise Bay, Sechelt's back door.

Although the highest ridge is out, the other two places I've found—the lower slash and the marsh—suit me down to the ground. Except for the swamp, which will probably dry by midsummer, there's no water on either site, and this is a plus. Marijuana growers, especially ambitious ones with many plants, often locate their gardens near creeks or ponds, where they can siphon water. Naturally, pot thieves home in on these places like camels drawn to an oasis. With barrels and a battery-powered pump, I intend to haul my own water.

The road is another plus. It's impassable without a four-wheel drive, and so overgrown that Henry the Ford has to plow through alder saplings like a pig in a briar patch. Once the pampered cream-puff of a weekend camper, my vehicle will end this season without an unscratched inch on its tinny hide. I'll not be bothered here by truck huggers afraid to scratch their expensive toys.

At the end of the first week in March, I am grounded by weather. Just as spring was nicely underway—forsythia, daffodils and crocuses in bloom; elderberry leafing out, salmonberry showing

scarlet along the creek banks, alder catkins snowing green pollen
—arctic air vaulted the Coast Mountains and came whistling
down the inlets. Ever since, sleet, snow and freezing rain have
made the slash too treacherous to walk through.

Rather than be housebound, I poke around in Sechelt for parts
I need to make my watering system. Unlike Gibsons, which has
fouled its nest with an ugly commercial strip, Sechelt is developing an attractive sense of itself. There are some good restaurants,
centers for the arts and Indian cultural activities, a new library
and, every August, a festival that attracts some of Canada's best
writers. But the Peninsula, even with 27,000 residents, is still thin
on hardware, and I find that I will have to get my parts in the city.
This is a chronic local complaint: too little selection and prices
inflated far beyond levels justified by "freight," the merchants'
perennial excuse.

One evening I visit with Ned, my mentor in all matters con-
cerning marijuana. He lives on a tidy little farm whose orchard,
huge garden, flowerbeds and lawns he carved from the bush, all
within the past fifteen years. The effort has made him so gaunt
that, with his shock of wild hair, he looks like a refugee from some
biblical famine. Ned is full of droll stories. Tonight it's an account
of a running battle with a large bear that was tearing up his
garden and orchard. Lurching around the kitchen, Ned acts out
the chase, the shot, the bear's charge, more shots, the dash to the
house for more shells and the final demise, all told with wry jibes
at his own shortcomings as a great white hunter. Before I leave, we
touch on more serious matters: Ned wants me to join him in a
marijuana-growing venture on Nelson Island, off the Peninsula's
western end. Troubled last summer by marijuana thieves, he sees
this island location as a solution, but he has no boat. Working with
Ned would be a lark and I could learn a lot; he's been growing pot

for more than two decades. But I ask him to wait a bit while I see how my own gardens come along. I expect they will give me all the work I can handle.

Day five of the arctic outbreak dawns sullen and grey, under an icy drizzle. At mid-morning an arch of lighter sky opens over Welcome Passage, a couple of miles across the bay from the cabin. Out of a dead calm, a blast of warm air comes sweeping across the open water and smashes into the gnarled firs along the shore where I've come to watch. Within minutes, rents of blue are torn in the lowering overcast and rags of sun-shot cloud are flying overhead. And then, just as suddenly, black clots of storm cloud roll up from the southeast and it begins to rain. The sky is wild with gulls and crows tossed like leaves on the turbulent air. The wind smells of earth and things growing. I turn my face up to the sky and lick fat raindrops from my moustache. Spring has returned, borne on a tropical exhalation from the southern oceans.

The unexpected holiday has given me a chance to step back and look at the kind of start I'm making here. I'm wary of my tendency to bull ahead too fast. Today, heading back to work on the mountain, I resolve not to turn marijuana growing into another of my addictive work trips. Yes, I expect a lot of sweat and toil; anyone who thinks this is a business for lazy hippies has never tried it. But I also intend to continue the pursuit of psychic health that made me a cannabis criminal in the first place. For this to happen, I have to make a choice. I can turn all of my attention to growing dope and making money, if that's all I want from the experience. Or I can open myself to the peace and sanity all around me on the mountain. It's like fly-fishing on river estuaries. As nature's busiest intersections, where the lifestreams of land and sea come together, estuaries are always fascinating places. For years I fished the local estuaries for cutthroat trout, whipping the waters with single-minded determination, all the while blinkering myself to the beauty and wonder on every side. Then one day, skunked, soaked and disgusted, I lifted my head and looked around. Ever since, my days on the estuaries have been magical, whether I catch fish or not. I know the delight I find in the stoop of an osprey or the green fire of a merganser's head will live on in my mind's eye long after the fish is caught—or, in this case, the crop harvested.

In practical terms, what this means is finding grow sites that are pleasing to the eye as well as to marijuana plants; places open to wind and sun and frequented by wildlife. Both the lower slash and the marsh meet this test. The clearcuts are small and the wounds left by logging have been bandaged by fireweed, bracken and swaths of young alders, which are even now showing a mist of green. From the lower slash I can look across a dozen miles of Georgia Strait to Vancouver Island, or down-strait to where the waters meld into a blue infinity of sea haze and sky on the southern horizon. The strait is never empty. A toy traffic of tugs and barges, ferries, fishboats, log carriers and occasionally the white fleck of a sail inches across the great sheet of crinkled water. On afternoons of wind and broken cloud, its surface becomes a moving pattern of silver and shadow. And on summer evenings, cruise ships steam north in the indigo twilight, the lights of their tiered decks blazing on into the night.

To my right, just before a wall of timber closes off the view, I can see the lighthouse on Merry Island, whose friendly winking I will come to watch for on summer evenings. The rooftops of Sechelt jut here and there above the trees, and beyond, I catch the sunflash of cars beside the blue bite of Davis Bay. At its eastern extremity, the slash tumbles into a ravine so steep its floor is lost to view, though on still days I can hear the rustle of the creek that runs there. And from the west end of the slash, just before the road dips into the timber, I can look back and see Vancouver's Point Grey way off to the southeast. By day it is barely visible, but after dark the university district becomes a streak of orange light, and I revel in the proximity of my primitive pot growing on a wild mountainside to all those seething brains.

The marsh is a very different kind of place. Enclosed by hills on three sides, it has no view of the sea, though to the east, from a rock outcrop where I sometimes sit to eat my lunch, I can look across a timbered bowl and through a notch in the hills to snow-capped mountains beyond Sechelt Inlet. Rising steeply to the north like a row of seated giants is a line of craggy-faced bluffs. There are still some old-growth firs up there, taking refuge from the chainsaws, their ragged crowns towering high above the monotonous stands of manmade second growth. Working here on days of southeast gales, I will learn to listen for these old-timers baying their ancient basso profundo to the winds. The marsh itself will become a place of encounters with birds, bears and a whole community of pond life hitherto unknown to me. Right now, in March, it is mostly water—pondlets black as onyx, punctuated by sulphur-yellow shouts of skunk cabbage—though by fall it will turn sere and brittle as cornflakes underfoot.

In time, I will come to think of all this—the lower slash, the marsh cupped like a palm within the hand of the hills, and the skyscraping ridge above—as simply the mountain. At about two thousand feet above sea level, my chosen bit of country doesn't amount to a pimple on the craggy face of British Columbia. But for me it is not only a mountain of rocks and trees but also a mountain of the mind, a place of hopes and fears, epiphanies and disappointments. For that, it is more than adequate.

CHAPTER 2

PRESENT AT THE CREATION

Cold drizzle from an oystershell sky brings in the equinox. After a lot of weighty cogitation over maximum sunlight and minimum risk of detection, I choose two garden sites on the lower slash and one on the side of the bowl above the marsh. Each will be home to about thirty full-size plants, plus as many again in smaller containers. This is putting a lot of eggs in a few baskets, and even as I do it I'm uneasy about the risk. But the work entailed in clearing and fencing a dozen smaller gardens is just too daunting. Growers who have this kind of arrangement expect to take two or three years to get all their plots in place. I've decided to roll the dice and shoot for a big crop in my first year.

In order to keep track of them in my diary, I have named my gardens. The Pocket Garden is just that—a pocket of salal, tucked into the western end of the lower slash and hidden from the road above by rock outcrops and a nasty tangle of logging slash. The Hillside Garden is situated on a narrow bench partway down the steep creek ravine that forms the eastern end of the lower slash. For want of inspiration, I have called the garden on the side of the bowl above the marsh simply Number Three.

The first two plots require little clearing. Between the young firs, the open space is covered with knee-deep salal and a brown mat of last year's bracken and fireweed, ideal for seating my five-gallon peat pots. But Number Three is a thicket of head-high cedar, springing from knotted roots and branches that were flattened by logging and have regrown like a pit of snakes. My elder brother, Noel, has come along to help, and I marvel once again at his prodigious strength. Two years his junior, I grew up in awe of his hardrock physique, his utter lack of fear, his capacity to run a hundred yards in under eleven seconds on sheer power without technique or training, his ability to build a boat or fix an engine even before he was old enough to shave. Now, spade beard swinging like that of an Old Testament prophet, he makes haystacks of limbs and saplings and heaves them into the bush. The cedar fights back. Repeatedly, its tough, limber branches (the Indians used them for cordage) get under the chain of the saw and flip it off. Three hours of such festivities produce a cleared space about fifty by fifty feet. Finally, we enclose the garden in a fence made of old herring seine net to keep out the deer. Unlike their mule deer cousins in the B.C. Interior, the coastal black-tails will browse marijuana down to the stalk.

By now, I'm beginning to appreciate how much work it is to grow from seed. Roughly half the plants will be males, which have no value as marijuana; it is the flower of the female plant, the bud as it's called, that packs the psychoactive punch. Two plants to get one female and, ergo, everything else doubles—plots, fences, pots, soil and, above all, work. I will have to water and fertilize them all until late July, when the plants can be sexed and the males yanked out. I'd pay dearly for clones (rooted cuttings from female plants), but to get them I'd have to know someone who has a heated greenhouse or an indoor marijuana setup, and I don't.

That said, I'm well satisfied with my gardens. They are nicely hidden from the road, and the fences are secure—eight feet high, with gates, no less. Made of fine black nylon, the netting should be impossible to see from any distance. And I've taken care to enclose a number of trees, so the plots won't be too conspicuous from the air.

When I get back to the cabin, there is a message on the answering machine from Carole, suggesting that it would be a pleasant change to see my face in North Vancouver for the weekend. Later, when we talk on the phone, as we do every night, there is an edge to her voice that tells me I've been away long enough. She knows me too well. Before we got together a dozen years ago, I used to stay on my little farm near Sechelt for weeks on end, making only occasional forays into Sechelt for supplies. Days, I wrote my film scripts and worked outside; evenings I read, carved masks and picked my banjo—a full life that left little room for anyone else. As Carole knows, the hermit within me is alive and well, and she's right to give me a prod now and then.

We talk about this country–city thing quite a lot. When we move here, the transition will be much harder for Carole than for me. All her adult life she has lived in cities, including a decade in New York. She uses a city in ways that have always eluded me, wandering the streets and shops, making discoveries, sampling the delights of the metropolis like a bee in a garden of a thousand blooms. I go directly to the theater, the store, the library, partake of what I want and leave. Sometimes it seems that this country–town dichotomy is a regional disease here on the Peninsula. Who knows how many marriages are riven by it; one partner dying of backwater boredom, the other thriving amongst the stumps. We've agreed to keep a toehold in Vancouver for concerts, for friends and family or just for periodic whiffs of the cosmopolitan air. In my anchorite days, I could not have imagined that I would ever acknowledge such a need.

Waiting for the Friday morning ferry at Langdale, I am force-fully reminded of my countrified origins. Right here, just across the road from these acres of recent blacktop, is the spot where I arrived on the Peninsula in August of 1943. I had just turned seven. We had come from the clipped and proper Little England of Caulfeild in West Vancouver, and the culture shock could hardly have been greater. Our new home was a damp and gloomy cottage without neighbours, near the end of a dirt road. There was no electricity, no phone, no running water, even, when the ram (a current-powered pump with a bulbous cast-iron head that resem-bled a cartoon octopus) in the creek got plugged with autumn leaves. There was no library, no theater, no hospital, no dentist, one cafe (certainly not a restaurant) and so few cars that you knew them all, though none would give you a lift. With the steamer calling only once a week (twice in the summer), Vancouver might as well have been a million miles away. Even Sechelt was little more than a rumour, reached overland by connected logging roads. We went there once, right after the war, two families pool-ing resources to hire the local taxi, a weary 1930s limousine with jumpseats in the back. I remember throwing up on Rat Portage hill and sitting on the long gravel beach at Sechelt, too dazed by the journey to eat our picnic lunch. The same trip today takes twenty minutes.

Thriving under the primitive conditions, perhaps even stimu-lated by them, was a remarkably diverse, if eccentric, community. Socialist-minded Finns had moved in around Gibsons in the early years of the century after being cut adrift by the collapse of their upcoast utopian community at Sointula. Their co-operative ideals blossomed into a store and a jam factory, and their pacifism split the community during the First World War. J. S. Woodsworth, later a member of Parliament and founder of the Co-operative

Commonwealth Federation, was a Methodist minister in Gibsons in 1917 and spoke eloquently against conscription from the pulpit, pleasing some of his congregation and outraging the rest. (More than sixty years later, I found the old sensitivities still alive when I began asking questions in Gibsons for a film based on a haunting story that had come down from the war. It concerned draft dodgers who had hidden in a camp on the mountain. One of them, who had had a change of heart, returned to the camp in uniform to bid his friends farewell. Mistaken at a distance for a military policeman, he was shot dead by his best friend, who later went mad and committed suicide. The community nipped my film in the bud by complaining to the CBC that I was a closet McCarthyite out to rake dirt from Gibsons' socialist roots.)

When we first arrived on the Peninsula, Lord and Lady Ord, insolvent but authentic English gentry, resided nearby in the local approximation of a manor house with their nephew, Lancelot Belovely Ord. The house was a gloomy barn of a place, built by the lord himself, though never finished. Invited for tea, my mother was served by Lady Ord from a massive silver service arranged on Okanagan apple boxes. Housekeeping in the Dominion was easy, her hostess said, pointing to a hole in the floor where all the sweepings went. Too soon, the Ords came into an inheritance and moved to Vancouver, where they were lionized by local society.

Within a year or two, we moved to Granthams Landing and new acquaintances. I delivered papers to a frail old couple who showed me the exquisitely illuminated scrolls the man had engraved for Queen Victoria. I remember them standing in the rain in their housecoats, clinging to one another, the night their house burned to the ground; there was no fire department on the Peninsula. Also on my paper route were a retired zoology professor, a judge who had sailed before the mast and specialized in marine law, and a man who had lived here so long he could remember rowing to Vancouver before the steamers came—all of them willing, even anxious, to talk to a curious kid. There was Andy Boyle, a recluse who sweated sacks of potatoes down from his mountain garden on his back—it was said that you could smell Andy long before you saw him—and sold them to my mother for a few dollars and some chat about their native New Brunswick. When the police found him dead in his shack, they uncovered wads of shares in the Panama Canal. There was a couple at Dog-patch, near Port Mellon, who tended their waterfront garden all summer naked as jaybirds, save for felt boot liners on their feet. Next door to us at one point lived a massive old Irishman with many rugby scars and a glass eye. Every few days, I'd take it out for him and swab out the socket. Sometimes I put it back upside down, and he'd phone me in the middle of the night to come and turn it over because it was hurting him. Meeting him in the near-dark with one eye peering at me and the other staring fixedly into right field killed any aspirations I might have had for a career in medicine. The first doctor in Gibsons was a violin-playing communist who had argued political theory with J. S. Woodsworth and passed his interests down to his sons. The incumbent in my time still played the violin but had traded in his communism for an egalitarian outlook that expressed itself in an unvarying first question to patients: "Well now, what do *you* think is wrong with you?"

As a backwater, the Peninsula caught a lot of life's sad flotsam. I remember the English remittance man coming every month to Hopkins Landing (just around the point from Langdale) for his cheque, head down and mumbling to himself. He lived alone, without friends or neighbours, in a filthy shack overrun by cats. And old Mrs. Olsen, who was said to have lost her mind after her son drowned, walking the trail to the store, toothless and absorbed in a plaintive monologue. Though I gave it little thought then, there was a lot of loneliness and pain that no one acknowledged, and much small-town nastiness. The Provincial Police constable regularly got drunk with his cronies and harassed the most vulnerable people in the community, among them an impoverished family named Rabbit with twelve children. Shades of *Watership Down*, the Rabbits eventually turned on their nemesis, leaving him unconscious in a ditch.

There weren't many occasions for people to come together, at least not until the early 1950s. There was a New Year's dance (women wore gowns fit for a coronation; men came in white shirts open at the neck, collars over their jackets), a ball game and maypole dancing on the Queen's birthday, and a turnout of veterans on Remembrance Day. The fall fair was a small one-day affair, highlighted by a dance that drew a menagerie of stumpies and recluses from their isolated shacks and goat pastures. Long before I was old enough to attend such free-boozing affairs on my own, I got to witness the shouting and stomping because my mother would be called out to play the piano, accompanying the doctor's violin and his brother's sax. I even took part in the fair, or tried to, persuading a neighbour to drive me and my Flemish giant rabbit to the competition. Alas, there was no blue ribbon for me or even a class for rabbits, and Bugs, as he was called, capped the day by pissing copiously in my lap on the way home.

A countervailing bent for arts and letters ran through the Peninsula, though it was thin and scattered. Here a painter, there a sculptor or writer, and rarely any contact between them. Hubert Evans, whom I didn't come to know until he was in his eighties and writing excellent poetry, raised a family at Roberts Creek, halfway between Gibsons and Sechelt, on the income from serials, children's fiction, plays and the classic Canadian novel *Mist on the River*. There was a stump-ranch pianist who developed the technical wizardry of a world-class performer, practising on a dummy keyboard. He came occasionally to our house on Saturday evenings and played devilishly difficult pieces by Liszt, Beethoven and Brahms, all without a trace of feeling or interpretation. The schoolteacher next door could barely span an octave (the dummy pianist's immense hands reached nearly an octave and a half), yet she played with such fiery passion Chopin's Revolutionary Etude made her sweat like a weightlifter. When she could be persuaded, one of my aunts sang "Danny Boy" in a soul-wrenching deep contralto honed during her time as a soloist in the churches of Toronto. The tiny community hall at Granthams was converted for a time to an artists' studio, where anyone who felt like it could come and throw paint at canvas. These were just the things I knew about; doubtless other artists and would-be artists were at work in their private spaces.

Almost straight out of high school, I left the Peninsula to work in newspapering, a curious choice for someone who could neither spell nor write, despite a habit of reading. But my literary shortcomings were the least of it; I came to Vancouver with a bottomless inferiority complex, partly of my own and my family's making, partly a legacy of my rustic hometown, and partly the tenor of the times. In those postwar years when millions of North Americans were moving into cities, rural meant crude, cloddish and dumb. City people jeered if I said I was from Gibsons, or worse yet, Granthams Landing, and I soon learned to disguise my origins with some mumbled circumlocution about "up the coast."

Time, the great healer, would mend all this. In television I became a journalist at last—though print purists might call this oxymoronic—and gradually shook off the stinking albatross of stunted self-esteem. I came to see my rural origins as a cause for pride and a source of skills that served me well when I began developing my little farm in the 1970s.

The Peninsula has changed, too, perhaps more than I have. If it's still a backwater, it is catching some very interesting drift—artists, musicians and writers, scientists, a lively publisher, and retired people from every conceivable background. A few of them I know already; many more I want to meet. But that will have to wait. I'm here to grow a crop and make a dollar, not gad about while my wife is hard at work in town, keeping this whole enterprise afloat.

Ned and I have a good thing going. We swap and share and help each other in the way that I've always believed a community should work. While I had the farm I supplied him with rare apple varieties for his orchard and taught him to graft and prune. I still lend him tools and give advice on plumbing or carpentry. He reciprocates with apples, vegetables, marijuana seeds and tips on growing. Trained in such things, he keeps an eye on my sewage treatment system. This morning, he's chipping in with a pickup load of topsoil.

Ned loads the topsoil with his tractor, a tiny, exquisitely engineered piece of Swedish technology. But even with four-wheel drive, it gets stuck in the late-March mud and looks a mess by the time we extricate it. I offer to wash it down, but Ned says forget it, the mud will fall off when it dries. When the job is done, he leans on the truck, yarning and rolling a smoke. He always tears the gummed strip off the paper and sticks the cigarette together with spit. "That glue is poison," he says with a grin. "Bad for the lungs."

I covet his tractor and say so. I had one, though not nearly as versatile as the Swede, as he calls it, but sold it with the farm.

"Yes," Ned agrees, "it's a good one, and it should be. It took me about a hundred years to pay for it."

Ned is chronically short of cash. In a way I admire him for this, because his penury is the price of his principles. He's that rarest and most obstinate of birds, a purist. As a floor layer, he won't stoop to anything lower than the very best hardwood. He'll apply tile only as a favour or under extreme duress, and linoleum never. As an organic farmer, he won't have a pesticide, herbicide or chemical fertilizer on the place, and he spends endless hours weeding and engaging in hand-to-hand combat with bugs. As a grower of marijuana (the best I've ever smoked), he's more interested in breeding the ultimate strain than in mass production for a big return. Though I don't envy Ned all that work, the world could use more people like him.

In a cement mixer borrowed from Ned, I combine four parts soil with one part compost and one part manure. To each batch (roughly three five-gallon pails) I add what Ned calls "the powders" —rock phosphate; bonemeal for phosphorous and calcium; blood-meal and canolameal for nitrogen; and greensand, a finely ground marl of marine origin, for potassium and trace minerals—about three cups of each. Peat or perlite can be included to retain moisture, though mulching with hay or bracken holds water much longer and keeps the roots cool. Last comes dolomite lime to adjust the pH to roughly 6.5. The mix is entirely organic, which, according to Ned, seems to produce a more resinous marijuana bud and a stronger, clearer high. There is nothing scientific about this formula—an agronomist would probably shoot it full of holes —but it works. A five-gallon pot of this soil will produce a plant of six feet or more, bearing from two to eight ounces of cured buds, depending on the variety. Except for a seaweed concentrate, applied with regular watering in August to enhance colour and add zap to the smoke, there is enough nutrient here to sustain the plant throughout its life cycle. If I had my druthers, I'd give the plants an occasional dose of fish fertilizer throughout the summer, but, as I learned last year, the stench attracts bears, and they raise hell in the garden when they find nothing to eat.

The compost I add to the mix starts in the city with the accumulation of vegetable scraps, mouldy bread and garden waste combined with ashes from our fireplace, all collected in two noisome garbage cans in the back alley. Periodically I haul the cans up to the cabin and layer their contents in a compost bin with equal portions of a fine black soil that I like to believe has special properties. Twenty years ago this soil was scooped from a swamp to make way for a pond on my small farm. It was sour and stank like rotten eggs. For a decade it slowly mouldered and dried until one day, as I was burning brush next to it, the soil caught fire, so high was its organic content. For a week I chased the smouldering embers, digging further into the pile each day and hosing down the ashes, only to find it smoking again the next morning. By the time the fire was extinguished, I had reached the center of the mound and discovered that the whole thing had turned into friable soil, rich in organics and water-retaining clay as fine as dust.

Over the years, I used some of this soil on the farm, mixing it into the gravelly earth around my apple trees, a collection of heirloom varieties I had scrounged from all over the continent. I dug it into the vegetable garden and into pockets of native soil in the timber, where I planted rhododendrons given to me by an old friend from his collection of more than a hundred varieties. It was my soil bank for the future; the farm was my home and refuge, won from the bush after years of toil, and I never dreamed of leaving it. But when Carole came along, there was no place for her there, nothing she could become part of that wasn't already shaped to my design. My orchard, my garden, my house, my everything. Moreover, the place had grown beyond me, demanding a ceaseless round of picking and pruning, mowing and upkeep. So with great relief we sold and moved to our weekend place here, bringing with us two enormous truckloads of the soil that remained.

I love this work. It's like being present at the creation. Topsoil is the foundation of terrestrial life on the planet, and here I am, making it! In nature, it takes centuries for erosion and decay to turn stone and organic matter into an inch of soil. Much of what I'm working with is already soil, of course, but even so, after six months, when I shovel the compost into the empty half of the bin, mixing and turning as I go, the stuff at the bottom is completely reduced to soil. Further up, tangled clots of earthworms are hard at work breaking down chunks of vegetable matter and shitting out the castings that make the richest of all soils.

Some things don't break down, and these surface periodically. The pricey Henckels paring knife that Carole gave up for lost. Sometimes an earring or a comb. A wheel-less Dinky Toy truck, consigned to the scrapyard by Devon, my six-year-old grandson who came to visit last summer and made his first triumphant solo swim from the shore below the cabin. Mussel and clam shells from the day Carole won sixty-five dollars in the lottery and blew it all on an epic bouillabaisse.

I've told Carole I want my ashes scattered in the compost so that I can finally make a positive contribution to the world. There's a lovely moment like this in *Wasn't That a Time*, a film on the 1980 Carnegie Hall revival concert of Pete Seeger's pioneer folk music group, the Weavers. Lee Hays, the bass singer, died not long after the concert, and the film included a sequence of the other three members of the group—Seeger, Ronnie Gilbert and Fred Hellerman—mixing Hays's ashes into his compost bin, as he had asked. There was a lot of laughter and also a muted message: today's decay is tomorrow's flower. Composting, of course, is all the rage these days. It's environmentally correct, though I wonder how many people see it as the flip side of death, especially their own.

Appropriately perhaps for April Fools' Day, I've started packing pots of soil into my plots. It's hard work, very hard. I begin with the Pocket Garden because I expect it to be the toughest haul—about seventy-five yards through the slash, which has to be the most god-awful terrain to negotiate on foot. In this rock-ribbed country of rampant growth, logging leaves behind a nightmare tangle of smashed trees, limbs, tops and discarded logs, ten feet or more deep in places. Fireweed, bracken and brambles then deposit a mat of dead vegetation that hides leg-swallowing holes between the logs. In time, the wood slips its bark and turns slick as snot underfoot, or it rots and then collapses when you least expect it. After a day in the slash, even with caulked boots, your legs look as if they've been hit by shrapnel. The coastal deer breeze through this stuff. Many times, I've watched them run flat out over slash that we two-legged animals would have to crawl through.

With chainsaw and axe, I make a trail of sorts, which I will hide when the packing is done. The pots are too heavy to carry full, so I shovel a third of the soil into buckets, making three trips for each two containers. By the time I've covered half the distance to the garden, staggering like a drunk because I can't see around the pot to where I'm putting my feet, my back is giving out. I split the distance, moving all the pots to the halfway point, then taking them the rest of the way. With thirty big tubs and thirty smaller ones, packing into this site alone will take about a day and a half. The Hillside Garden is farther from the road, though downhill and easier going, and Number Three, while closer, is at the top of a steep bank. Altogether, I can expect nearly five days of steady packing.

Even though I'd rather be sinking a beer on the sundeck, I no longer dislike this sort of hard, boring work as I once did. The secret, I have found belatedly, is to free your mind to be elsewhere. That means adjusting the load and pace of work so that your body isn't constantly screaming for attention. My only regret is that it took me forty years to learn something so obvious.

Taking a break from my labours at Number Three Garden, I happen upon a tiny pond in the marsh, a circle of tea-coloured water no wider than a long spit downwind. Its surface mirrors an inverted tracery of marsh grasses and bare willows, etched black against skudding clouds. At first glance the water looks dead. But kneeling by the edge I notice clusters of bubbles under the surface, which turn out to be nests of frog eggs. Gently, I scoop out one of these masses; it fills both hands and is surprisingly firm. The egg masses I remember from schoolroom aquariums were dull things, clouded with green algae and mud. This is like soft crystal, clear right through and shot full of pea-sized bubbles. The eggs are exactly the size and colour of black peppercorns, and when I turn them over each shows a grey spot like a pinhead on its underside, perhaps an eye of the nascent tadpole. Bound together by skeins of invisible molecules, the eggs are rocked in a watery womb as elegant as a piece of Steuben glass. Returning the mass to the pond, I notice that the surface film, which I thought was lifeless, is actually swarming with black insects so small as to be barely visible. They act like water dropped onto a hot griddle, bouncing about so quickly I can see them only when they are momentarily at rest. Some physicists think that as much as 90 per cent of our universe is made up of a mysterious substance known simply as "invisible matter." From that perspective, these minute creatures are giants in a universe of the small that may telescope down and down forever. Hunched low over the water, I wonder what worlds and what pond-watchers lie hidden within one molecule of one wing of one of these insignificant gnats.

Packing pots into the Hillside Garden, I keep hearing the screech of a red-tailed hawk from the ridge above me. Twice it swoops down to harry passing bald eagles, diving at their backs and calling its harsh *chiirr-chirr-chirr* until the invaders cross the ravine to the east and rise on updrafts over the bluffs. The red-tails have a nest somewhere in the lofty firs atop the ridge, and just as I'm thinking of climbing to look for it, the pair glides out from the trees, high over the slash. They ascend for a while in slow circles, diminishing gradually to mere specks against the blue. I've gone back to my work and forgotten about them when I hear more loud screeching overhead. I look up in time to see the hawks plunging together down the sky, tumbling and swooping in balletic free fall, though never quite touching. Below the treetops the female breaks away and describes a lovely, looping glide up onto a limb. Close behind her comes the male, settling softly onto her back to mate.

Later, as I'm looking overhead for birds, I step into a hole between the logs and pitch headlong down the hill, spewing soil over the ground and goring my shins on sharp knots. Enough of this freeing the mind from work. Better to watch where I'm putting my bloody great feet.

CHAPTER 3

THE PLANTING MOON

The geese are flying. Once or twice in the night I hear them pass high over the cabin, and again at dawn, cackling faintly above the thump of waves on the beach. By the time I climb up onto the mountain the sky is full of them, Canadas, white-fronts and huge flocks of snows winging northwest from the Fraser River delta with a southeast gale under their tails. The migration has been underway for a week or more, though for most of that time the wind has been against them, and it seems that only the most impatient birds will buck it. With destinations as far off as Wrangel Island, beyond the Bering Strait, they can't afford to waste energy.

A couple of days ago, with high stratus still moving out of the west, broken storm clouds came galloping up Georgia Strait from the southeast, outriders of an approaching storm. Geese caught the leading edge of the changing weather and rode it like a wave. Standing on the highest ridge, I could hear them coming long before I saw the first wavering lines. They were staying low where the wind was strongest, fading in and out of the mist. At times they disappeared altogether, and I could follow their passing only by the chorus of honks and cackles, rising as they approached, then trailing away like a train in the night. I wonder if there is a purpose to all this noise. Could it be mutual encouragement, a sort of work chant for the field hands? Maybe it's just staying in touch, as most biologists suggest, but I like to think it is something less prosaic, perhaps a shout of joy for one of the greatest adventures on earth.

This morning they are high, way up thousands of feet, the Canadas in inky silhouette against the clouds and the wings of the snows flashing white where they cross patches of blue. Birds fly high to find favourable winds, and some ornithologists believe they also seek out lower temperatures to cut the loss of body fluids used in cooling their muscles. Geese that nest in Tibet are believed to reach heights well above twenty thousand feet on their migrations to and from India across the Himalayas. Migrant shorebirds have been seen by pilots at similar elevations over the Atlantic off the southeastern United States. Flying once in a small plane at ten thousand feet over Kenya, I saw barely visible Vs of birds far overhead. Storks, the pilot said, returning from their wintering in southern Africa to nest on the chimneys of Europe. He estimated their height at eighteen thousand feet.

Many Canada geese are no longer migratory, and there's a daily parade of them past the cabin. That's a big change. I don't recall ever seeing a Canada goose or snow goose up close in the wild when I was a kid; relentless hunting had made them scarce and exceedingly wary. Although it's good to have them back, to my mind the resident Canadas that now reduce city parks to expanses of mud and shit are semi-domesticated bums. I wonder to what extent these two populations, the migratory and the earth-bound, have become discrete, because the survival of wild geese is not as secure as their rejuvenated populations suggest. Their winter habitat in the United States and Mexico is being steadily co-opted for human purposes, and the day may come when the great migrations will falter and die unless the city birds once again take to the skies.

By the middle of April the migration is pretty well over, though I haven't been on the mountain to see the last flocks. With my gardens ready for planting, there is little to do until the weather warms. I've been working on the bluff above the cabin, sawing up trees blown down by last winter's gales. I split and stack the wood to dry until fall, when it will be much lighter to carry, and pile the limbs and tops to rot. I used to burn them until it occurred to me, more recently than I care to admit, that I could return their nutrients to the ground instead of contributing to Earth's burden of greenhouse gasses. This is the up side of our incessant winter rains: five years in this climate of creeping mould will reduce a mountain of wood to mush.

With time on my hands, I've relapsed into reading newspapers, an old habit that leaves me vaguely dissatisfied, like half a meal for a hungry man. Is it that the news is mostly bad or that the stories never change, just the names and addresses? This morning one report quotes an RCMP spokesman who calls marijuana "the most dangerous narcotic in Canada today." It's dangerous, he says, because it is many times stronger than it used to be and it triggers aberrant, even criminal, behaviour. This doesn't jibe with my experience; I remember Thai sticks in the 1960s that were as high-octane as any marijuana around today.

I call Ned for his opinion. "That's bullshit," he says. "There used to be a lot more crappy grass around, weak stuff with seeds, but the good weed was as strong then as it is now. If there's a difference, it's the chemicals you get now in hydroponic pot. They're rough, hard on the head. But the THC content hasn't changed all that much."

Actually, this matter of THC levels—Delta-9-tetrahydrocanna-binol, the psychoactive component of cannabis—is just the latest in a series of questions I've had over the years about marijuana. I was curious about what I was smoking, though I did no serious research. But now, as a grower and purveyor of pot, I feel I have some kind of responsibility to acquaint myself with the facts. Getting at the truth hasn't been easy, though. There's no shortage of information—more than a thousand studies have been done on the effects of cannabis. But almost all of them have been designed to demonstrate the dangers of pot. That's where the research grants are available, spun off by the war on drugs.

The charges against marijuana fall roughly into the areas of health and behaviour. Studies have tried to prove that cannabis causes damage to brain cells, the reproductive and immune systems and the lungs. Yet as Lynn Zimmer and John Morgan have shown in an invaluable recent book, *Marijuana Myths, Marijuana Facts*, except for evidence that pot can be harmful to people with chronic lung disease, science does not support any of these claims. Cannabis smoke does contain tars, including carcinogens (but not nicotine), yet it has never been shown to cause lung cancer. In fact, no death has ever been attributed to marijuana. Opponents have also tried to link marijuana to everything from addiction, highway accidents, "amotivational syndrome" and psychosis to violent and criminal conduct. But again, no study has been able to demonstrate a causal relationship. (These findings have recently been confirmed by an Ontario court case in which the judge exonerated marijuana of thirteen of the most common charges against it.)

Lack of scientific evidence about marijuana's dangers has done little to dampen the hysteria created by years of drug war propaganda. Millions still believe that getting stoned means entering an alien state in which people spin wildly out of control. Remembering the fondness of hippies for pot, many conclude—quite rightly —that the drug is a catalyst for intellectual dissent that could threaten existing power structures. And judging by the crazed ranting I've seen on the Internet, there is also a religious component to this dread and loathing. It seems that puritans feel threatened, perhaps even tempted, by the sensual pleasures, especially the sexual ones, offered by the devil's weed. I suspect that Christian fundamentalist outrage may be fed by a Calvinist hostility to a spiritual free lunch. Admission to the higher planes is supposed to be reserved for the righteous, and then only after a lot of soul-searching, flagellation and probably death. Fundamentalists can't abide the thought of someone lighting up and achieving a spiritual insight through the back door.

Whenever I think a discussion of marijuana with friends or neighbours is going nowhere, I fall back on a couple of telling numbers. Fewer than 10 per cent of those who try marijuana ever go on to take up the habit, and of those who do, only 1 per cent use it daily. No matter what you happen to think of pot, that doesn't sound like a very large problem. I also take comfort from the comment of America's first drug czar, Harry Anslinger, who told a congressional committee in the late 1930s that the pacifistic effect of cannabis is so strong it would destroy the will of American youth to fight in foreign wars if were to be legalized—a potential boon, it would seem, to societies prone to violence, not least the United States.

After much reading and research, I'm convinced that marijuana is a relatively benign drug with significant therapeutic potential, certainly much safer than alcohol or tobacco. So my conscience rests easy and I sleep well at night, secure in the knowledge that I'm not setting loose some demon drug that will wreak havoc in the land. I suppose if I had a personal concern about pot, it should be for my lungs. When I was eighteen I came down with tuberculosis, which would have killed me within months had I contracted it before the discovery of streptomycin just eleven years earlier. My X-rays still show the scars, and I have some searing memories of the experience. The night I began my seven months in Vancouver's Pearson Hospital, the man in the next bed died. Death from TB is not pretty. As the disease advances, the lungs break down into what medical texts describe as "cheesy masses." It eats through blood vessels, releasing hemorrhages (red phlegm had been the warning flag for me), and the end often comes with the bursting of a major artery. You literally drown in your own blood. I'll never forget the strangling sounds from behind the curtain next to me and nurses scurrying away with plastic containers heaped with paper towels drenched in blood. The next morning, the sepulchral old man across from me (it was a four-bed room) intoned the theme song of the wards: *TB or not TB / That is Congestion. / Consumption be done about it? / Of corpse, of corpse.*

Once burned, twice shy, I read with considerable interest a 1995 California study that compared the effectiveness of various methods of smoking pot in screening out tars. Regular and filtered joints were tested, along with three types of water pipes (often called bongs), and two kinds of vapourizers, devices that heat marijuana electrically to produce smoke-free psychoactive vapours. Both the water pipes and the filtered cigarette captured THC more readily than tars, producing smoke that is actually worse for the lungs than a regular joint. One of the vapourizers, a hotplate device made in Canada, delivered less tar but fell down badly on what's called the THC transfer rate, the percentage of THC in the marijuana that actually gets through to the smoker. The study concluded that the easiest way to avoid harmful toxins may be simply to smoke stronger marijuana, so that less is ingested. And the plain, unfiltered joint came through looking as good or better than any of the whiz-bang modern devices.

If my occasional toking is clogging my pipes, I can't say that I've noticed. I wheeze and hack a bit climbing hills, which I attribute to advancing years and a phlegmy nature. Would I breathe any easier if I quit smoking dope? I don't know, and I have no intention of finding out, at least not for many years to come.

Waiting still for planting weather, Ned and I finally make a much-discussed but long-deferred boat trip to Brittain River, a fishy little stream in Jervis Inlet, the fjord that cuts forty-five miles back into the mountains north of the Peninsula. When we set out from Secret Cove the sun and wind are already well up—short of a house fire, Ned is not an early riser—and we take a pounding before turning into the sheltering slot of Agamemnon Channel. From there it's easy going. A half hour sees us past Egmont and into what I think of as the inlet proper, long reaches with regal names—Prince of Wales, Princess Royal, Queens Reach—swinging east, then north, then east again beneath spires of ice and snow that loom higher and higher over the dark water. Up there above timberline, winter still holds the country in its grip, squeezing the waterfalls down to wispy threads on the glacier-planed cliffs. But down here at tidewater, we can see Brittain River's grassy estuary glowing luminous green in an elbow of the inlet for miles before we come to it.

All over the coast, these inlet creeks seem to be stamped from the same exquisite mould: an alluvial fan rising suddenly out of black depths, a strip of saltgrass and wildflowers broken by drifts of clam and oyster shell, glades of Sitka spruce giving way to densely regrown forest and, finally, an enclosing ring of peaks at the valley's head. As we nose into a blind channel, big male mergansers bolt for open water, white and greeny-black rockets flashing feet of hot vermilion. Even the requisite black bear is in its customary place, grazing for all the world like a contented cow in a lush meadow between the spruce.

We've come here for two reasons: to fish and to hunt up an old man who splits cedar shakes that Ned might buy for his out-buildings. Ned's youngest son, Danny, has skipped school for the day to try out his first fly-fishing outfit, a nimble little rod and nicely matched line that Ned bought for him in Vancouver. He scrambles out of the boat as soon as we touch the beach, anxious to get at the lunker trout he imagines lying like sunken logs just offshore. I recognize myself at his age, mustard keen but also impatient and ripe for disappointment. The trick with cutthroat trout, I've been telling Danny, is not catching them so much as finding them. A month ago when newly hatched salmon fry were dropping down this stream to begin their seaward migration, the trout would have been waiting in the estuary, eager to come to any silver-bodied fly. But now, in the third week of April, the fry have scattered and cutthroat could be anywhere along the mile of beach. Or, for that matter, gone elsewhere in the inlet.

We work the creek mouth first, letting the current sweep our flies over the drop-off into deep water. But there is too much competition—three harbour seals cruise just beyond my casts, and a river otter surfaces once in the current, then dives and vanishes. These are portents of fish but not of good fishing; predators spook the trout and make them lie low.

Leaving Danny to search for the cutthroats, Ned and I go look-ing for the old man. As soon as we are out of sight, Ned stops to roll a joint. This dissembling is meant to hide from his son the fact that he grows and smokes marijuana. It's silly. At thirteen, Danny is much too bright and observant not to have noticed the signs and smell of pot on every side. Though I've never broached this with Ned, I wonder whether he's afraid that his son would disapprove. Or is it that he thinks Danny would start smoking? Ned's told me that he was no older than Danny when he began toking, and he would be the first to say it did him no harm. But what was fine for Ned is not all right for his son.

Maybe I'm being too hard on Ned. Although I smoked pot openly in front of my own kids, that was in the permissive sixties, well before kids like Danny were routinely dosed with anti-drug propaganda in the schools. Even so, I don't think any purpose is served by Ned's skulking around; marijuana is so readily available, Danny has probably tried it already. My own kids showed little interest in pot, and I wonder if that was because it never had the allure of forbidden fruit. At least it never became an issue between us, as it would have if I'd tried to hide my own toking and warn them off with hysterical scare stories about marijuana. Sooner or later they'd have learned the truth and dismissed me as a liar or a fool or both. Open as we are with each other about most things, though, I say nothing of my thoughts to Ned. Since he separated years ago from Danny's mother, his relationship with his son is a delicate thing he nurtures carefully, and my gut feeling is to leave it alone.

We find the old man outside his trailer, which sits crookedly on the bank above a waterlogged float a few hundred yards around the point from the estuary. He's a little troll, probably in his eighties, glasses bleary with grease and fly shit, snaggle teeth caked by snoose, fisherman's brown tweed pants hitched up with both belt and suspenders nearly to his armpits, so stiff with dirt they look as if they're holding him upright.

We tell him we've seen a bear feeding on the estuary. "Bears!

Christ almighty, bears, bears, bears," he croaks, his voice high and peevish. "The buggers must be starving. I've never seen so many. One of them, a great big bugger, come after me, and would have got me, too, if it hadn't been for that dog." "That dog" is eyeing us suspiciously from under the trailer, not deigning to come out and make friends. He's big and tan-coloured, with a smooth coat and a dark head the size of a bucket, a pretty good semblance of a bull mastiff, were it not for little floppy ears that he wears at half mast with an air of perpetual embarrassment.

The old man shows us where the bear appeared suddenly when he was splitting shakes, bursting into the open-sided building and chasing him around a pile of cedar blocks before the dog came to the rescue. Gimping about in laceless shoes run over so far at the heels they make him bowlegged, he acts out the struggle: dog and bear rolling together out of the shed, old man making for the trailer to get his gun, bear nearly catching him in the open, dog to the rescue again, and finally the shot from the doorway.

In his gnarled and querulous frailty, this fellow reminds me of numberless other old men I've met over the years on the B.C. coast, utterly isolated and solitary as bears gone off to die in mountain caves. I believe they become trapped in the roadless immensities of the inlets by the habits of a lifetime; this old man is dragging cedar out of the bush simply because that's what he's always done. But they're not just casualties of overwhelming geography. There is self-indulgence here, too, a turning away from the accommodations to other people necessary for a social life. I've felt that same tug of reclusiveness; living alone on my little farm, I became more and more reluctant to venture into Sechelt, only ten minutes away. The old man tells us he lives in the inlet and splits shakes to supplement his pension, but in truth there's no money to be made here; the valley was worked out by shakers years ago. His shakes are poor, narrow things, so badly corrugated (from cutting too close to the butt of the tree) that I know Ned won't take them.

The three of us walk together to the end of the gravel beach a half mile from the estuary, where the old man shows us a smooth granite pool the size of a big hot tub, carved by a waterfall that drops thirty feet over a cliff. Trout are sometimes trapped here by the dropping tide, and the old man tells us he has seen bears swatting them onto the beach. Danny has followed us and found the cutthroat, hooking two bright fourteen-inchers just off the waterfall. He's excited and pleased with himself, though a bit deflated when the old man tells him he catches three- and four-pounders trolling a spoon over the drop-off in front of the estuary. Another day, I tell Danny. Another day, we'll be back.

The trip home is fast but wet, eating spray from steep chop in the inlet, then surfing down Malaspina Strait on a heavy westerly swell. At home, I take an after-dinner stroll out to the point, just a hundred yards or so below the cabin. The scene resembles a Tom Thomson painting: pines contorted by wind, sheets of lichen-mottled granite, dark water streaked with windlines and whitecaps, hills of deepest blue across the strait. Here, unlike Thomson's Algonquin, hundreds of surf scoters ride like a black snake over the waves. All this augers well the morrow; it will be a planting day.

April 22. First planting—a date worth noting in my diary. Seasoned dope growers say it's important to keep a record of such things for future reference. I poke the seeds—three per pot to allow for germination failures—a half inch into the soil, water lightly and cover with inverted plastic glasses to trap the sun's warmth and fend off slugs. Ever since I planted my first garden at age eight or nine—a few doomed beans in the hardscrabble behind the house at Granthams—putting seed in the ground has given me a wonderful sense of anticipation. Every gardener must feel it. It's the promise of so much to come from so little. Latent in the hundred or so seeds cupped in my hand is the power to stone half the population of Vancouver.

How-to books for marijuana growers recommend sprouting the seeds between layers of wet paper towel, presumably to avoid planting unviable duds. This makes sense if you are buying seed and can't afford to plant more than one per pot. But growing your own seed means you can sow as much as you want. Marijuana is a profligate seed producer. Last year I pollinated only two colas (branches of female flowers) and harvested too many seeds to bother counting. And I've never had any difficulty getting them to germinate in the ground. Incidentally, the word "cola"—Spanish for "tail"—applies properly only to the flowers on the tip of the branch. In this part of the world, though, it has come to mean a continuous, dense mass of flowers. Thinly budded branches lower on the plant are still called just that, branches.

Ned says I'm pushing the season and should wait until May to plant, when the soil is warmer. Maybe so. But if my seeds don't germinate now, I'll just plant again. It seems to me that the longer the growing season, the bigger the plants will get and the earlier they will mature. (How little I knew! Marijuana grows so fast, I've since learned, plants seeded as late as the beginning of June will catch up to or even surpass April plantings. And maturity is controlled by light, not the age of the plant.)

By the time I've finished sowing the Pocket Garden—180 seeds under sixty glasses—I no longer fear that I might be jumping the gun. Even though the icy westerly is still howling this morning, down here behind the wall of timber at the end of the slash, the air is hardly stirring. By mid-morning the sun is hot, drawing eddies of steam from each pot, like cauldrons at a gathering of witches. And when I go back to the first glass I put on, the soil beneath is already warmed by its tiny greenhouse.

Deciding *what* to plant has cost me a bit of anguish. Ned offered me seeds, and I was sorely tempted to accept because his varieties were all bred and acclimated here to local conditions over many years. But in the end I decided to stick with the purple strain that served me so well last year. I know its habits and preferences, things like yield, odour, size and tightness of the buds, time to maturity and mould resistance. It originated in high-elevation gardens in a dry part of the southern B.C. interior, hardly ideal conditioning for low elevation on a rainy coast. Nonetheless, it seems quite happy here, perhaps because the variety has a lot of the *indica* marijuana strain in its breeding, the source of its deep purple hue at maturity. *Indica* is a northern plant, used to much harsher conditions than *sativa*, the equatorial strain.

When I finish sowing Number Three Garden, the pill bottle in which I keep my seeds is still half full, and there are hundreds more seeds at home. If I were a true devotee of the weed, I'd cook them up somehow and eat them. Although they are not psycho-active, pot seeds do have a lot of nutritive value and are much praised as food in the drug culture press. To my mind, they taste like a mouthful of gravel and would be more appropriately writ-ten up in books about how to survive in the wild by eating skunk cabbage, bushes and stumps.

At dusk, as I'm nursing a beer on the deck and thinking about all those hundreds of seeds swelling in the ground, a full moon rises into a green sky over Turnagain Island. Although I certainly didn't plan it this way, the timing could not be more propitious. Ancient cultures planted their crops at the time of the full moon to ensure fertility and a good yield, and just to set the right example some of those peoples also copulated in the newly plowed fields.

Later on the phone, when I tell Carole about this astronomical conjunction, she says she's glad of the moon, but as for the humping between the pots ... well, my plants will just have to make it on their own.

CHAPTER 4

COSMIC
WINDS

All through these weeks of hard work, I've tried not to forget that I am here on the mountain to cultivate a healthy psyche as much as a crop of marijuana. Every day after lunch, weather permitting, I sit quietly for up to an hour on an overturned bucket, doing what I call "getting out of my head." The routine is simple: I make myself comfortable, hands resting loosely in my lap, eyes closed. Breathing deeply and exhaling slowly, I pause at the end of each breath, relaxing as if my very bones had gone soft. I concentrate on the warmth of my body, visualizing all my billions of cells glowing with slow, luminous fire. A deep heaviness comes over me, as if I could sink into the ground. And within five to ten minutes, I lose touch with my body, withdrawing first from my extremities and working in to the center of my chest, until all physical sensation has narrowed to the regular coming and going of my breath.

At this point, which I usually reach without difficulty, I am conscious only of smell and sound—the tang of fir pitch from a tree I've been limbing, the sough of needles combing the wind, small rustlings in the underbrush, ravens croaking far off. I concentrate on the red light filtered through my eyelids and on my breathing. Gradually, smell and sound move away to distant corners of my mind, and I am left with my thoughts.

Now comes the hard part: shutting down my conscious mind and allowing the unconscious to come to the surface. I try to let my mind relax into a quietly passive state and concentrate on creating a mental vacuum. As thoughts occur, they are pushed gently off to one side. On good days, I can indeed get out of my head and into the awareness that I am part of a universe as immortal as all time and limitless as all space. I have the sense of entering another dimension, a realm of existence fully as real as the rock-solid tangibility of everyday life. Invariably, I return from these journeys rested and at peace.

I can remember when I first felt the ground of reality move beneath my feet. I was twelve, visiting with a kid named Steve who lived at the far end of my paper route. I'd stop in most evenings before the long ride home in the dark, and Steve usually had some diversion ready. When he caught the mumps, he displayed his bloated testicle every evening for a week. He held cat races (his father had been a horse trainer), firing up the two family felines by throwing them in the oven for a few seconds before releasing them from a starting gate he had constructed. He shot arrows from his bedroom window, puncturing the washtubs hanging outside the neighbour's back door. On this particular evening, three or four adults had also stopped by, and one of them suggested that we play a parlour game called Mental Telepathy. One of us was to leave the room, while the others decided on some action the person would be expected to perform when he or she returned. We were to visualize the action and silently repeat to ourselves the precise words of instruction. Steve went first, and when he came back into the room, we all sat dead still with our heads down, intoning to ourselves, "Water the plant, water the plant." After several minutes of apparent confusion, he fetched water from the kitchen and poured it into a potted plant on the coffee table in front of us. Right away I was on my guard. Steve was full of dirty tricks, and I was wary of being set up. Two or three others took their turns, and I seem to recall that at least one person couldn't carry out the instructions. Then it was my turn. When I left the room I was surprised that I could hear nothing being said beyond the door, as this was my first line of suspicion. Called back, I stood around for a minute or two, feeling embarrassed. Then I saw a pencil and pad on a card table, and picking them up, I wrote my name. The unspoken instruction had been "Write your name."

For nearly twenty years that one encounter with the paranormal haunted me like an island of mysteries in a sea of conventional reality. I'd been marked indelibly by the experience, and yet I couldn't fit it into my belief that the world, both out there and inside my head, was just what it seemed to be. But all of that was to change forever on a day in May of 1963, when I took LSD for the first time.

In the late 1950s my father, Ted, had become involved in exploring the psychedelic drugs then emerging, some of them synthetics such as LSD, others plant-based chemicals long used by aboriginal peoples. Ted was interested in psychedelics both as agents of enlightenment and as therapeutic instruments for the treatment of addictions, particularly alcoholism. He worked as a therapist in a Vancouver clinic that did pioneering work with psychedelics until it was shut down by federal drug laws in the 1960s.

LSD was getting a bad name at that time, thanks to its misuse by young people who had no idea of its power. I suppose the horror stories had made me a bit apprehensive, though I could not have been in better hands. By trial and error, Ted had learned about dosage, combinations—in my case, a blend of LSD and mescaline, a derivative of the peyote cactus—and how to create the right set and setting for an LSD session. (As I learned later, "set" is what you know about a drug and what you expect to happen when you take it; setting is just that—the locale and ambience for your trip.) Though he had no formal training in psychology or pharmacology, Ted had a great deal of personal experience with psychedelics and possessed the gift of being able to accompany a drug taker on a trip without ingesting any of the drug himself.

This LSD session was an interesting conjunction for Ted and me. After a few years of newspapering, I had taken a degree in journalism at an American university and come back to Vancouver in 1960, primed to do great things in my old job as a reporter at the *Vancouver Sun*. But my job was scotched by an economic recession, and with a young family to support I found myself doing public relations for a dairy company and editing a magazine preposterously called *Butter-Fat*. While my self-esteem was being ground down by the bum-kissing and flackery of PR, Ted was flying high, growing his hair long and identifying more and more with the sixties counterculture. All through the 1950s, he had struggled as a writer to promote many of the same iconoclastic values. When he saw his vision suddenly emerging all around him, he instantly recognized the coming upheaval and it recognized him. Young people came from all over to sit at his feet. He travelled to the mountains of Mexico in search of magic mushrooms; lived at Rochdale, the co-op college in Toronto that turned into a hippie drug tower; did sensitivity training for executives in California; immersed himself in the cultures of Native people; helped establish a Native Indian publishing venture and then wrote for it. Struggling financially, I envied his freedom and resented the fact that any number of people my age had more rapport with him than I did. The sixties were passing me by. Now, about to take LSD,

I was going to the psychic heart of the decade. If it accomplished nothing else, I hoped it would take me at least a little way into his world and bring us closer together.

Within an hour of swallowing the drugs, my understanding of reality was crumbling fast. The first sign was an overpowering scent of flowers, emanating from a bouquet in a distant bedroom of the house at Granthams. Neither my mother, Marj, nor my brother, Noel, both in the living room where I was lying, could smell them. Before long, the lid seemed to be blown off all my senses: colours glowed as if lit by some inner fire. Whatever I touched felt alive with electric energy, and I heard the Verdi *Requiem* throb and soar in my skull as if in the vaulted ceiling of a great cathedral.

Over the next four or five hours, all connection with my body and conscious mind unravelled. There was a sense of departure, of rising effortlessly and looking down on myself lying there in the May sunshine. Gradually I drifted away, losing touch altogether with my surroundings, sinking with indescribable bliss into a boundless sea of being. Patterns and colours streamed past, complex and brilliant beyond anything I'd ever known or imagined, and yet there was a sense of coming home, as if I had been here many times before. After what seemed like hours, I found myself ascending into a night sky ablaze with stars. Higher and higher I went, rushing onward towards a distant star far brighter than any other. Larger and larger it grew until its light filled the sky and finally the entire universe, enveloping all creation. In a flash of blinding white, I felt myself disintegrate and scatter to the remotest corners of space, glowing with cold, unquenchable fire in billions of celestial bodies. The imagery was breathtakingly, achingly beautiful, and the sensation was one of a psychic explosion, like an orgasm that goes on and on forever. Overwhelmed and melted by ecstasy, I became a disembodied soul, floating free in time and space, living eternity in a day. I was filled with a towering certainty that the universe is one, a serene and perfect unity of all things. The long coming down to earth was drawn out for hours and marked by feelings of profound tenderness, reverence and love so intense as to be almost painful.

More than thirty years later, I still think of that day as the greatest revelation of my life, as if the shutters of a darkened house were thrown open, letting the sun stream in. Ever since, I have felt the constant daily presence of the great tide of the unconscious—intuitive, creative and immortal. I carry it with me like a talisman.

Even after my LSD trip, I used to believe there was a normal waking consciousness, the state we all walk around in. Now I'm not so sure. Every day, we go through so many changes of mood and perception, anything from a runner's high to a jolt of booze or rush-hour rage. Even here in the quiet of the mountain, my state of mind shifts with the weather, the work and countless other things I'm unaware of. I think the fact that we're mostly oblivious to this process, feeling the changes in mood but taking no active part in shaping them, often makes us yearn to break out of the prison of our minds, or at least to look over the walls. A while back I came across Andrew Weil's fine book *The Natural Mind*, and I was intrigued by what he had to say about consciousness:

> Ultimately, [consciousness is] the only problem worthy of total intellectual effort. It is the concern of all the world's philosophies and religions, other problems being less precise statements of the same thing. All of us are working on the problem of consciousness at some level, and the conclusions we come to determine what we think about ourselves and the universe, how we live, and how we act.

For me, that's the real significance of the psychedelic experience —it expands our consciousness to the point of awareness that we and the universe are one. Our understanding of that, or the lack of it, will determine the ecological fate of the planet. Without the knowledge that abuse of the earth is abuse of ourselves, no amount of technical or economic wizardry will prevent the collapse of life as we know it.

Sitting on my bucket on the mountain, I'm aware of my place in the universe. It's breathing that makes the connection, realizing that every breath I take contains molecules shed by trees, rotting wood and swamp muck; spores of fungi; pollen from willow, alder and wild currant; the breath of birds and animals; and the briny exhalations of the sea below me—all borne along on a life-giving tide of oxygen. Bits of this atmospheric soup lodge in the olfactory receptors of my nose. Other fractions, mainly oxygen, pass through the walls of my lungs into the bloodstream in exchange for carbon dioxide. As molecules pass back and forth across the alveoli, millions of minute sacs whose walls are only a single cell in thickness, I become composed, quite literally, of the world around me, and the world in turn is composed of me. As the only bodily function that is both voluntary and involuntary, breathing is the link between the conscious and unconscious minds, and almost all systems of spiritual practice see breath as the key that grants passage into the realm of the spirit. In fact, the words for "breath" and "spirit" are identical in many languages, including Sanskrit (*prana*), Hebrew (*ruach*), Greek (*pneuma*) and Latin (*spiritus*).

But much as I value my quiet times here, I don't have any illusions about plumbing the depths of my unconscious solely through breath control and meditation. I'm not sufficiently dedicated. Like most people seeking access to the inner cosmos, at least in the Western world, I'll continue to rely on what Aldous Huxley called the "gratuitous graces" of psychedelic drugs. Huxley believed that whole populations could be turned on to psychedelics and changed thereby to peaceful, loving and spiritual citizens. I don't think so. Psychic change of that magnitude can only grow slowly, most likely from a nucleus of enlightened people. Some observers see this kind of psychic shift as the next stage in human evolution. But I expect that if it happens at all before we commit ecological suicide, it will result not from an evolutionary advance but from turning back to the spiritual practices of our ancestors.

Although the archaeological evidence becomes pretty thin at about the 10,000-year mark, there's every reason to believe that people were getting high long before that. Certainly the plants were there, as were human appetite and curiosity. We know from diggings in Texas caves that Native Americans were tripping out on mescal beans (*Sophora secundiflora*) 9,000 years ago. In Siberia and India, linguistic evidence traces the use of the brilliant red fly agaric mushroom (*Amanita muscaria*) back 7,000 years. And analysis of the mummified body of the pharaoh Ramses the Great confirms that the Egyptians used marijuana at least 4,000 years ago.

There is also evidence that psychoactive plants hold the key to some of history's most enduring mysteries. It seems likely, for instance, that the secret of the Grecian cult of Eleusis was a decoction of psychoactive mushroom or fungus, possibly rye ergot, the natural form of LSD. The rites of purification and initiation were held in autumn, the season of mushrooms and ripening grain in Europe. Initiates drank a potion and saw awe-inspiring visions that sound today very much like an LSD trip. Plato, who contemporaries believed had been to the Temple of Eleusis, wrote that beyond this ephemeral and imperfect existence is an ideal world of "forms," where the original, the true, the beautiful patterns of things exists.

The secret of soma, which so intrigued Aldous Huxley, was cracked by the careful scholarship of banker–turned–drug researcher Gordon Wasson. At least that's the conclusion I draw from *Soma: Divine Mushroom of Immortality*, his analysis of the Rig-Veda, a series of sacred texts left by the Aryans, a soma-using people who entered India from the northwest about 1600 B.C. Among their hundreds of references to soma, the Vedas allude to a plant that grows without seed, which Wasson takes to be the fly agaric mushroom. Hindus consider the Vedas to be *apaurnsheya*, Sanskrit for "not of human origin"—in other words divinely inspired, most likely through the medium of a psychedelic.

Although neither cannabis nor the opium poppy grew in the New World before Columbus, the aboriginal peoples of the Americas had discovered nearly a hundred other indigenous psychoactive plants, perhaps ten times as many as were native to the Old World. And these were just the known species; many others may have gone undiscovered or been tried and rejected as too dangerous or unpleasant. In Mexico and Central America the Spanish conquistadors, barred from psychedelic knowledge by their own faith, walked into a bewildering world of trances and rituals. Native peoples were mind-altering with several kinds of psilocybin mushrooms, morning glory seeds, peyote cacti, psychedelic vines, various members of the deadly nightshade family and even psychoactive toads, all of which are still used by Indian people today.

Even tobacco was a psychedelic in the pre-Columbian world. Scrapings from ancient ceremonial pipe bowls have yielded tobacco traces six times stronger than the leaf that is grown today. Tobacco of such potency, thrown by the handful on fires in a sweat lodge or tent, must have produced mental states unknown to any contemporary smoker. Yet there is nothing in the earliest records to suggest that the aboriginal use of tobacco was casual or addictive. Before it was taken from its ritual context by Europeans, it was a sacred drug, strictly reserved for ceremonial purposes.

European intervention has had the opposite effect on coca, making it much stronger. Cocaine was first extracted from coca leaves in 1860, and by the end of the century occasional abuse of the new drug caused it to be outlawed in Europe and North America. Ever since, aboriginal South Americans, who have used it as a stimulant and medicant for millennia, have been under increasing pressure to destroy their perfectly harmless coca plants. Although taken to enhance the capacity to endure physical hardship—Inca runners chewed coca leaves in the high Andes, and their descendants still measure journeys in terms of the *cocada*, the period of time that one chew will sustain them—coca may also have had psychic purposes. The coca high is much more subtle than the soaring rapture of a powerful psychedelic, but who knows what it became in the hands of a shaman skilled in the arts of trance, ritual and native pharmacology?

After pot trips that came close in their intensity to an LSD session, I've had similar questions about marijuana. Could it be that under the right conditions pot can have a psychedelic punch equal to that of mescaline, psilocybin or other powerful hallucinogens? Pharmacologically, this seems unlikely; cannabis contains none of the alkaloids that are the active principle in many strong psychedelics. On the other hand, in its long history marijuana has often had a sacramental role that implies formidable power to invoke religious visions. Middle Eastern priestesses of the shamanistic cult of Ashera burned it in caves and on hilltops at the time of the Old Testament prophets. The Scythians ("cannabis" is a Scythian word), a nomadic people who wandered between Central Asia and Europe seven centuries before the Christian era, burned marijuana in urns filled with hot rocks from their funeral pyres. The oracle at Delphi delivered her prophecies through a cloud of intoxicating smoke. Did these people get higher than we do because they *believed* in marijuana's mystical powers and used it in powerfully evocative settings? Certainly the Greek historian Herodotus was impressed. He wrote that the Scythians inhaled pot smoke in skin tents (reminiscent of the North American sweat lodge) and danced and sang and howled with joy.

Cannabis resin, in the form of an infusion known as *vijaya*, was said by ancient Hindus to be the favourite drink of the god Indra, who gave it to the people so that they might attain elevated states of consciousness, ecstasy and fearlessness. To this day, Hindus celebrate the end of the festival of Durga pooja by imbibing *bhang*, a drink containing milk, cannabis resin, cucumber and melon seeds, sugar and black pepper. In the Muslim context, Allah himself is implicated in the use of hashish, according to the Arabian epic *The Thousand and One Nights*. Perhaps because of its prohibition of alcohol, Islam has been more tolerant of cannabis than have either Christianity or Judaism. The water pipe is believed to have been invented in North Africa, and Muslim families in the region still gather to smoke in a room designated for the purpose, known as the kif room, after the Arabic word for marijuana. Christianity's antipathy to marijuana is perhaps to be expected, given its stress on sin, repentance and mortification of the flesh. Judaism's hostility, on the other hand, seems to have more to do with religious politics than morality. Hebrew kings worshipped the Canaanite goddess Asherah, the marijuana-loving Queen of Heaven. Her devotees inhaled pot smoke from urns or open fires. (Was Moses's burning bush a cannabis plant?) Such practices were condemned by King Hezekiah; he started a housecleaning that was completed by his grandson, Josiah, who, in the words of the Old Testament, "slew all the priests of the high places that were upon the altars, and burned men's bones upon them." Asherah and cannabis were out, and monotheism and an all-male priesthood were in, with marijuana and the goddess banished permanently to the fringes of Jewish mysticism.

The vision quests of our forebears were rites of passage designed to integrate the individual into society. In a psychedelic trance, the ego-self died and a person was reborn in a state of cosmic consciousness as a full-fledged member of the tribe. Today, in Western industrial societies, rampant individualism and emphasis on the intellect have turned direct, personal experience of the unconscious into something threatening, even immoral, and the drugs that facilitate the process have become objects of fear and hostility. With so little sense of a shared identity, most people who experiment with psychedelics take them over and over again for personal gratification and enlightenment. We've strayed a long way from the Temple of Eleusis, where initiates drank the potion once or at most twice, or from the mushroom eaters of Mexico, who normally make their vision quest only once in a lifetime. In the original religious context, multiple trips are redundant, because once you've experienced the cosmic epiphany you are changed forever.

But despite our ecological peril, I feel strangely heartened some days by what I see from my bucket perch. In this first-ever aspiritual civilization, more and more people seem to be hungering for a sense of connection to the human family, if not the cosmos. If Earth's collapsing life supports will allow us time, there's at least a chance that this process will reach critical mass and reverse our apocalyptic ways. I'd like to think I'm part of that movement, cultivating enlightenment here on the mountain. Enlightenment in my meditations and enlightenment in the ground, for it's possible that someone, somewhere, will come upon an enlarging insight through my pot and make some small contribution to the growth in human consciousness. Even if that never happens, I can be content in the knowledge that the fruits of my labours will provide many thigh-slappers, glorious pigouts and jolly good romps in the sack, pleasures as necessary to our survival as the air we breathe.

My seedlings are up! Ten days after planting, I plow through the dew-drenched slash and arrive, soaked to the ass, just as the first of the morning sun is slanting into the Pocket Garden. The inverted plastic party glasses on each pot are beaded silver with condensation, hiding whatever may be growing within. Lifting the first of them, I find three seedlings of the most vivid green imaginable, standing an inch above the black soil. Between the two round, rubbery seed leaves, the first true marijuana leaves are just beginning to show their distinctive saw-toothed edges. Quickly, I go through the rest of the patch and find seedlings in every one of the sixty pots, most of them doubles or triples.

Without further thought, I begin pulling up the surplus plants, leaving the biggest, one to a pot. But I haven't gone far before I begin to question my choices. Is biggest necessarily best? Since it's the females I want to keep, maybe I should be selecting the shorter, thicker seedlings, as those are female characteristics. Just as I'm becoming annoyed by my dithering—I know full well that marijuana doesn't show its sex for months—another thought occurs: why not save these perfectly good plants? Rather than murdering them, surely there is some place I can heel them into the ground and keep them alive in case they are needed.

Within an hour I'm back on the mountain with buckets of soil and boxes of four-inch plastic pots, and I begin transplanting the surplus seedlings. By mid-afternoon, I have them all together in the back of Henry the Ford—a total of nearly 170 plants from all three gardens. The size of my marijuana enterprise has suddenly doubled, and I have to find a home for my new charges. I remember an overgrown skid road east of the swamp, which I had rejected as a garden because the trees were too small to hide mature plants. For a nursery, it proves to be ideal—level ground, well hidden from the road, with water nearby to keep the seedlings from drying out. In these tiny pots the plants will need constant attention, and they'll have to be transplanted into larger containers within a few weeks. Over the coming months they will be the bane of my existence and, in the end, my salvation.

Checking my gardens a couple of days later, I receive two sharp reminders that I'm an intruder on foreign ground, where the permanent residents hold sway. Sixteen seedlings in the Pocket Garden have been mowed down by slugs, and there is some lesser damage in the other gardens. Although I could have thwarted the slugs, at least for a few days, by leaving the plastic glasses over the plants, I was afraid the seedlings might "damp off" from mildew-rotted stems caused by excessive moisture. So I replaced the glasses with inch-wide strips of copper sheeting, bent into rings four inches in diameter, encircling each seedling—a sure-fire slug-stopper, I'd been told. Well, I've just added copper bands to salt, iron filings, lime, broken glass, gravel, oyster shell, axle grease, ambergris, acids of every kind, beer, ball bearings, Grapenuts, fish hooks, dog piss and spent nuclear fuel rods on the list of foolproof slug remedies that don't work worth a damn. (I have since discovered—no guarantees, mind you—that slugs will avoid diatomaceous earth. Trouble is, it's expensive, and you have to lay down a broad swath to keep the buggers from crossing.)

Sharp reminder number two awaits me in the Hillside Garden. I arrive to find it looking as if it had just been strip-mined. Many pots are dumped and soil is strewn everywhere. Fresh bear tracks are all round, and there are two gaping holes in the fence where my visitor came and left again, as easily as passing through smoke. By the gate, which I'd rather he had used, the bear has left a calling card—a heap of fat, green turds, so full of vegetable fibers they look like pot cleaners. Scraping about in the spilled soil, I find that I can recover all but one of the plants, and when the soil is back in the pots, things look much as they were.

Later, it's Ned who comes up with an explanation: the bear smelled the bone meal in the soil and, finding nothing to eat, swatted the pots about in frustration. The answer, he tells me, is to set out your pots early in the spring, so that the bear can do his thing and the smell of bone meal will dissipate long before the plants go in.

Lesson by hard lesson, I'm learning this trade.

CHAPTER 5

HAZARDS
OF
THE LAW

Every year towards the end of May I feel a persistent twitching in my right arm and wrist. It's the return of an old urge to cast a fly over some limpid lake or stream, revived by the annual flight of black ants. On the mountain, the air is full of them, inch-long queens winging down the rays of the late afternoon sun in search of places to land with their cargo of fertilized eggs and start new colonies. They flop onto the hood of the truck, crawl over my back and arms and litter the road. I cast my mind, if not a line, westward to Sakinaw Lake at the Peninsula's end, where cutthroat trout would even now be rising to the hatch, dimpling the lovely six-mile sheet of water like rain.

The ant hatch is a feast for the birds, though only the insectivores are adept at catching them—violet-green swallows mainly, and olive-sided flycatchers. The flycatchers perch on the topmost spikes of cedar snags, piercing the sky with their three-note silver whistle—*quick-three beers, quick-three-beers*—the last note trailing down and away. Robins fly up to intercept the incoming ants but make a hash of it, missing half the time and fluttering clumsily back to the ground. Better than any bird are the dragonflies, large black ones and mid-size models in luminous blue that rise from the pond like Spitfires to seize the ants from beneath.

The birds I listen for most at this season, Swainson's thrushes, make no appearance here, keeping to their shady haunts at the forest edge. Russet-brown, with a whitish ring around the eye, they are shy, nondescript little creatures. And yet, when they begin to sing in late May (they arrive a month earlier but remain silent, except for a low whistle), their rising fountains of song set the hills to ringing. Now, in the gathering dusk, I can hear them calling from the timber atop the ridge and all across the broad swath of forest below the slash. If there is an archetypal summer sound in the coastal forest, this is it.

I haven't had much chance to hear the thrushes yet this year. They avoid the open rock bluff around the cabin, and since they began singing I've been on the mountain only briefly to water my transplants and replace the few plants still being taken by slugs. It's just as well that I'm not busy with my gardens, as this morning on a trip to Vancouver Henry the Ford breaks down, and I have to be pushed ignominiously off the ferry and towed to a garage. The offending part, my mechanic tells me later on the phone, is worth about twenty-five cents, but getting it out and replacing it will cost as much as a brain operation. "Seventeen hours' labour," he says cheerfully. Through my stunned silence, I hear muffled sniggering coming down the line. The bastard has his hand over the receiver, enjoying his little prank. My mechanic fancies himself a joker, but his talents would be better employed in the interrogation cells of some dictatorship.

After three days I give up waiting for the missing part to arrive from Timbuktu, and without wheels I head back up the coast, worried that my transplants may be dying of thirst in their tiny pots. As the ferry nears the Langdale terminal, the ship's loudspeakers belch the news that the bus I had planned to take to Sechelt has been cancelled. A lean, craggy-faced man, whom I guess to be in his late sixties, offers me a lift. As we settle into his Cadillac, he extends a hand as hard as an axehead and tells me he is a judge on his way to preside over the provincial court in Sechelt.

Passing through the trashy outskirts of Gibsons, we chat about crime, crowded court dockets and his career (RCMP, followed by eighteen years on the bench). As we take to the open highway, the judge asks what I do for a living. *Thunk!* My stomach clenches and I'm gripped by the kind of fear you get on a cliff top or skyscraper, fear that you might lose control and jump. I imagine blurting out, "Your Honour, I can't tell a lie. I confess, I'm growing marijuana." But I choke the words back and launch into a recitation about my years in filmmaking. After a mile or two he cuts me off: "But what are you doing now? What are you doing up here on the Sunshine Coast?" His manner is peremptory. I imagine myself in his courtroom, pockets bulging with grass, cringing under his vulture's stare.

"Well, I spend most of my time writing, and I've been building a house up towards Pender Harbour."

"Writing what?"

"Scripts. I still do some scripts for other filmmakers, and I'm working on a book."

"A book? What about?"

For a moment I hesitate. Like many writers, I don't like discussing work in progress, except perhaps in generalities. With this guy and this topic, we'll be into the particulars very quickly. But what the hell, I decide, raise the red flag. This could be interesting. So I tell him the book is about marijuana.

"What's your slant?" he demands.

Carefully, I explain that my interest has more to do with civil liberties, consciousness and other matters that surround marijuana than with the drug itself. "As a society, we treat cannabis as mainly a legal matter," I tell him, "but it's really none of the state's business what people do in the privacy of their own homes. You can't have a responsible democracy unless citizens are responsible for their own conduct."

"Well, how widely do you define responsibility?" he wants to know. "If you legalize marijuana, do you think the people who use it should have to pay the costs to society?" The costs to society are the result of the law, I tell him, adding that I'm not aware of any significant harm done by marijuana itself. "Health, addiction, automobile accidents, loss of productivity at work. Those are real costs," he says. "Legalize marijuana and we will have the same situation we have with tobacco. People are free to smoke it but they don't accept any responsibility for the burden it places on the Medicare system."

How much responsibility, I wonder, is the judge prepared to accept for the environmental cost of his gas-hogging Cadillac? But I keep this thought to myself; a debate about penalizing people for their pleasures will get us nowhere. Instead, trying not to proselytize but succeeding only in sounding dreadfully earnest, I say that except in the hands of addictive personalities who will abuse almost anything, marijuana seems to be pretty safe. Driving stoned doesn't strike me as a good idea, I add, even though traffic accidents attributable solely to marijuana are rare to nonexistent. He confirms the latter; in his courtroom he's seen that other substances, usually alcohol, are almost invariably involved. As for all the rest, the judge isn't buying it. He offers no facts, no examples, no evidence of any kind. Marijuana is against the law and it's bad stuff. Period.

As we coast down the hill through Selma Park, our conversation lapses. I can see the slash beyond Sechelt where my plants are even now reaching for the morning sun. I think of the lacy leaves, heavy with dew and stirring in the first puffs of the day's westerly. The judge has been thinking too.

"What I can't understand," he says, "is why anyone would want to smoke marijuana. Why would they want to just blank out their minds? They must be trying to escape into some kind of oblivion." Until now, I'd felt that the judge and I were having a useful talk, even if we disagreed. But this statement opens an unbridgeable gulf between us; he hasn't the remotest idea what turning on is all about. In his experience, getting high means getting drunk, zonked, blotto. By the time psychedelics came along, he was already a conscript in the war on drugs. Now, on the bench, he believes he passes judgement evenhandedly, when in fact his decisions are driven by drug war propaganda and the laws he applies are a fabrication of politics and prejudice. I want to respond, to tell him that a pot trip is not about oblivion, not about getting stupid and sick. It's about thinking and seeing differently; it's about euphoria, ecstasy even, about wondrously enhanced taste and smell and music and sex and laughter. But I know better than to try.

As we pull up to the courthouse in Sechelt, he says something about the book paying for the house Carole and I are building. I have to laugh. "I'll be lucky if it pays for lunch. Unless you're a name in Canada, writing doesn't pay for houses."

"Well then, you must be doing it for altruistic reasons," he says. To this point, the judge has been forceful but strictly judicial in our conversation. This remark has a sarcastic edge.

"I'm doing it because it's interesting. And because I believe there are some things worth saying about marijuana and our drug laws."

He pauses at the base of the stairs to the courtrooms. "Why don't you write something like ... what's his name? Berton, Pierre Berton. He must make money."

"Judge," I want to say, "to come up with an idea like that, you've just got to be toking on the sly." But I settle for a good day and thanks for the lift.

Driving to the city before Henry let me down, I had heard a radio commentary about the hearings underway in Ottawa on Bill C-7, legislation to replace the Narcotic Control Act of 1961. That act, passed at a time when relatively few Canadians had any personal experience with marijuana, reflected the prevailing "reefer madness" hysteria. More than three decades and millions of smokers later, one might expect legislation more in keeping with the times. But it is apparently not to be. Under the new legislation (since passed into law as Bill C-8), police will get even greater powers of search and seizure; the constitutional right to trial by jury is to be limited; convictions for cannabis offences will still get people a criminal record, severely limiting foreign travel and employment; and there will be no provision for the medical use of marijuana.

Later, at the risk of bringing on Ned's first heart attack, I told him what I'd heard. "Christ almighty," he erupted, "for thirty years we've been trying to get the bloody government to accept the truth: marijuana's safe as churches and it should be legal. What's it going to take to get them to listen—a goddamned war?"

Ned is too much the pacifist hippie to advocate violence. What he—and several million like-minded Canadians—really want is a key to the corridors of power in Ottawa, something to counterbalance powerful lobbies such as the pharmaceutical multinationals, who see marijuana as a threat to their largest market, the users of tranquillizers; the alcohol barons, who must also feel threatened by a potential competitor; and the hundreds, perhaps thousands, of drug enforcement agents and prison personnel who would be in the unemployment lines if pot were legalized. Together, these groups have managed to get drug laws written that protect their interests, despite the findings of the government's own polls that nearly 70 per cent of Canadians support decriminalizing marijuana.

But public opinion has never counted for much in our drug policies. Canadian laws are formulated through a back-room process controlled by senior bureaucrats in the departments of justice and health, and particularly by the RCMP, which has had a choke hold on drug policy since the 1920s. The only liberalizing change in marijuana laws in living memory happened in the late sixties, when pot arrests were soaring and the public was becoming restive about the jailing of young people for simple possession. The Liberal government of the day responded by appointing the Le Dain Commission on the Non-Medical Use of Drugs, which recommended decriminalization. Mindful of angry parents and possible lost votes, Ottawa amended the law to allow conditional and unconditional discharges, causing the number of convictions ending in jail sentences to fall rapidly from 50 to 3 per cent, where it remains today. As for decriminalization, the government introduced legislation in 1975 downgrading possession to a minor offence, but then lost its nerve and let the bill die on the order paper. It was never revived.

In the United States the National Commission on Marijuana and Drug Abuse recommended decriminalization in 1972. The following year Oregon became the first of eleven states to reduce marijuana possession from a felony to a misdemeanour punishable by a ticket and a fine. Both President Jimmy Carter and Prime Minister Pierre Trudeau came out in favour of decriminalization in 1977. But despite an announcement three years later by Trudeau's justice minister, Jean Chrétien, that new laws would soon be on the books, nothing happened. Public attitudes towards marijuana began to harden in response to the rising din of anti-pot propaganda south of the border. Ronald Reagan had launched his "zero tolerance" drug war, which would achieve zero results and cost $30 billion annually by 1995. In lockstep with his U.S. presidential pals (George Bush continued his predecessor's policies), Prime Minister Brian "Me-too" Mulroney proclaimed a drug crisis in Canada in 1987, even though marijuana use had been dropping all through the decade.

Whenever I find myself waxing rancorous about Canadian drug laws, I'm reminded that things could be worse: I could be living in the United States. While the average time served for murder in the U.S. is less than nine years, at least thirty people are serving life sentences, without possibility of parole, for growing or selling marijuana. An Oklahoma man is in jail for life because a fraction of a gram of cannabis was found near his foot on the floor of a friend's apartment. Property—land, vehicles, houses, boats, bank accounts—has been confiscated from persons found innocent or sometimes not even charged. A Vermont family lost a forty-nine-acre farm for growing six pot plants, and in a case currently before the courts an Alabama couple will lose custody of their two young children if convicted of selling clothing made of hemp fiber. U.S. police forces are allowed to retain seized assets for their own budgets and use them for anything from buying new cruisers to raising their salaries. When evidence is insufficient for a criminal conviction, some accused have been assessed an "administrative" fine; a Kentucky man found not guilty of cultivating marijuana still had to pay $12,500 to get his farm back. Under a law recently passed by Congress, anyone convicted of growing more than sixty thousand plants can be *executed*, even for a first offence. Growing one plant in Virginia can get you thirty years behind bars; in Oklahoma, life. Parole for incarcerated drug offenders, a quarter of whom are there for simple possession of marijuana, is blocked by mandatory minimum sentence laws passed by Congress. Pre-empting the discretionary sentencing power of U.S. federal court judges has resulted in such gross miscarriages of justice that many now refuse to try marijuana cases. Killers, rapists and other violent offenders are actually being given early release from overcrowded jails to make room for drug offenders.

Although Canadian law is less draconian, there are definitely places to avoid if you smoke or grow marijuana. Nova Scotia judges still hand out two-year sentences for cultivating forty to fifty plants, and Alberta is pretty tough on cannabis offences. The RCMP spokesman in British Columbia can still call marijuana "the most dangerous narcotic in Canada today" without attracting laughter and finger-pointing on the street. But the average jail sentence for all pot offences in B.C. is less than a day, and a hundred-plant indoor grow show (which will generate $10,000 a month) will cost you no more than $5,000 to $7,000 in fines if you are caught. A criminal record remains the most onerous punishment, though even that is avoidable if the judge can be persuaded to grant you a discharge. In fact, from the grower's standpoint, the present state of marijuana law in Canada is close to ideal. Criminalization keeps prices high and excludes such potential competitors as governments or tobacco companies. With some regional exceptions, Canadian consumers of marijuana have little to fear from police or the courts, and they are still unlikely to be tested for drugs at work, though this odious invasion of privacy is beginning to creep in from the U.S.

It's been said that American drug laws are fostering civil, judicial and penal procedures normally associated with police states. While Canadian policies may be more temperate, they have still been used too often as an excuse to run roughshod over civil rights. From 1929 to 1977 hundreds, perhaps thousands, of law enforcement officers held writs of assistance granted by Canadian courts, giving them carte blanche to conduct searches of any property or person, at any time, without a warrant. Although the writs were declared unconstitutional by the Supreme Court in 1985, untold numbers of Canadians are tagged for life with criminal convictions obtained under them. In 1988 Parliament passed a law making it illegal to advocate or even comment favourably on the use of illegal drugs. Possession of pro-drug literature became a crime. This legislation, without parallel in the Western world, was struck down by the courts in 1994. Police still act as if it were on the books, though, most recently carrying out seizures of drug literature in Saskatchewan. Contrary to the practice enshrined in centuries of common law, police officers on drug raids are not required to knock and announce their presence before entering premises. They say they need this exemption to avoid giving a warning that will allow evidence to be destroyed. But one practical effect of their actions was the death in 1992 of twenty-two-year-old Daniel Possee of North Vancouver, who just happened to have a harmless target pistol in his hand when police barged in. He was shot dead on the spot, his only crime the possession of a few grams of marijuana. Courts normally grant search warrants only on the basis of "reasonable and probable cause" to believe that an offence has been committed. But when it comes to drugs, warrants can be granted even on the basis of anonymous tips, opening the door to all manner of abuse. Bill C-8 extends the power of a drug search warrant to everyone on the premises; a warrant for Toronto's SkyDome, for example, would empower police to strip search all fifty thousand patrons.

To justify these powers, police do a lot of bragging about the quantity and value of the drugs they seize. With marijuana it's tonnage that matters, not arrests, as the judiciary have little enthusiasm for court dockets plugged with pot cases. Busts are tallied in numbers of plants, which the police convert to street value at wildly inflated rates that would be the envy of even the most successful grower. The U.S. Drug Enforcement Administration (DEA) has taken a similar tack, though it is still in hot pursuit of arrests and jail sentences. In 1994 it reported eradicating 508,631,008 pot plants, 99.2 per cent of which were "ditch weed," wild marijuana descended from 300,000 acres of hemp grown during the Second World War under a U.S. government program to replace Asian fiber supplies cut off by the Japanese. As a hemp variety, it has almost no psychoactive content, which begs the question why the DEA would bother trying to eradicate it. Surely they know enough about marijuana to tell rope from dope. Are they simply trying to justify their budget with impressive numbers? Or might they be looking ahead to the possibility that potent psychoactive varieties of pot could hybridize with ditch weed and cover the American hinterland with untold billions of marijuana plants, fecund as flies and free for the taking?

Criminal lawyers specializing in drug cases speculate that a radical change in Canadian drug policy may be in the works, though not because of any moral or philosophical shift on the part of government. Cost-saving will be the motive: the war on drugs is becoming unaffordable. Ottawa admits to spending $270 million a year fighting illicit drugs, but that figure ignores such ancillary costs as courts, judges, counsel, jails, guards, parole services, social workers, treatment, drug-related crime and support for families of jailed offenders. Eric Single, a professor of preventative medicine and biostatistics at the University of Toronto, calculates the full bill for the drug war in Canada at $1.4 billion a year. (His figure for the annual cost of problems generated by alcohol and tobacco is $17 billion.)

To my way of thinking—and many others share this view—drugs themselves do not damage society; the damage is done by laws that force the distribution and use of drugs into a criminal context. By any measure—physical well-being, financial costs, crime rates—the harm done by drugs can be dealt with far better by strategies that treat drugs as a health problem rather than a criminal matter, as other countries have demonstrated. To judge by the rumbles of discontent, this is also the conclusion of more and more of Canada's frontline troops in the drug war. In 1993 the Canadian Police Association, representing forty thousand cops, urged Parliament to remove possession of marijuana from the Criminal Code and make it a misdemeanour—a ticketable offence, no more serious than a traffic infraction. According to my friend Mike Brandt, a former RCMP officer, it's the police forces who have the addiction problem. "They are hooked on the money and career opportunities created by the war on drugs," he says. "They're indoctrinated, not trained in what drugs are really like. Then they are put in this unenviable position where they are looked upon by the public as experts, when they really aren't, and they have no business pretending they are. So they develop a mythology about drugs that will justify their actions. Now, some officers go along with all that for career or ideological reasons. They're gung-ho drug fighters. But a growing number don't. I mean, how often can you arrest the same skid road heroin addicts and still believe in what you are doing? What's the point in busting people for marijuana when the courts don't want them and the law is held in contempt? In my experience, a good many police officers would rather look the other way."

British Columbia's chief coroner, Vince Caine, for twenty-five years an RCMP officer, made much the same argument in his landmark 1995 report, *Illicit Narcotic Overdose Deaths in B.C.* "The war on drugs is an expensive failure," he told a Vancouver newspaper. "We should not be hiring more police. We should not be direct- ing addicts into the courts. We should not be building more jails. Addicts don't need jails. They need *care*. What we have now is a system that's persecuting society's victims."

Prohibitionist politicians frequently cite three international drug treaties, to which Canada is a signatory, as a reason why our drug laws cannot be moderated. But countries of a more tolerant bent, such as Spain, Italy and the Netherlands, have interpreted these treaties much more liberally, so that people there can possess and smoke marijuana without interference. Federal government documents obtained under an access to information application by the magazine *Cannabis Canada* indicate that the treaties in no way prevent us from applying a harm reduction approach to drugs instead of criminal sanctions.

Perhaps if we were less in the shadow of the American elephant, we could learn from other countries. The Dutch, for instance, depenalized marijuana possession in 1976, meaning that they stopped enforcing the law and allowed coffee shops to sell mari- juana and hashish. The rules include a ban on advertising, a min- imum user's age of eighteen, a five-gram limit on transactions, and strict prohibition of other illicit drugs. With more than twelve hundred coffee shops now operating, cannabis use in the Nether- lands remains similar to that in other European countries with much harsher prohibitionist policies. This approach has driven a wedge between sales of pot and so-called hard drugs, reducing heroin and cocaine use to one of the lowest rates in the Western world. If there's a flaw in the system, it's the failure of the Dutch to legalize trafficking or growing in large quantities; coffee shops must still buy their supplies through the back door while the police look the other way. By creating a sanctioned market for an illegal product, the government has provided an irresistible opportunity for organized crime to take over marijuana production and distribution. With so much money on the line, corruption spread to the police, unleashing a scandal in the early nineties that rocked the national government. Dutch officials see full legalization as a remedy, but opposition from prohibitionist countries makes that politically impossible.

Despite the difficulties, the Netherlands has managed to create a refreshingly civilized atmosphere around marijuana. Passing through Amsterdam on a film trip a few years ago, I went to Sensi Seed Company, one of Holland's leading cannabis breeders and seed exporters, to buy a variety that Ned wanted to cross into his own strains. I paid $50 for ten seeds and went on my way. No secrecy, no skulking around in back alleys with dubious characters. Retiring to one of the city's pot bars, I selected a fine Hindu Kush from the marijuana menu and sat back to contemplate the difference a few thousand miles can make. For the harmless diversion I was pursuing, a hundred people are convicted every day in Canada and saddled with criminal records. For the same offence in the United States, there are people rotting in jail until they die.

After a week of waiting for two sets of parts that didn't fit, Henry the Ford is finally ready to resume his duties on the mountain. And none too soon. With the summer solstice in sight, the sun is strong enough to dry out my plants in a matter of days. Although I've been dipping water from the pond for the transplants by the skid road, without the truck there's nothing to be done if the other gardens begin to wilt. But in the Hillside Garden this morning, I find my charges standing straight, their leaves lush and beaded with dew. Marijuana puts out a huge root system, and these youngsters have likely already plumbed the depths of their five-gallon pots, where the moisture will last for a week or more.

On my way back from the garden, I sit for a while on a stump by the road to watch for the red-tailed hawks whose mating I witnessed in April. They built, or perhaps refurbished, a nest on the ridge in a dense knot of limbs just beneath the crown of an old-growth fir, a vantage point commanding a broad sweep of slash below. Red-tails don't appear to use these lookouts as hunting sites, as bald eagles do. All along the coast, eagles can be seen perching close to their nest for hours at a time, ready to swoop down on any likely meal. The hawks hunt on the wing, silently quartering the open ground or sometimes calling loudly, perhaps to startle small animals into movement that will give them away.

Even though the nest is too high and well hidden to see, I can hear the rusty peep-and-croak of young chicks, like the cracking voices of adolescent choirboys. They must be old enough by now to be left alone, as both adults are away foraging this morning. It seems, though, that no matter where they are on the mountain, the parents keep a sharp eye on the nest. Ten days ago when I was here a young bald eagle came gliding past, and both adult hawks plummeted down from the ridge with their talons extended, harrying the intruder all the way across the valley.

Aside from rubbernecking for birds, I'm hard at it today transplanting my extra seedlings, now more than a foot tall and bursting out of their four-inch plastic pots. These orphans are making a lot more work than I expected when I so blithely rescued them from early extinction. First, I've had to mix another whole truckload of soil. Then pack it, a gallon peat pot under each arm, into the gardens along the old skid road above the pond. And this is not the end. Since these containers are too small to support a big root system, I'll have to transplant them all again, either as replacements for males in five-gallon pots or into their own big containers.

In the course of replacing plants that succumb occasionally to slugs or causes unknown, I've devised a transplanting technique that I like to think is ingenious. Transplanting four-inch pots is easy: wet the soil, pack it down firmly, turn the pot over, tap the bottom and out pop plant and soil as a cube in your hand. But when it comes to transplanting from gallon peat pots, there is too much soil to handle without it crumbling and disturbing the roots. My invention employs two lengths of stove pipe, one six inches in diameter and the other four. Pressing the larger pipe deep into the pot around the plant, I lift out a solid plug of soil containing the plant with roots intact. If the soil is damp, the plug will not crumble away at the bottom. In the five-gallon pot where a plant has died, I dig a hole a bit larger than the plug. Then, taking care not to crush the transplant, I slide the smaller stovepipe down inside the larger and push the plug out intact. To keep the smaller pipe from cutting into the roots I tin-snipped half-inch slits around its bottom end, bent tabs at right angles to the pipe, and presto! a new plant in the big pot, with nary a trace of the wilting and delayed growth that often follows transplanting.

Nothing, it seems, can hold marijuana back for long, so indomitable is its will to grow. In the last days of May, less than six weeks after seeding, my largest plants are two feet tall, with stalks as thick as my thumb. Plants confined by the four-inch pots are smaller but show their expansive drive by massing roots across the bottom and up the sides of the containers, like prisoners trying to break down the walls of their cell. You wonder what these plants could do, given unlimited feeding, space and sunlight. Ned, whom I tend to believe, told me of harvesting more than a pound of buds from a twelve-foot giant he once grew on top of a pit containing a pickup load of manure. An American, whom I met in an upcoast inlet and tended not to believe, claimed to have grown plants on the Kona coast of Kauai that took ten months to mature, reached a height of sixteen feet and had trunks as thick as a man's thigh. The largest plants I've seen were about ten feet tall, though they were leggy and sparse, more like hemp varieties than psychoactive marijuana. I've toyed with the idea of growing my own whopper, but I guess I'm too sceptical to try it. The result, I fear, would be the cannabis equivalent of those bloated pumpkins that are now all the rage with competitive gardeners—a thousand pounds of sagging mush with the flavour of cork. Anyone can grow a big pot plant, but I suspect there's a price to be paid in the quantity and size of buds or quality of the high. It was ever thus: no free lunch, and more's the pity.

CHAPTER 6

BUMMERS
AND
BENDERS

There are few things I enjoy more in this province of contrasts than driving from Vancouver to the Interior on a day of rainy coastal gloom. When I crest Allison Pass, an hour east and five thousand feet above the Fraser Valley, it's as if I had just landed after a flight to some distant part of the country. Within miles, the drizzle abates, the choking rainforest gives way to open parklands and the air is suddenly dry and keen in the nostrils, making me feel like bounding over the surrounding peaks. Then, somewhere in the high country along the road to Princeton, an arch opens in the clouds ahead and I burst through into sunlight, cobalt skies and far-off vistas of golden grass, rolling east like heaving seas to the horizon. At Keremeos, well and truly in the Interior now, I turn south and follow the Similkameen River, coiling as smoothly as its spoken name through ranchland and orchards. Across Richter's green pass, I drop down to Osoyoos in the desert country of the southern Okanagan, a transition so sudden that my jacket in the back seat is still damp with Vancouver's morning rain.

My destination is the Kettle River Valley, an hour east of the Okanagan. My youngest son, Raul, lives there in a house my parents built in the early 1970s on a high, dry bench of bunchgrass and ponderosa pines. He runs a one-man guiding outfit, drifting the Kettle and teaching people how to cast a fly or handle a canoe in the river. As lovely as any river in the province, the Kettle is an eastern sort of stream, gliding with a summery sigh through jade fields of alfalfa, pine forests and cool cottonwood tunnels, dappled with sunlight. Accompanied by Devon, my young grandson, Raul and I pass long, languid days on the river, drifting flies over green pools, lunching on sandbars and snoozing to the soughing of the hot west wind in the pines. Many happy hours I spend with Devon, reading aloud, trading jokes, flopping in the tiny swimming pool by the house and contemplating the wisdom of those aboriginal cultures that turn the first-born child over to its grandparents to raise as the joy and consolation of their old age.

It is mid-June by the time I return to the Peninsula, and I'm on the mountain early, eagerly anticipating prodigious growth in my plants. Cresting the knoll above the Pocket Garden, I see that the gate is ajar, and just inside, a pot is tipped over and its plant missing. My first thought is "bear," but as I come down the hill, wading through a sea of dewy salal, I can see more empty pots and others overturned. No bear has done this. Only the human animal is capable of such methodical destruction. One glance inside the fence tells all: every last plant has been yanked out by the roots and carted away, sixty in all.

This, of all my gardens, is the one I least expected to lose. It is farthest from the road, and the slash—a hell of thorns, brush and pitfalls—the worst to cross. So who found it, and how? It's too late in the season for some other grower to blunder onto the garden while looking for a place to plant his own dope. And it is months too early for pot thieves to be on the mountain; there's no crop yet to steal. That leaves only one possibility: a pilot must have spotted the patch from the air and reported it to the RCMP.

So, what did he see? Probably not the plants; they are still pretty small to show from any distance, and their colour blends well with the new foliage on the salal. That leaves the deer fence or the pots, or both. From the side, the fence is all but invisible; from above, it might appear as a black rectangle. Which means that the fences will have to come down, every fence in every garden. Other than a great waste of time, this is no loss, for Ned tells me (now he tells me!) that deer usually don't eat marijuana here on the Peninsula. It's on the Gulf Islands, where food is severely limited and the deer overpopulated, that fences are a must. My pots are also suspect. Sun-bleached to a silvery grey, they can probably be seen from a thousand feet. More work: I'll paint them flat brown—all one hundred and God-knows-how-many of them. As for the Pocket Garden, it's a write-off, the first place the cops will check from the air come harvest time.

A long day takes care of the fences and pots, but I'm not through yet. Losing a whole garden sticks in my craw, and I don't intend to lose another. On the powerline, where they have no future, I cut a tottering truckload of alder saplings eight to ten feet tall. These I jam upright into the ground between the pots, creating a canopy that will provide camouflage, yet still let in the sun when their leaves wither after a few days. I gather armloads of bracken and pack it around the plants to hide the soil, which turns conspicuously black when wet. Draped over the edge of the pots, the bracken makes my painting largely redundant, though it has an added benefit as mulch to slow the evaporation of precious water when the hot weather comes. Finally, I go back once again over all the trails I made when the gardens were first developed, training bracken and fireweed across the paths and dragging in brush to discourage anyone from passing. This, too, is probably wasted effort, for I haven't used these trails in two months (I get to the gardens by roundabout routes, changing them frequently), and they are already heavily overgrown.

On the evening of the solstice, I sit for a long time on the deck, taking stock after an eventful week. The sun at this season sets way to the north around the point so that I can see only its fiery corona, caught in the ragged old firs on the bluff, and insects milling slowly against the light. In the stillness, distant voices come thin across the water, and somewhere out in Malaspina Strait I can hear the sleepy mewing of gulls.

I realize now how tired I am. Ever since the Pocket Garden was ripped off, I've been flying around like a fart in a gale, trying to make my little enterprise secure. I've become jumpy and suspicious, conjuring up cops or thieves every time I see a footprint, which usually turns out to be my own. These are symptoms of pot grower's paranoia, a disease endemic to the trade, for which the treatment, if not cure, is frequent repetition of the following homily: growing marijuana outdoors is a game, not a business, and, as with all games of chance from roulette to racing, you shouldn't play if you can't afford to lose. Losing entails more than mere money. It means being able to take your lumps with a grin and a shrug. There's no harm in creeping around like some latter-day Natty Bumppo, hiding trails and looking for footprints. Men are, after all, just small boys grown large. But come police or pestilence, I tell myself, never forget that dope farming is only an adult version of cops and robbers. If it seems more serious than that, then it's time you smoked a fat bomber and put things back in perspective.

Good medicine, though I don't seem able to apply it to myself with any consistency. As the plants shoot up and I see promise of handsome returns for my labours, I've become fiercely protective of my gardens. My stratagems for camouflage are harmless enough;

it's the feeling of hostility towards strangers that I don't like in myself. I meet them often on the main logging road at the bottom of the mountain, men with kids usually, out looking for firewood or somewhere to fish. Stopping to shoot the breeze, I manage to be friendly, though I have a nasty sensation of skating on thin ice over an undercurrent of suspicion. If they say anything about going up the mountain, worry will twitch for days at the corners of my mind until I return to check my plants. I should worry less about my gardens and more about the law. When the police scooped the Pocket Garden I thought only of my lost plants, while Carole's concern was that I could have been caught and charged with cultivation for the purpose of trafficking. With the plants on public land, I'd have to be found *in flagrante delicto* for a charge to stick. Even so, Carole is right when she says I'm too blasé about the police. I'm like a frog in a pot of water; turn up the heat slowly enough and the frog will sit there without moving until it's cooked. The enemy is gradualism, danger that comes on so slowly the defensive mechanisms of fear and flight are never triggered. That can happen, *is* happening to me as I tend my marijuana with no more thought for my own security than a farmer among his turnips.

Out of some warped sense of social obligation I've accepted an invitation to a party tonight. I should know better. For me, "let's party" are two of the most dismal words in the English language. When I arrive (late), I can hear the shouting and stomping from the nearest parking spot, half a block away. Shouldering through the crowd, I recognize a few people and try to talk. But the hog-slaughter music is so loud conversation is reduced to mutual bellowing. After half an hour, things are going downhill fast. Someone spills a bowl of chili and everyone walks it into the shag carpet. There is a fight on the patio, and one of the combatants puts an elbow through a window, cutting himself. A girl has been sick in the bathroom and passed out on the floor, so no one can get at the toilet. This is all known and familiar, a scene I once revelled in, drunk and stupid as anyone here. But what really throws me is the dope smoking, great fat joints going round and round between people so hammered they can hardly find their mouths. Short of a public hanging, I can't imagine a worse place to be stoned.

I get out as the cops are coming in; the neighbours have had enough and phoned in a complaint. At home, feeling a bit of a wet blanket, I make myself a cup of tea and sit mulling over the way marijuana seems to be misused so often. It is a psychedelic, after all, which comes from Greek words meaning "mind-expanding." When you're stoned you are wide open, all your senses picking up the most subtle nuances. In that state, I want to be damned sure my surroundings are as pleasant as I know how to make them.

Over the years I've cobbled together my own rules and ritual, mostly borrowed from friends with a long and healthy relationship to pot. First, I try to smoke for positive, not negative, reasons. If I'm in a lousy mood I'll take a drink, not a toke. Second, I've watched myself closely to learn what smoking regimen works best for me—the times, places, frequency and dosage—and I try to stick to it like glue. Me, not marijuana, has to be the boss. Third, although pleasure is its own sufficient purpose, I endeavour to go quietly and make space for wonders of a different order that marijuana can reveal. As for my ritual, it's grounded in the recognition that I can't be stoned and function intellectually, or at least I have no desire to try. No reading, no complex tasks. Which means that I don't smoke unless the track ahead is clear—an afternoon on the water or at the beach, or an evening of good food, music and carnal delights. No phone calls, no work. If there's a problem this regimen doesn't address, it's the munchies; for an aging and incipient porky, I eat too much when I'm stoned, though I do try to keep a tight rein on the booze. Mixing dope with a lot of alcohol is like trying to run in opposite directions at the same time. One is a sensitizer and the other a depressant. Admittedly, the first thing I do after lighting a joint is open a beer, preferably one of my mud-brown Bass. But one is enough; any more and the alcohol gets in the way.

Toking up has a sense of occasion for me. Once or twice a week, more often on vacation, I like to clear the decks and make an evening of it. I don't enjoy smoking casually between times, a puff here, a puff there, so that I am neither stoned nor straight. But that's just me; I know people who smoke all day every day and handle it as well or better than I do. Ned, for instance. He takes a puff every hour or two, keeping his mood exactly where he wants it, and yet he is probably never really stoned. He manages this with a kind of control over his appetites that I can only envy. He will nurse a single bottle of beer over an entire evening. Though he's never without his tobacco and papers, he seems to go through no more than half a dozen cigarettes a day.

Recently, I watched this process when Ned and I were working together, setting up a small marijuana garden on Nelson Island. (I've finally succumbed to his blandishments, agreeing to lend a hand until he finds a boat.) Ned is so paranoid about thieves he insisted that we locate the pots a quarter mile inland and several hundred feet above sea level. It was brutal work, carrying eighty-pound loads of soil in a back pack all the way from the beach. Before we got started, Ned lit up a joint and offered me a drag.

"No thanks," I told him. "It just makes me more conscious of my complaining body."

"Funny," Ned said, "it has just the opposite effect on me. If I keep a little buzz on, I can put my body on autopilot and let it do the work. Then my head is free to bugger off and think of something else."

"Sort of like coca leaves?"

"No, I don't think it gives me any more energy. It just closes a door somewhere in my brain so that I don't hear all the bitching and complaining coming from the rest of me."

I notice that there are limits to this. When Ned gets really tired, he collapses like a pricked balloon and moans pathetically. Nor does marijuana do anything to insulate him against the cold, to which he is unusually sensitive. Messing around in the bush too long, we failed to keep tabs on the rising tide, so I had to peel off my clothes and swim out to the anchored boat in bitterly cold water. By the time I got back to the beach, flushed an angry pink, Ned was hunched on a log, looking as if he was about to succumb to vicarious hypothermia.

On occasions like this, alcohol has no substitute. Years ago, when over-proof rum was sold in B.C. liquor stores, it was a staple on all my canoe trips, the jolt (with brown sugar, hot water and lemon) that stood me upright after a killing day on the water and a plunge in a glacial stream. Alcohol is wonderful stuff, as stories and songs from every land in every age will attest. For thirty years I drank as much and often as I could, and I would still be at it, were it not for bottomless morning-after depressions that welled up and threatened to engulf me in the early eighties. Much as I revelled in the wild, uninhibited energy of alcohol, I was always conscious that boozing is like trying to ride the crest of a wave—it's great while you're on top but impossible to stay there for long. One drink too few and your high goes flat; two or three too many and the whirlies begin. The penalties for getting it wrong are severe: green-bile mornings, wasted days and the nagging five o'clock tug of impending addiction. When I set that against red eyes, a dry mouth and a slightly increased pulse rate—the only acute symptoms of marijuana use—it's no contest: pot is a better deal. Short of death, there are no limits to alcohol's effect; the more you drink the drunker you get. With pot, there's no such incentive to overindulge. When the receptors in the brain are plugged with THC—and this takes only a few tokes of good weed—you can't get any higher. You may get sleepy or muzzy in the head, but when you are stoned you are stoned, and that's it. You are on top of the wave and can count on staying there for at least a couple of hours.

I make one exception to my rule about never mixing marijuana with work: if I'm groping for a way to break a logjam in writing, smoking will often do the trick. But it's not something I set up in a calculated way, lighting a joint and waiting for the divine afflatus to descend. It usually occurs quite unexpectedly in the course of a relaxing evening; after a few tokes a solution to something I've been struggling with just pops into my head. I suspect this happens to many people. The idea for one of the best Canadian novels of 1997 originated in this way, and its author even credited me in the book's acknowledgements with "material inspiration" for the marijuana I had given him.

Deane, a friend who's a philosophy professor, put me on to this. Three or four times a week he tokes up and takes a long walk in the woods. "The motion is meditative," he told me when I asked him about it, "so my body can be exercising while I think, usually about my work. I find that if I've been concentrating on a particular problem for a while and then I get high, I am able to see it in different lights, find creative solutions."

Any rhythmic physical activity, such as running, sawing wood or rowing a boat, can have the same effect. Jogging used to give me some useful insights. But it wasn't as reliable as marijuana. Pounding along some seawall or trail, I'd get an idea, though rarely more than its bare outlines; stoned, I'm free of distractions and can explore the inspiration in detail. A while ago, when I was searching for a descriptive key to the cryptic iconography of Northwest Coast Indian design, a set of vividly evocative pre-European images came to me after smoking. I found myself in an abandoned Haida village on Haida Gwaii, the Queen Charlotte Islands, where I had once camped, only now I saw the place in all its aboriginal splendour, massive cedar houses lining the cove, women drying herring roe, children playing at the water's edge and men at work on a great sea-going canoe. I don't believe for a moment that marijuana is the source of such images; it is merely a facilitator, opening channels to the subconscious. Ideas rise spontaneously like wine bubbling from a fountain, though they are sometimes more plonk than Chateauneuf du Pape. Since when I'm stoned they all seem brilliant, I make a habit of jotting them down and reserving judgement for the cold light of day.

Once or twice I've tried to write on pot, and the results were garbage. Stoned, you're in an intuitive mental gear; giving form and substance to stoned ideas requires a different, in fact opposite, state of mind. One is inspiration, the other execution. Any creative act —building, writing, applying paint to canvas, composing or playing music, cooking—is a rational process of highly developed craftsmanship. Some artists have chosen to ignore this, striving while under the influence to capture the wild imagery of psychedelic trips. The results are usually a mess. Although I know a few artists who do exquisite work while mildly stoned, I suspect that, like Ned, they smoke to maintain a comfortable buzz, rather than looking to pot to guide the hand that shapes the perfect line.

At the end of June hot weather arrives, and with it a plague of biting flies that make working on the slash a little hell. By mid-morning the sun brings out the insects and the old skid road is humming like an aerodrome. Carrying water from the pond to my transplants, I'm soon soaked with sweat and set upon as an ambulatory banquet for deerflies and horseflies. The bug repellent with which I'm smeared from head to boot tops (I've been wearing shorts since April) only serves to attract them, like bees to nectar. While the horseflies bite hardest, it's the green-eyed deerflies that drive me nearly mad, swarming around my head with an unnerving whine, perfectly pitched for psychological warfare. Both kinds of flies bite through my shirt with ease, pitting my back as if I'd been hit from behind with a charge of birdshot.

More fun with the bears as well. I've been piling up plastic garbage pails in my gardens as containers for water, once I begin hauling it in the truck. At the Hillside Garden, I find the pails scattered every which way and punctured with tooth and claw holes, apparently the work of a suburban bear used to foraging for garbage. He is also a collector, for one of the garbage pails has disappeared altogether, lugged away into the bush. Perhaps he imagines it will be miraculously filled with things to eat, much as South Seas cargo cults built airfields in the hope that planes would land, laden with chocolate bars and cigarettes. As a parting gesture, the bear knocked over a large plant, which has continued to grow quite happily on its side so that all the branches are turned up to the light. Some growers do this deliberately, forcing their plants to throw extra shoots and grow closer to the ground, where they are harder to see from the air. But I could never humble my plants this way; I glory too much in their green energy reaching for the sun.

Order restored, I'm climbing back to the road when I turn to see seven mature bald eagles wheeling together over the slash, their white heads and tails gleaming against the ultramarine waters of the strait. For long minutes, the group hangs together, holding their positions as if tethered like kites. The attraction, perhaps, is a dead deer or carcass of some other animal, though I can see nothing below them, no ravens, vultures or other scavengers. Eventually, five of the eagles rise and go their separate ways, while the last two launch into a flat glide, shearing wing to wing across the wind towards Vancouver Island, diminishing finally to black specks against the towering cumulus.

Aggregations of eagles are common on the coast, though not in this place or season. Adults like these should normally be closely tied to their nests for another month by the food demands of their chicks. But the behaviour of bald eagles in B.C. has been anything but normal in recent years. Surveys by the Canadian Wildlife Service have found that the production of chicks, which usually averages one to three per nest, is far below that level, even in some of their most pristine habitats. In Clayoquot Sound on Vancouver Island's west coast, for example, only one chick is being fledged for every ten nests. There are at least two possible explanations. Over-fishing of everything from herring to halibut has stripped these waters of most of their aboriginal abundance, leaving perhaps too little food for eagles to mate and raise a brood. Pollution could also be the cause. Bald eagles are thriving in B.C.'s Lower Mainland, the most heavily settled and grossly contaminated part of the province, largely by scavenging dead farm animals and garbage dumps and by preying on waterfowl attracted to farmers' fields. So productive are these eagles, their offspring have moved out to colonize unspoiled areas, possibly taking with them contaminants that prevent them from breeding successfully. Or, as some scientists suspect, hormone imbalances inherited from their parents may render them barren for life. Could this explain the gathering of eagles I have just witnessed?

Later in the day, walking in the green tunnel of alders below Number Three Garden, I hear the screech of a red-tailed hawk, and I stop to listen. The sound seems to be coming from low down in the dense foliage just ahead, not a place I'd expect to find a large hawk. Again and again it calls, and then I hear a tiny bell-like sound at the end of each vocalization. As I move closer, there is a fluttering, a glimpse of upright crest and a flash of deepest blue. It is, of course, a Steller's jay, the greatest mimic in the western forest. This bird moves with sly furtiveness, following you unseen, appearing when you least expect it and speaking in strange tongues. Under the straight-down winter rain, its plumage turns nearly black, as if touched by the stain of melanism that runs through many species west of the mountains. Though these are characteristics of the supernatural beings who haunt the coastal mountains and inlets of Native imagination, the Steller's jay has no place in the Indian pantheon—or at least none that I know of. The role of conniving joker belongs to its close cousin, Raven.

June 28. My fifty-eighth birthday, and a fine day it is. After a soft morning on the mountain I go for a long swim and loll like a seal in the sun on the deck, thinking what a momentous year this has been. After forty years as a slave of overweening ambition and fear of failure, I've been set free. I have been given back my life, and what am I doing with it? Growing dope on a mountain like an aging hippie. Ten years ago, or even five, I would not have believed it possible. But here I am, happier and healthier than ever before. Sweet are the fruits of noble endeavours.

CHAPTER 7

GREEN GENES

First watering. Growing as they are in peat pots, my plants are close to wilting after two hot rainless weeks. This is to be the test run for the Rube Goldberg system I've rigged up for hauling and pumping water from the truck.

I have joined four 40-gallon plastic barrels together with polyethylene pipe to make a reservoir that can be filled and emptied through a single outlet. This, in turn, is hooked up to 250 feet of hose on a homemade reel mounted at the back of the truck. Downhill, the water will be gravity-fed; uphill it is to be lifted by a 3,500-gallon-per-hour bilge pump, powered by the truck battery. All of this paraphernalia is hidden beneath a canopy with the windows blacked out to discourage prying eyes, because no one could mistake this for anything but a dope-watering system.

At the Hillside Garden the water flows swiftly down the ravine, and within an hour all my plants get a welcome drink, two buckets for each big pot and one each for the smaller replacement plants. An hour to drive home and refill, and Henry the Ford is once again labouring up the mountain with 1,500 pounds of water aboard. On the highway, my day is made by a discreet sign on a septic tank pump-out truck: "Your shit is our bread and butter."

At Number Three Garden, there are difficulties. The patch is up a steep bank, so I have to use the pump. But I haven't made the wires long enough to reach the truck battery, and I have to jury-rig an extension with rusty jumper cables that make a poor, sputtering connection. Up among the plants, the water takes forever to come through the hose and then runs very slowly. The pump is supposed to lift twenty vertical feet but seems near its limit at what I estimate to be no more than fifteen above the intake. Two hours drag by before everything is watered and the tanks pumped dry.

Wearily in the gathering dusk, I unhook the wires and shut off the truck, which I've left running so as not to get stuck here with a flat battery. As I step out into the evening quiet I hear a sound that freezes me in my tracks: there is a vehicle on the road, and it's coming this way. At almost the same instant, headlights begin to show beyond a screen of alders overgrowing the road about a hundred feet away. Sweet Jesus! I'm caught with the hose out and wires running everywhere like spilled spaghetti. Scooting around to the back of the truck, I start cranking furiously on the reel, bringing the hose hissing through the underbrush like a scalded snake. I stuff the last of it into the canopy, slam down the door and run for the front of the truck, hoping to intercept my visitors before they are close enough to figure out what's going on. The advancing headlights have slowed to a crawl (the driver is trying not to scratch his pickup) and are just now pushing through the last of the alders. Yanking the jumpers off the wires, I throw them under the hood and walk towards the lights with a palms-up shrug that I hope will say, "Aw shucks, fellas, sorry to get in your way."

There are two good old boys in the truck, with matching beer bellies, baseball caps and cans of Kokanee clenched in meaty paws. "We're lookin' for huckleberries," one of them says, though that's obviously just an excuse to cruise around and sink a few cool ones on a hot evening. The huckleberries won't be ripe for another month. I feed them a cock-and-bull story about taking pictures, and they seem convinced, probably less by me than by the film company sign on the door of my truck. (Filmmaking is my cover, complete with tripod and 16 mm film cans on the front seat.) "Nope," I tell them, "I haven't seen a single berry, and there's nothing I'd like better right now than a huckleberry pie." Unless it's one of the cold beers I can see in an ice chest behind the seat.

After they've gone I sit for a while on the tailgate of the truck, counting my lucky stars and taking deep breaths of the cool breeze dropping out of the timber on the ridge. Tomorrow, for sure, I'll buy a battery so that I don't have to leave the truck running to pump water.

A few days later, after a morning weeding grass, buttercups, potato seedlings and gluttonous squash plants (survivors from the compost) out of the pots, I walk down from the skid road through head-high bracken to eat lunch by the pond. Every day, I pick out an attractive place to nosh—a boulder looking east to the mountains, a stump facing onto the strait, green shade under the alders —and sit quietly watching the passing scene. The menu is an unvarying fat boy's special: sliced tomatoes and tofu with balsamic vinegar and olive oil, nine-grain bread as heavy as sliced porridge, and green tea, a pricey variety called pinhead gunpowder.

Except for hasty visits to scoop out water for the transplants, I haven't been to the pond since I saw life stirring here in March. It is much changed. A forest of water plants has grown from the bottom, spreading yellow water lilies and pondweed with leaves like purple spearheads on the surface. Grasses and reeds bend low over the tannin-stained water, roofing dark caverns under the banks. As I watch, in part through eight-power binoculars, a tapestry of life unrolls before me in sharp closeup.

Black whirligig beetles are spinning frantically on the surface, pairs swinging their partners like square dancers. There are two kinds of water boatman (perhaps one of them a backswimmer), rowing with hairy, oarlike legs just beneath the surface film. A brown newt (or is it a salamander?) gulps an air bubble at the surface, flashes an orange belly and fades again into the murk. A spider with a body as round and white as a hailstone scampers over the surface film, while another, narrow-bodied and surphur-yellow, spins its web in the grass at the water's edge. As I'm watching a tiny green frog climb a reed, an inch-long brown beetle pops to the surface for air just beneath it. This creature I recognize as a water tiger, a fearsome apparition of hooked forelegs and shell armour, one of a family of voracious diving beetles that are the scourge of life in ponds. Here, too, are dragonfly nymphs, armed like the beetles with sharp hooks, though these hooks are appended not to their legs but to a deadly "mask" that they shoot forward from beneath their jaws to spear their prey. Down deep—which is only about three feet—I glimpse the occasional two-inch fish darting through the weeds. Sticklebacks, I suspect, and wonder how on earth they ever got to this oversized puddle, which is too small to have either an inlet or an outlet. Cruising for mosquitoes over the pond are at least five species of dragonflies, a delicate sky-blue variety and another in hot vermilion (actually damselflies, close cousins of the dragons), a large kind dressed in darker blue, an even bigger black model, and a short, thick-bodied species with yellow sides and head.

Absorbed in all this, I fail to notice a black and red ant on my bare leg until it gives me a sharp nip. I swat it away and it lands in open water, well out in the pond. Four or five feet away, a group of water striders take no notice at first. But when the tiny ripples made by the ant's impact reach them, they home in quickly for the kill. One strider seizes the ant and dashes away in a series of eight-inch leaps—the equivalent of Jesse Owens broadjumping a hundred feet—with two other striders in hot pursuit. Under a microscope, you can see the hairy pads at the end of their middle and hind legs that prevent water striders from breaking through the surface film. My guess is that these pads also act as sensors for vibrations that come like Morse code along the tympanic membrane of the surface film; how else could the striders differentiate the ripples created by the struggling ant from all the other activity that keeps the pond in constant motion?

Beneath its open face the pond is largely a closed book to me, a stage for secret lives I will never understand. And that's fine. As a fly fisherman, I've aspired to some small understanding of aquatic life. But half of the twenty-five major groups of insects on the planet, embracing some 751,000 known species and at least as many unidentified, live in fresh water. Making analysis and identification a condition of my enjoyment would be a recipe for frustration. Sometimes it's enough simply to watch and wonder.

Heading home after a hot afternoon, I pull on my T-shirt and see the brand name on the label. "Beefy," it reads. It's one of those little gifts that Carole is forever giving me. "Strange brand name for a shirt," I told her. "Listen, stupid," she said, "that's not the brand, it's the size."

By mid-July, after a month of almost unbroken fine weather, my plants are well advanced in the stage that indoor growers call "vegging." This is the time before the flowers begin to form, when marijuana maximizes long hours of sunlight and nitrogen-rich fertilizers to put on its most spectacular spurt of growth. In the big pots, the plants now average four to five feet tall and as much as three feet in diameter.

Marijuana is an exquisite plant—graceful, symmetrical, tough enough to make rope, delicate enough to dip its elegantly serrated leaves to the slightest breeze. Its green is so vividly alive it stands out like cold fire against all the other hues and shades on the slash. Sometimes I thrust my face into its foliage just for the pleasure of inhaling the exotic perfume. Taking enormous satisfaction in seeing my plants respond to the care I give them, I like to imagine that they do this not just as dumb vegetables sucking up water and fertilizer but as sentient beings that can be stimulated by my affection. This may not be as nutty as it sounds. I've been reading up on a controversy that I remembered vaguely from the late 1960s. Cleve Backster, a New York expert on polygraph (lie detector) testing, hooked electrodes from one of his machines to a dracaena plant in his office and recorded some astonishing responses. The plant reacted, not only to Backster's actions, such as burning a leaf, but also to his *thoughts* about doing so. The discovery led Backster to a long series of experiments and finally to the conclusion that plants are sentient, sharing some kind of cellular consciousness that is common to all life. His findings, published in 1969, made newspaper headlines around the world and touched off a spate of skits, cartoons and lampoons, not to mention people chatting up their plants.

One of the more interesting responses came from the Russians, who pooh-poohed Backster's work as old hat. (The Soviets, in those years, were claiming to have invented everything from the telephone to the hot dog.) In the 1950s they had monitored plants with instruments sensitive enough to tell them when a plant wanted to drink, whether it craved nourishment or was too hot or cold. In partial support of Backster's findings, a Soviet scientist said: "That plants are able to perceive the surrounding world is a truth as old as the world itself. Without perception, adaptation does not and cannot exist. If plants had no sense organs and didn't have a means of transmitting and processing information with their own language and memory, they would inevitably perish." This endorsement of his theories must have pleased Backster, though it stopped short of affirming his most bizarre claim, that plants can detect human thoughts and emotions and reflect them in metabolic changes.

Backster's work, and that of others who followed him, is chronicled in a fascinating 1973 book, *The Secret Life of Plants*, by Peter Tompkins and Christopher Bird. After close perusal, I have decided to reserve judgement on the question of whether my plants are reading my mind. But I intend, like the lifelong atheist who undergoes a death-bed conversion just in case, to think nothing but kindly, nurturing thoughts in the presence of my charges. Banished for the nonce is all contemplation of the coming day of execution, when I will chop them all off at the ankles and hang them upside down to dry.

Back in June when they were about eighteen inches tall and just beginning to surge ahead, I pinched out the center leaf bud of some plants to force more growth into secondary branches. The immediate effect was impressive: a bushier structure with three to five leaders, instead of just one dominant central stalk. But over a whole season, I question whether this practice makes any difference; each marijuana strain seems to revert to its own genetically programmed conformation as it matures. Pinching or pruning late in the season is not a good idea, as the plant's hormonal balance shifts from vegetative to reproductive growth, and it is unlikely to respond.

Mid-July, the peak of vegging, is also the time when the guessing begins: which are female plants and which are male? Telling them apart is no trick once the sex organs are formed. The males have small, pendulous five-petalled flowers with pollen-bearing stamens, and the females develop calyxes with a pair of spiky pistils. But waiting that long—into August or even September with some plodding individuals—is costly. The sooner the males can be identified and replaced with females, the more time the chosen plants will have to put on growth in the bigger pots before flowering begins. Unfortunately, male and female flowers both form in the same spot, at the nexus of branch and trunk, and for weeks they can look confusingly alike even to the most experienced grower. There are other sexual indicators. Male plants tend to grow tall and spindly, females short and bushy, though a month or more after your plants are sexed that enormous fat mother you were counting on to produce eight ounces of buds can still turn out to be yet another cursed male.

The uncertainty is compounded by the bewildering proliferation of marijuana varieties. As Ned explains, all these strains have been crossed and recrossed so many times you can't predict how a plant will grow or mature until you've worked with a variety for several years. Even then, you can get big differences between individual plants of the same variety, because they sometimes throw back to traits bred into them generations ago. Experts in marijuana genetics don't consider a variety to be stable until it has been bred back to itself for three successive generations.

Ned should know. He's been messing about with marijuana strains for more than twenty years, crossing and selecting and crossing again, until he gets something he likes. In his quest for the perfect smoke, he is in the company of untold thousands of pioneers who have made marijuana one of the greatest success stories in the annals of modern horticulture.

Twenty-five years ago, virtually all the marijuana consumed in North America was imported. Most of it came from Mexico, then increasingly from Colombia, with lesser quantities from Thailand, Panama and elsewhere. While a few of the imports were excellent, most were ordinary at best, often badly cured and always mixed with seeds, as much as 50 per cent by weight. Even so, imported weed was still considered to be better than "home grown," a pejorative for pot that no one smoked if they could avoid it. This was, in part, a bum rap. By the early 1970s breeders, mainly in California, were producing some excellent new varieties, with names like Purple Haze, Polly, Eden Gold, Maui Wowie, Kona Gold and Bur Sur Holy Weed, though they supplied only a tiny fraction of the booming North American market.

The breakthrough for domestic growers came in 1975, thanks to a chicken-brained idea hatched by the American Drug Enforcement Administration. The United States and Mexico joined in a program to spray Mexican marijuana fields with paraquat, a highly toxic herbicide that causes lung fibrosis and death if swallowed, even in small doses. With imported marijuana suddenly suspect, millions of Americans went looking for safer alternatives. At the same time, the U.S. Coast Guard and the paramilitary Border Patrol stepped up efforts to cut off the flow of imported drugs. In response, many smugglers turned to cocaine, which was much easier to conceal, leaving the domestic marijuana market to local growers. The track was clear, and the fledgling American marijuana industry never looked back.

To this point, marijuana in North America, whether imported or locally grown, was all *Cannabis sativa* (literally, hemp useful), an equatorial strain of tall, sparse plants with narrow leaves of green to yellowish-green. At its best, it was superb dope, characterized by a clear, cerebral high, but it had one serious limitation: *sativa* could not withstand frost and would not flower reliably north of about 30 degrees latitude.

Fanning out across the globe, American growers sought hardier strains that would flower at higher latitudes. In Afghanistan, they found what they were looking for: *Cannabis indica*, a hardy, early-maturing variety selected over many centuries by Afghani farmers for its disease resistance, large buds and heavy load of resin, which they converted to hashish. *Indica* was shorter and bushier than *sativa*, its leaves thicker and dark green to purple, and the high was a heavy "body" stone, prized by many smokers for sex, eating and deep relaxation. From these two strains, *sativa* and *indica*, growers around the world would revolutionize marijuana breeding in just two decades, producing thousands of new varieties.

It began in Hawaii and northern California. Before the end of the 1970s, growers had made hundreds if not thousands of crosses, weeding out undesirable characteristics and selecting progeny for potency, colour, odour, taste, growth habits and especially the high they wanted. Breeders gathered at secret harvest festivals to exchange seeds and growing tips. A legendary underground group call the Sacred Seed Company began distributing the remarkable new hybrids. Names like Skunk, Early Girl, California Orange and Mendocino Purple became known and sought after by growers and consumers alike. By the early 1980s Dutch seed companies were taking the best of the new American varieties home for hybridizing with strains from Asia, the Middle East and Africa and returning the best of the crosses—collectively known as Nederweed—as seed to pot farmers scattered from Alaska to Australia. Once in place, the new pedigreed varieties could be reproduced, true to type, generation after generation, by growers who had learned how to clone their female plants.

In 1983 the DEA gave marijuana yet another timely boost by expanding its paraquat spraying from Mexico into the U.S. Already under intense pressure from state and federal dope cops, growers began to move their operations indoors, sparking a new round of research into plant potency, size and early harvest and a raft of technological advances to create a whole new growing environment. By the end of the decade the efforts of hundreds of growers working independently coalesced to produce the ultimate in high-tech marijuana culture: the Sea of Green. Under a blaze of lights, hydroponically grown plants no bigger than a table lamp were induced to ripen a single thick cola in less than two months. Thirty plants could be jammed together in a space the size of a phone booth, yielding two pounds of prime buds. Dozens of new indoor varieties were created, many of them crosses with the famous Northern Lights bred by a Seattle grower. Potency increased and time to maturity diminished steadily, leading to super strains like the Dutch-bred AK-47, named for the number of days to harvest. When it first came on the market, AK-47 reportedly fetched $250 for a single seed.

Some growers believe marijuana breeding, at least indoors, has reached the point of diminishing returns, where gains in things like potency or early maturity may be offset by losses in other characteristics, such as yield or quality of the high. Be that as it may, there are other fields to explore. Marijuana contains more than 460 known compounds, at least 60 of them elements with a molecular structure similar to THC, the only cannabinoid that is both highly psychoactive and present in large amounts. A few other cannabinoids are just as potent as THC but occur only in traces and only in a few marijuana strains. Given this chemical complexity and the thousands of genetically unique varieties now available, marijuana offers growers an almost infinite opportunity for experimentation, especially with different types of highs.

Many smokers recognize a spectrum of marijuana trips, ranging from the robust physical effects of the archetypal *indica* to the clear, bell-like high of a *sativa*. By manipulating the proportion of *indica* genes to *sativa* genes, breeders can design strains with precisely the effect they want. There is also scope for selective breeding and better cultural practices to clean up unwanted side effects —headaches, muzziness, harsh taste and throat-rasping smoke— of chemical traces left by fertilizers or undesirable components of the plant itself. Aroma and flavour are also open to further manipulation. There is even talk in the trade of trying to design varieties for therapeutic purposes: a particular strain for glaucoma and others for high blood pressure, epilepsy, chemotherapy nausea or any of the ills for which marijuana is known to be an effective treatment.

Looking at my own variety in light of this history, I can limn the rough outlines of its provenance. Its six-foot height at maturity and relatively clear high both speak of *sativa* origins. Its dense growth, reddish pistils and purple leaves are *indica* traits. Otherwise I know little about this plant, except that it came from the southern B.C. interior and was given to me by a grower called Dieter, after whom I have named it.

While breeders on the U.S. west coast and in the Netherlands were getting most of the attention in the 1970s and '80s, people like Dieter were quietly working away in their gardens, crossing, selecting and crossing again, year after year. By the 1990s their efforts would earn B.C. Bud, as it has become known, a reputation as the equal of any marijuana in the world.

When I went looking for seeds for my first garden, Dieter was the obvious choice. I knew him slightly, a hard, barrel-chested man, wonderfully fit from years of growing marijuana in the mountains. And I'd sampled his dope, which was strong, aromatic and beautifully tinted with the purple of an archetypical *indica*. But he had since pulled stakes and moved on (because of pot thieves and a neighbour who finked to the police, he told me later), and I had not seen him in years.

When I tracked him down in the Okanagan Valley, Dieter was living on a tidy little farm, close by the bank of a quicksilver creek. "Yes, of course, you can have all the seeds you want," he said, opening two of the beers I'd brought. I explained that it wasn't just the seeds I wanted. "I've developed an interest in the whole story of marijuana," I said, "and I'd like to hear about your part in the breeding revolution that went on in B.C."

Dieter smiled and took a pull on his beer, as if preparing for a long story. "I started in 1973 with seeds from Mexico," he said. "But of course all they showed for flowers were a few little hairs, because they just weren't hybrid enough to go into their reproductive cycle this far north."

"But in those days," I said, "you couldn't have known exactly what the problem was."

"That's right. There were no books, at least none that I knew of. No one around here I could turn to. But knowledge was shared and it travelled everywhere by word of mouth. One of the things I learned—we'd be talking about the early 1980s by this time—was that the plant was sensitive to the seasonal light cycle. It wouldn't flower until the days got short enough. I thought, well hell, if a person can make the daylight decrease early enough in the year, then you'll have something. So I got some of those black plastic sheets, and along about the twentieth of July I tried covering just a few plants. I pounded some stakes into the ground, took some string and tied the plastic down tight all round. I'd put it on about seven o'clock in the evening, after the sun was down, so they wouldn't cook. Leave it on twelve hours and take it off about seven the next morning."

"Did it work?"

"Holy smokes, did it work! After about ten days—that's all it took—they were starting to flower, and they just kept on going when I quit covering them. They made beautiful flowers, and by early September we were harvesting big, juicy, sticky bud. It was incredible. People couldn't believe it. They'd say, 'How do you do that? Where does this stuff come from?' People were driving up from the coast with suitcases full of money. Marketing was no problem whatsoever. It went real quick. It was beautiful."

At about the same time, Dieter switched to a variety from Chile that had been crossed with an *indica* in Northern California. It flowered earlier but still too late to beat the frost at the 3,000-foot elevation where he had his gardens. "If you didn't have good flower by early September, well, forget it. The nights would be getting too cold, and bud formation wouldn't happen." So for the next six years he covered all his plants to fool them into flowering. "It was a tremendous amount of work," he told me. "You had to be very dedicated."

It was not until 1989 that Dieter found a variety that could make it on its own. "Somebody gave me a couple of seeds—just two seeds, and I don't know where they originated—and said they were very good for early maturing. Both turned out to be females. I crossed them with my Chilean variety and got a whole bunch more seeds, and the next year, for the first time, I had a great harvest without covering a single plant. That was real progress." What Dieter had created was the variety I am now growing. Although we'll never know, Dieter's two seeds may have contained genes of *ruderalis*, a Russian strain that matures very early and has widely spaced buds, valued by some growers for mould resistance. Other growers avoid *ruderalis* like the pox because its THC content is low.

All over British Columbia, from the timbered valleys of the Kootenays, the Gulf Islands and deep coastal inlets, the hot, windy canyons of the Fraser and Chilcotin, to the sprawling Peace River country in the north, growers were hybridizing, selecting and swapping, just as Dieter had done. Out of these years of work came dozens of new varieties with names like Island Spike, Mighty Mite, Piney, A-3, B.C. Skunk and Kootenay Mountain Red, all fine-tuned to local tastes and growing conditions. Here on the Sechelt Peninsula, Ned was in the thick of this. Year after year, he nursed along his best strains, bought or bartered for new ones, and painstakingly concocted hybrids from the cream of his collection. Finally, in the mid-1990s, he came up with Rasta, the best outdoor dope to pass my lips, and the variety that I will surely switch to if I grow another year.

Nothing speaks more graphically of this horticultural revolution than the marijuana seed catalogues. Names and descriptions ooze promise like the glossy seed and flower publications of companies such as Burpee, McKenzie, or Thompson and Morgan. Among the pages and pages of listings, one finds Skunk Passion (strong, pungent smell), Durban Poison (sweet anise-licorice flavour), Smokey Bear (sticky, stinky and fruity), Swazi (exotic flavour from Swaziland), Night Queen (orangelike aroma), Lambsbread/Skunk (very special Jamaican taste and high), Jolly Rancher (sweet, yummy bubble-gummy smell), Dutch Treat (elusive connoisseur strain) and Slyder (strong, lethargic stone that enables a person to slide across the room without lifting his or her feet, usually from the television to the kitchen, i.e., refrigerator, and back again).

You can see it coming, the slick mags for dope snobs, with adverts for exotic strains of cannabis. "Sierra, a bright, bold yet unpretentious *sativa*, spiced with hints of mountain thyme and notes of frost-touched juniper berries. Quality cannabis that lifts the discriminating smoker to a high, wide plane of consciousness, crystalline and far-seeing as the alpine air." Or "Swami, direct from the ashrams of India. This musky saffron- and mango-flavoured *indica* induces a deep, meditative trance, opening the doors of perception to peace, harmony and the timeless wisdom of the ancients." Or "Fug, a rough, tough jungle weed for studdy men who like their smoking down and dirty. Not for the faint of heart, this sticky, stinky blend of Bordello and Cape Clap goes right to the crotch. Two-toke dope to blow your rocks off!"

Already, some self-proclaimed connoisseurs distinguish between heavy "blue collar" dope for the working man who wants a stone suitable for drinking beer and watching drag racing on television, and a more cerebral "white collar" pot for the lofty discourse of urban professionals. Meantime, lo the poor consumer! How to penetrate this smog of flavours, colours, odours and highs when all you want is a good stone at a reasonable price?

I've consulted with experts on this question, people like Ned and Dieter, who are knowledgeable not just as growers but also as sellers who have been subjected for years to the iron discipline of the market. If your dope isn't good, no one is going to buy it. First and most obvious, they say, insist on clean pot—no loose leaves and no buds more than two or three inches long. Otherwise the stems get too thick, and you can buy lumber much more cheaply at the building supply store. Don't accept damp "asbestos" dope that you have to light with a blow torch; it weighs more and the extra you pay for is water. Nor should it be crackly dry, as resin glands turn brittle and fall off when you handle it. Don't be fooled by the frosting. Some highly resinous indoor marijuana is as white as a wedding cake but still a second-rate smoke. Try before you buy. Unless you've bought the same dope from the same dealer before, always toke up before you put your money down. And when you bring it home, don't leave it in a Baggie in the dresser drawer. Seal it tight in a mason jar, with as little air space as possible, and keep it in a dark, cool place.

If you are thinking of growing your own stone, even just a plant or two on the balcony, smoke some of the parent variety before you sow. Marijuana normally grows very true to type, which means that if the plant from which your seeds were taken was a donkey, they won't grow up to be racehorses. To avoid genetic throwbacks to inferior strains, get your seed from an established seed dealer. Your local hemp store will have names and addresses, or you can select from the listings in cannabis magazines.

It's insidious how quickly the perfidies of marketing have crept into a marijuana culture that got its start in anti-consumerist hippiedom. As with those tasteless red apples in the supermarket, appearance is becoming the be-all and end-all. Some dealers now pay less for outdoor marijuana than indoor because it's not as "showy" with resin, even though it may offer a superior high. The standard of manicuring now requires that the narrow bud leaves (bracts) be almost entirely removed, even though they are often plastered with resin. This doesn't make for a better smoke and it's wasteful, since this "shake" usually goes into the fire or compost or down the toilet. Which brings to mind a mythical variety called Manhattan White, believed to grow in the sewers of New York from seeds flushed down the john when the police came calling. Hidden away from the sun, its leaves are said to be pale as rolling papers. And, by the way, only the brain-dead put tell-tale pot leaves in the garbage.

With the disciplines of marketing and science now firmly in the saddle, it's unlikely that we will ever again see anything like the wild and wonderful proliferation of marijuana varieties of the early 1970s. Hundreds, if not thousands, of strains were created serendipitously by pollen blowing from one garden to another.

When sinsemilla culture began—most likely in Marin County, California, around 1975—male plants were destroyed, except for a few isolated individuals kept for breeding, and the number of accidental hybrids fell off sharply. Before long, leaving males in the ground to seduce your neighbour's sinsemilla crop became something close to a killing offence. By the late 1980s many outdoor growers were using clones rather than seed, eliminating males altogether from their operations. Finally, with the move indoors, marijuana breeding has almost stopped, as most growers clone the same variety year after year. With millions of dollars to be made, the seed companies, especially the Dutch, are still turning out new wonder varieties every year. As creations of hot-shot horticulture, they are no doubt superb. But there is something missing from these new super buds, some resonance of the old excitement and spontaneity experienced by growers like Ned and Dieter, who cobbled together genetic mud pies and came up with dope as good as dope can be.

Climbing through a wasteland of smashed wood at the old landing (where logs were "yarded" to a spar tree and loaded on trucks) above the Hillside Garden, I hear the high-pitched whine of wings and look up to a male rufous hummingbird hovering directly overhead. The slash is wide open here, no trees, no brush even, and the hummer hangs alone against the open sky, its vermilion throat patch iridescent in the morning sun. Directly above it, scribing a chalk mark across the blue, is a big, four-engine passenger jet. The juxtaposition is striking: the bird of nature superimposed on the bird of humans, the miracle against the machine. Impressive as it is, the plane is no more than a jumped-up Meccano set when compared with the complexity of the hummingbird.

The heart of a hummer beats 1,200 to 1,400 times a minute, powering fifty wingstrokes a second, wingtips cleaving the air at something like 250 miles an hour. Slow-motion photography reveals that, when hovering, the bird's wings move horizontally, parallel to the ground, and are rotated with a kind of sculling motion, so that the *top* of the wing angles *down* on the backstroke, providing lift, just as the bottom of the wing does on the fore-stroke. When the rufous hummingbird arrives in the spring (males a few weeks before females), sometimes as early as the first days of March, there are few flowers in bloom, and these tiny birds may have difficulty gathering enough food during the day to carry them through the night. To conserve energy, they have evolved the capacity to drop their body temperature by as much as 10°C. The high-altitude Andean Hillstar hummingbird can knock an incredible 30°C off its temperature, slowing its metabolism by 75 per cent. To enhance their foraging capabilities, hummers are attuned to the full range of colours that we see, plus ultraviolet hues strongly reflected by flowers. They may even use ultraviolet light, which will penetrate light cloud cover, as a navigational aid to orient themselves to the sun. And I have seen the males engage in a kind of sexual semaphore, flaring the feathers at their throat to catch the sun, sending sharp stabs of colour through the forest shade to attract mates or deter rivals. By the end of July they are gone from the coast, wending their way from flower to flower, all the way back to Mexico.

After a searing week of record temperatures at the end of July (global warming?), my plants are parched and I'm hauling water yet again. Crossing the open ground of the powerline that girdles the base of the mountain, Henry the Ford is rocked by dusty gusts from a black scowl of thundercloud building in the mountains to the east. Fine gravel rattles on the windshield and roadside alders bend low before the wind, turning up the pale undersides of their leaves like supplicants raising their hands to a wrathful god.

The steepest pitch of road through the timber is sheltered by high ground to the east. Here, in the stillness and gathering dusk, a summer snowfall of fireweed seed cotton is settling silently down through the trees. I stop the truck and get out to watch it fall, billions of spiky pinwheels glinting in the headlights, collecting like a dusting of snow along the road and over the underbrush. For weeks the slash above this stretch of forest has been turning mauve with firewood bloom, and now this blizzard of down has been set loose on the wind.

Cresting the hill on the slash, I find the valley beyond the Hillside Garden lost in tumbling cloud and twitching with lightning, as if a celestial welder were at work. Ragged silhouettes of old-growth trees flicker and die on the ridge. Just as I'm getting out of the truck, the first fat drops splatter on the windshield, and by the time I have pulled the hose down to the garden, the rain is coming sideways. Climbing back to the truck, I sit for twenty minutes, waiting for the squall to pass and listening to a radio series on the Beethoven string quartets. The critic, who has written a book on the subject, ranks the last five as Beethoven's "most profound," which is fair comment, though I find some of them pretty dark. But he gets under my skin when he dismisses the middle quartets as lightweights and calls the final movement of No. 9, one of my favourites, "a bit of tub thumping."

In a pet, I snap off the radio (the lightning was making it crackle anyhow, like a 1930s crystal set) and stomp off down the hill to my watering. For a miserable hour I stand around in the flickering dark with a garbage can lid on my head, wondering what I am doing here watering when it's raining anvils. But in truth, even this downpour will do little to quench the thirst of plants that soak up two buckets of water a week.

Naturally, the rain stops just as I reel the last of the hose into the truck. The cloud shreds like wet paper and stars prick through. Over Georgia Strait, the rain curtain is raised on a necklace of faint lights along the Vancouver Island shore. But I have eyes for none of this. I'm soaked to the skin and still pissed off with that condescending twit of a critic. What really annoys me is the sneaking suspicion that he's probably right.

CHAPTER 8

PROFITS
AND LIES

July makes its exit under torrential rain and August arrives swaddled in clammy marine cloud, blown inland from the summer fog banks of the open Pacific. As if stimulated by the change in weather, my plants suddenly open their overcoats and flash their private parts. Pistils emerge from the calyxes of the females. Male flowers reveal themselves as tiny nodules, for which offence the plants are promptly pulled up by the roots. A few modest individuals hang back, forestalling their salvation or execution to a later day.

Other than watering—the rains have taken care of that for a while—there is little that has to be done at this season, and I plan to use the time to meet a genuine marijuana farmer. By that I mean a veteran grower who makes his living exclusively from dope. Ned doesn't count because he has always had other work. And I consider myself a dilettante; real growers don't depend on their spouses to keep the wolf from the door.

Actually, I began this quest months ago, roaming the strait in my boat and on the car ferries, calling in at Gulf islands, from Quadra and Cortes in the north to Salt Spring in the south, making discreet inquiries. It's a delicate matter. You can't just clomp up the government wharf, waving notebook and tape recorder and hollering for the local pot growers to line up and present themselves. You need a lot of time and, above all, contacts—people who know that you are not a narc (an RCMP undercover narcotics officer), people who know other people and can ease you into the community. I have recently found such a person, a woman who has lived more than twenty years on an island near the top of Georgia Strait, four or five hours' run from home. I've been there twice, and last night she phoned to say she has someone who will talk with me.

An apricot dawn is climbing the eastern sky as I launch the boat. During the night the wind came round to the west, and here in the cove flags are snapping and sailboats monotonously clanging their aluminum spars. Outside, in Malaspina Strait, a heavy sea is running. Clearing the point I take the first spray, shocking as a slap, full in the face. I'm wearing rain gear and rubber boots, standing above the windshield, the better to see drift logs and deadheads. The boat is open and sixteen feet long. With seventy horses behind, she's fast enough in calm weather. But her badly designed hull pounds so hard into waves, I have to throttle back to a wallowing crawl.

It is past noon when I tie up to the float at the island. The boat is rimed with salt, and my hair and eyes are gritty with it. I rinse off under a fresh-water hose on the dock and go looking for my lady friend. She is otherwise occupied. Finally, late in the afternoon, we connect, and she draws me a map to the home of Jim and Sara, the people who have agreed to see me. A ninety-minute walk through green tunnels of alder and maple brings me, at the end of a network of diminishing roads, to a grassy trail leading down through dense brush to the coast of the island.

The clearing at Jim and Sara's opens suddenly, a burst of light and colour at the end of a dark trail. In the right foreground sits a house of vintage hippie design, neatly crafted and faintly reminiscent of a pumpkin. From there, the ground slopes gently down to lawn, beds of mixed flowers and vegetables, a little grove of fruit trees and finally a bank dropping away steeply onto a gravel beach at the head of a narrow cove. Framed between the points of the cove, a string of indigo islets steps away towards the setting sun. The wind has died away, and a glassy swell is washing on the beach with a sound that hangs like a whispered conversation over the clearing.

I find Jim stacking next winter's firewood in a woodshed joined by a breezeway to the back of the house. He is compact and fit as a greyhound. After a minute or two, Sara appears at the door. Instantly I am her captive, her slave. Her face radiates such peace and kindness I want to walk right up to her, a total stranger, and give her a hug. Of course, I am too old-fashioned and reserved to do any such thing. Instead, I give Jim a hand stacking wood until Sara appears again at the door and tells us, "Enough, enough, it's time to come in."

While Jim douses his face at the sink and Sara kindles a fire in the kitchen range, I poke around, admiring their house. So far from powerlines, I'm surprised to see lamps, a stereo system, television, even a cell phone—all powered, Jim tells me later, with electricity they generate themselves. The house is on three levels and finished with loving care, like a piece of furniture. From the compact and comfortable kitchen, I step up a foot onto a living-room floor of yellow cedar that glows like amber in the gloaming light from windows facing onto the garden and sea. The room is made to seem larger than it is by a high ceiling opening at the rear into a loft with skylights, faintly dusted now with the first stars of evening.

Jim and Sara came to the island in the early 1970s, city kids full of back-to-the-land idealism. Sara was from Vancouver via

Toronto, where she had been working as a therapist in a clinic doing LSD research for the Le Dain Commission. Jim came from Ottawa, where his father was a mandarin in Trudeau's Privy Council. Any career expectations his family may have had for him had gone up in smoke years earlier.

"My marijuana experience started when I was sixteen or seventeen," Jim remembers. The three of us are sitting at the kitchen table, sipping homemade blackberry wine the colour of garnet and looking out through the leaded windows of a dining nook at the darkening orchard and forest. "The door opened into what was to me truth. All of a sudden I saw that most of the world was telling lies, serious lies. That the whole place was bullshit, and fucked-up and corrupt. I was just a nice suburban kid, but the drug experience showed me in plain, obvious detail what was true. It was like a religious experience, not done casually in public; it was serious business. Seeing what was true and what was not—that put me on the road that ended with me living here. Looking for a community of like minds, where people had the same sense of 'That's bullshit and this is wholesome.'"

Like many marijuana growers, Jim got into the trade with little forethought, growing a few plants on the side to supplement his income. "I was a deckhand on the ferry one week out of three," he tells me. "The first year we made sixteen, seventeen hundred dollars from our dope, which was wow! a lot of money. Incentive to do it again, maybe expand to another plot. A bit later I was doing carpentry and cabinet-making. But steadily, marijuana grew in economic importance. And then at some point, a bumper crop finally came in, more than ten pounds. I don't know what a pound went for then—twenty-five hundred dollars or thereabouts. That was wealth beyond anything we had ever imagined. It was almost a problem: do we have responsibilities with this kind of money?

What should we do with it? Although we weren't sure, one thing was clear: the time had come when I could quit work."

Jim started too late to grow the legendary monster plants of pure *sativa*, though he did see some of those early gardens. "Originally, there was no blossom. I remember going to a plot around 1977; I helped a guy harvest. Those were twelve- to fourteen-footers, and they were just for leaf. So marijuana with buds hadn't happened yet, at least not here. The people who were into pot commercially were growing vast quantities of leaf. But also their expectations of profit were tiny. By the time we started, there was seed available to grow plants with big fat colas, and so you had a dual product, bud and also leaf. You'd hang the plant upside down, sort of like curing tobacco, then cut all the leaves off with scissors to get rid of the stems. They'd end up kind of leathery, not brittle, so you could roll them. Leaf went for about two hundred dollars a pound, and it gave what most people felt was a more pleasant high than what you get now from the knock-your-socks-off stuff. A much more dependable level. Workers' pot. You'd smoke a whole joint, rather than two tokes like you would today, when you have to sit back for five minutes to see how you can handle it. If you felt like more, you could have another whole joint because you had bags of this stuff."

Like hippies everywhere, the island population was extremely mobile, travelling widely and returning, often as not, with seeds from exotic strains of marijuana in their pockets. For Jim, those were exciting years. "Oh my God, how the varieties proliferated! There was *ruderalis* from Siberia, strains from Afghanistan, Lebanon, Thailand, Colombia, Hawaii—you name it. Seeds were arriving from all over the world and getting bred into new varieties. Everything was becoming mixed and homogenized, and the smoke was getting much stronger than ever before."

"With all this activity," I ask, "wasn't the island beginning to attract the attention of the police?"

Sara sighs eloquently. "Ah yes, the police. How can we ever forget the police?"

Smiling wryly, Jim draws a deep breath. "There had been a few very cursory raids, though nothing organized or sustained. But it took only two or three years before the industry blossomed in this area and people were growing very large gardens. A hundred, two hundred plants. Plantations, big open tracts that were very visible from the air. At about the same time, the helicopter raids began in earnest. It takes a long time to learn how to make a garden so that it fits in with the landscape. That's a real art. A lot of people don't have that at all. And to make matters worse, there were a lot of loudmouths on the island, raving about our local strain of marijuana; it was important to their egos that it got broadcast that they were attached to a special product.

"We had a helicopter come here; it hovered low over our vegetable garden and buzzed away around the next point. A while later this policeman arrived in his city shoes, plowing through the bush from the next bay. I guess from the air it looked like about three minutes' walk from where they could land. It took him at least fifteen, and he was all sweaty and mopping his brow. A horrible walk. He arrived like the inquisitor in *Crime and Punishment*, who always twisted the guilty one's mind. He was full of police psychology, trying to trip us up—these two sweet, innocent hippies out in their garden. He wandered around saying things like, 'What's that hanging up drying?' 'Well, that's mint, actually.' We couldn't figure out what the purpose of this was. There was nothing to see from the air. We grew nothing at that time. But we were assumed to be guilty."

Up to this time, in the early 1980s, island growers had their plants in the ground, where they were easy pickings when the police helicopters came. As the surveillance became more rigorous, they began to grow in containers. The moveable garden.

"In August," Jim remembers, "you moved all your plants and your fence under cover of the trees nearby. You moved everything and waited for the raid to come. And when the raid was over, you'd move everything back out. That was the idea. Believe me, that was labour-intensive. It worked wonderfully for a few years. But then things began to change. First it was one week in the shade. Then two weeks, then three weeks. The plants would be starting to flower, getting real leggy, reaching for the light. And the police still hadn't come. No raid, third week in August. Where in hell are they? Sometimes there'd be a rumour: they're coming on Thursday. And that would pass through the island, *whoosh*, in about three hours, and everyone would stash their crop. And a couple of times the helicopter actually did come when it was supposed to. It was a leak from someone close to the police. But the second-guessing was overwhelming. You'd go into town, hear a rumour—so-and-so was talking to so-and-so and they know someone who works in the RCMP office. And I'd think, Oh God, I can't be bothered worrying about this. And then I'd decide, well, I can't afford to ignore rumours, and I'd rush home and move everything. That went on and on and on.

"You hear talk about lazy hippies in their hammocks. But this is a high-stress business, there's so much anxiety built up over the crop. In the spring everything's fresh, everything's light, it's another season's promise in the ground. It's like the Stan Rogers song. You love the land, you love the earth, you love the sky, you love life itself, but God, it's hard. And you're just hoping and hoping and hoping that everything works so you can pay off your debt to the bank, so that your kids can get the orthodontic work, so that ... It's the heart of the farmer. Except with dope you've got the police against you, you've got rip-offs against you, you've got crop failure, potency failure, your drying shed burns down, it rains all summer and your plants get mould, the market dries up—there are so many things that can go wrong. That's a farmer's reality. You love growing it, you love the contact with the earth, being out on the land—something is immense and eternal in your growing. Then you wake up and you're listening to the morning news, and the next moment you're hearing *booda-booda-booda-booda-booda*. And they're not going straight and high overhead. They're coming in low and they're circling. And you know exactly where they are. And you know they've found it. And you know that it's gone. Just like that. And your knees are trembling, and you feel weak. If you are a smoker, you roll a cigarette real fast. And your son says, 'Let's go, maybe we can still save some.' And you answer, 'No, it's gone, it's gone.' That's real heavy stuff."

While the police were becoming more vigilant, the growers themselves were upping the ante by increasing production; every year there was more to lose. "Everything was becoming very methodical, controlled, uniform," Jim tells me. "You were now creating the soil entirely, rather than relying on the native soil. You'd pump it heavy with bone meal, phosphorous, potash, manure, and every watering you'd pump it heavy with more fertilizer—pump, pump, pump, pump. You'd change your watering from casual to every five days; you'd never let the plants dry out. Every year you'd increase the yield off a potted plant—five, six, sometimes even eight ounces."

At about this time Jim also made an important breakthrough in plant breeding. He was growing a variety from Oregon called Larry, which shows its sexual characteristics by the end of May. "I use a fifteen-power geologist's magnifying glass to look for the male sex organs—just like balls and dinks—in the crotch of the branches," he says. "All the plants are still in gallon pots at this season, so I can eliminate the males and transplant all females into my gardens."

Due to some genetic quirk, about five in every hundred Larry plants go into flower in June and are ready for harvest in July, nearly three months before the normal plants. Mighty Mite, as the mutant is called, is very small but yields excellent pot. "I started playing with the plant," Jim recalls, "selecting the biggest ones and breeding them back to each other. Gradually, the strain grew bigger and bigger and later and later in the season, until I got a plant large enough to bear a worthwhile crop and still mature before the end of July, before the police came. And that gave us a summer crop that we could sell before the market got plugged in the fall."

But the police were also making changes. In this game of cat-and-mouse with the RCMP, Jim was about to feel the claws of the law. "It had been pretty cushy for several years; the raids slacked off and they hadn't come to this part of the island. I became more and more casual about my growing, putting more and more plants in each plot and moving them right out onto the open bluffs. Wide open—you could see them from ten thousand feet. When the grass around them dried out in the summer, you got dark blue-green against a golden background. Totally visible. Two big plots only a hundred yards apart. And then the police came early, just before we would normally start thinking about moving the plants under the trees. Twenty-sixth of July; they'd never come that early before. How could they do this? They're not allowed to do this! So I had sitting ducks. We had done really well the year before—big crop, big profit. About eighteen pounds, and the price had gone up to thirty-two hundred dollars a pound. I had grown plenty of backup plants; every pot was full with a female. Greed, greed, greed on the bluff tops. Running water to each plot. Cushy, cushy. And they took them all. And they macheted up the pots, threw them over the cliffs, just a mess. It took two days to clean it up. Fortunately, we still had Mighty Mites elsewhere, but we lost all the full-season crop of Larrys."

The next year the police didn't come until the middle of September, which was even worse than the July raid. By then, some growers had been hiding their gardens in the shade for more than a month. Others had given up waiting and moved their plants into the open, where the cops scythed them down, like peregrines set loose in a flock of pigeons.

For Jim, it was time for a major change. "I had to retool," he remembers, an echo of resignation in his voice. "It no longer made sense to hide our plants because we didn't know when the raids would come. So the solution was to make much smaller gardens in more subtle locations. Not so wide open and exposed. I would have to sacrifice some full sun exposure for better security. And the plan was that I wouldn't move them at all. They'd be in a pocket, surrounded by trees, packed close together so you didn't have to build too much fence to keep the deer out. It would be a green zone that blended in with the trees around. Just fifteen to eighteen plants, crammed together in a bowl. Pocket gardening."

It was an enormous undertaking that would cost him two years of gruelling labour. The soil that Jim had been accumulating in his old gardens had to be moved to new plots, usually high up on the bluffs. There were no roads, no trails even, and only one means of transport: Jim's strong back.

"I'm a Sherpa. I use a plastic mesh sack, a rice sack. I packed all the soil from way up on those hills, back down in the valley and way up on other hills, moved it all because it's valuable stuff. Good earth. I imported fifty sacks of manure, dumped it off on the beach and packed it four hundred feet uphill and half a mile inland. It rained and the sacks got very heavy. That got mixed in with compost and seaweed, also packed from the beach in sacks. And, of course, there are fences to build. I put chicken wire for six feet up from the ground and barbed wire above it, then paint the whole thing black, and it vanishes. Such a lot of work. It takes me a couple of days just to fence a small garden."

Sara has been sitting quietly most of this time, interjecting only the occasional comment. It is apparent from the way she looks at Jim that she admires and cares for him deeply. "I watch him and I know how hard he works and how much energy he puts into this really good product," she says. "And I also see how painful it is for him to have to be so secretive, and I see how that wears on him. And I see how he's not doing some other things he'd like to do, things that would give him other means of creative expression, because growing marijuana consumes so much of his life. I always feel that I want to be able to help more." Sara puts in hundreds of hours every year manicuring the finished product, but other than watering when Jim is away, she takes no part in the bull work on the land.

Retooling has paid off for Jim and other growers on the island. A friend of Jim's with a radio that picks up RCMP channels reports that the police have had slim pickings in recent years. "They fly around for days and they see pot everywhere," Jim says, "but it's all in pockets of six, eight, maybe ten plants, way off in the boonies, way off on the bluff tops, far from any place the helicopter can land. No big scores of forty or fifty. It's in bits too small to bother to pick up. For a whole day's work, including three, four thousand dollars in helicopter rental, they get maybe sixty plants. At one time they'd get almost a thousand in a day. So times are tough for the police. They didn't even put an article in the newspaper this year to brag about their seizures."

Unlike many growers, Jim and Sara harbour no resentment of the police, though they believe the campaign against marijuana is a waste of money. Years ago, before they were in commercial production, they were hauled into court for growing seven plants in their garden. After they were given an unconditional discharge, they invited the two RCMP officers who had busted them in for tea. "Their names were Tap and Lively, like a vaudeville team," Jim says, clearly enjoying the memory. "They stayed a couple of hours and we had a lovely chat."

Jim has taken a lot of the ongoing heavy labour out of growing by switching to concentrated organic fertilizers, a cocktail of powders much like I used in my own soil mix. He packs it in, fifty-five pounds to a load, which will do for about twenty pots. "After two or three years," he says, "I introduce new organic matter to add micro-organisms to the soil. If you don't do that you are going to have problems with fungus, disease. I find it right around the gardens—leaves and rotting vegetation—so that's a lot easier than packing in sacks of manure, though we're not averse to sticking our hands in shit around here; it's not a bad feeling. It's a farmer feeling."

No one has figured out a way to take the work out of manicuring marijuana. It's a tedious job and, done to Jim and Sara's lofty standards, seemingly interminable. I ask Jim to show me one of his buds. What he brings me looks more like a piece of sculpture than a dried flower—a perfectly symmetrical cone, with every leaf cut back to the stem and the sparkling resin intact.

"It's green gold," Jim says. "Any movement deteriorates marijuana if it's dry. The crystals get knocked off and fall to the bottom of the bag. If you want the very best, the less you handle it the better. Delicate, delicate, delicate."

Pruning is also slow, slow, slow. Jim hires help, and sometimes there may be as many as eight people working in the living room to process the Mighty Mite crop. "All of a sudden you have an immense quantity that you have to prune in a hurry to catch the summer market while it's hot," he says. "It can take a whole day for one person to do a single plant. Before you know it, your summer is consumed by harvesting, drying and processing. Last year was wet, and three pounds of buds moulded in the drying shed. When I brought it down here into the light, it was actually a joy to see the rot and know that we wouldn't have to prune it. Endless hours and hours of pruning. At that point it was like, fuck it, that's it—the end of summer pruning! Hurrah, a break at last!"

I had expected that long before now we would be sampling Jim's product and getting rapidly stoned. But neither Jim nor Sara smoke marijuana any longer, except rarely on social occasions. "It's like working in a candy factory," Sara says. "When you are handling it all day, month after month, you lose your appetite for it."

Jim keeps meticulous records for quality control. Each plant is numbered and processed separately and marked with its date of harvest and the name of the garden it came from. Samples then go to a tester for grading on a scale of one to ten. "It's tested by a heavy smoker who has it for his first smoke in the morning when he has a really clean palate," Jim explains. "He takes it very seriously, and his pay is the dope. Seven out of ten is totally saleable for the full market price. Under seven, well, it's marginal. Eight, dynamite. Nine is spectacular, and ten, well, the sampler buys all that for himself because he also deals. For a six, I have to be prepared to take less. But in the summer there are people who are willing to take anything, even a six that's two years old. Last summer, the dealers were desperate. They came to the island with thirty thousand dollars in cash and took everything we had."

I stay overnight at Jim and Sara's, sleeping in the guest house attached to a cavernous boat works that opens onto the beach. The next morning we linger long over a breakfast of omelettes with tea and homemade toast and jam, while Sara talks about her life beyond the demands of marijuana and keeping up their home and garden. Her talent and passion is for helping people in need, especially the terminally ill. Recently, she has been spending a lot of time with a woman on Vancouver Island who is dying of AIDS.

"She was abused sexually by her father," Sara tells me, "and has really felt abandoned all her life. She's thirty-five now and had a third child a while ago, which was born with AIDS. Her doctor knew she had HIV and hadn't told her. So she cared for the child and I became part of that. Then the child died. Now she is getting very sick. Recently, her mother packed up and left her, which has rekindled the pain of abandonment. The kind of love that I receive from my family is not available to her, so I carry within me something that she has never experienced. I have become a kind of connector for her. Just last week she said to me, with tears, that she thought she would have died long before now were it not for the feeling that someone cares about her. I tell her that we are mirrors for each other. This life of ours allows me to serve her in some way, but it also serves my desire to become more compassionate. That's what she gives me. And that's what I long to practise in a much more full-time way. I see very clearly where I am called. And I can go there because the marijuana generates enough money to allow me to do that. It's a great gift.

"Ever since I was a kid I have had this hunger to be inside other people, to know what's in their hearts and why they suffer. That's what led me to LSD studies. In helping people who are dying, all I have to offer is a space for them to do their death, however they have to do it. It's exhilarating for me to think that I might be able to facilitate a space of peace, a space that someone could walk peacefully through. So that they would not be afraid to go. It's a mutual exploration or exchange. I'm doing it for myself as much as for them. You can't tell people to not be afraid if you are afraid yourself. When the space is there, there is an ease that drains away the fear. I sit at the bedside and I think how people sing to babies when they are born, so in certain circumstances I have begun to sing, and it has been absolutely clear that that was the perfect thing for me to do for that particular person. To make certain sounds for them that allow them some kind of melting."

Within the past year Jim and Sara's son has finished high school, leaving her time to pursue her volunteer work. "I've wanted to do this for years," she says, "and I've always felt that I couldn't fully give myself to others because I so fully gave myself to my son. I'm devoted to him. But I've heard myself say to him in the past year that it is time for me to give myself to others. Working with these people may be a place where I can learn to be present for others, to be quiet in my mind."

Marijuana farmers lead a schizophrenic life, split between their clandestine activities and a front of some kind. Many island growers do a bit of mariculture—oysters or clams, usually—as a cover for their income. But Jim's carpentry storefront dried up years ago, and the division in Jim and Sara's lives has long been seasonal rather than occupational. After eight or nine months of hard, stressful work with their crop, winter frees Sara to do her volunteer work and Jim to pursue a passion for mountains that has taken him to the roof of the world in many countries. His eyes sparkle with excitement when he talks about it.

"It's such a rush. Climbing the big mountains in Ecuador you have to leave the hut at one or two in the morning, so you are doing the whole first part at night with headlamps. Because the coastal plain is on the west and the Amazon Basin a very short distance away on the east, clouds rise every day and fill the skies. But at night it cools and the clouds drop down into the valleys. So if you are climbing in the middle of the night, it is all stars above and you look down thousands of feet through holes in the clouds, and you see lights of little villages. You're very alive and excited, and where you are is just awesome. You are full of awe. And it is so good to be alive. If you are acclimatized, you feel strong and vital. And you watch dawn come up in this place, the light slowly growing over this surreal landscape of ice and snow. You feel something the Incas must have felt, because they did a lot of ritual sacrifices on the tops of mountains, all up and down the Andes. I read Sir John Hunt's *The Ascent of Everest* when I was a kid and dreamed of going to this magic land, and I have. That's what the green energy gives: some dreams can come true. I don't have to wait until I retire and no longer have the energy to climb in Nepal. Years before I had a dream: what a neat thing it would be to go with my wife and son to the foot of Everest. And we got to do it."

A big part of the appeal of travel for Jim is escaping, even for a month or two, from the corrosive climate of secrecy that marijuana growing imposes on everyone who does it. "I've always had a bit of a problem with feeling that it's not a very noble occupation," he says. "Maybe because my father is a highly moral person, a highly placed civil servant, a real Kennedyite—what can you do for your country? Seek out the position where you can be of most service. So I'm growing *dope* to make a *buck*! And it's something about taking my son with me to the gardens, seeing his bit of nervousness and worry. Seeing him growing older and worrying about police raids. And him learning to tell a lie. The lie, the implicit lie. The secret. That's the stressful part. I can handle the police, the bad crop—all of that. It's the lie, the secrecy. I moved way out here because there's less chance of getting ripped off, but I'm alone all the time in the bush. I go to my drying shed and it's deep and dark and deathly quiet in the forest. Year after year, I'm all alone. It's very closed in. It's not something that opens your heart up, makes you grow towards other people. It becomes you. The secret, the hidden places you don't talk about. That's the burden, not the work.

"That's one of the reasons I love travelling—soon as I'm out of the country, I'm free of that. Other travellers ask what I do, and I say, 'I'm a farmer.' Totally nonchalant. I don't have to lie any more. They ask, 'What do you grow, wheat?' And I say, 'No. I grow marijuana, high-quality marijuana.' 'Really! How interesting! I never met one of you people before.' Because they've all smoked, they all know what it's about because it's part of the world's trip. They get to meet a grower, and I get to be totally open about it. Proud of it. It becomes a point of engagement; they share their stuff with me and I share my stuff with them. It's wonderful because it's a release from skulking around. But that can never happen here at home."

Jim and Sara's marijuana-based life has reached a plateau of sorts. They have achieved a relatively stable income, based on turning out twenty pounds of buds or more a year at prices that are still worthwhile, though somewhat depressed by the burgeoning supply of indoor pot. Jim has absolutely no doubt that marijuana growers are here to stay.

"We are everywhere. You chop down one of us, tomorrow there are eight of us. There's nothing the police can do about it. Give up. And that's exactly what's happening—it's everywhere. If it's not in the bush, it's in houses. It's in warehouses, barns, bunkhouses, garages. Everywhere. It's so big they don't dare break it, because it has got to the point where the cash flow in many communities depends on it. It's bigger than mining, bigger than tourism—it's approaching forestry. It is a major business, and it is so intertwined with the people and the culture of this province. And yet no one talks about it."

The Canadian government estimates the value of the domestic marijuana crop at a billion dollars a year but, in fact, it has no way of knowing what the industry is really worth. British Columbia growers alone probably generate that much revenue. Increasingly, this money comes from sales to the United States, export dollars injected directly into local communities, where they stay, unlike the profits of resource industries that are siphoned off to shareholders elsewhere.

For me, the real significance of the marijuana industry is not so much its dollar value as the *kind* of economic activity it represents. In a country increasingly dominated by globalism and corporatism, it is perhaps the best demonstration we have of the advantages of small, local enterprise. Prices accurately reflect supply and demand, free of rigging or subsidies. Even though the market is global, growers retain their independence and contribute to the local economy—Jim pays manicuring help two hundred dollars a day—where the money goes round and round and everyone profits. It works for the grower, the dealer, the consumer, the community, the environment and, I think, even for the country, given the handsome returns from export sales and the social benefits whenever pot replaces booze.

In its localism and equity, the economy of Jim and Sara's island is similar to the one I grew up with. When I finished high school in 1954, this country had a tacit agreement with its young people: acquire some skills (a trade would do), work hard, and you can count on a job and a fair share of prosperity. Prosperity meant owning a home and a car, money to educate your kids, to travel a bit and to retire in modest comfort. That promise has gone, but not because Canada can no longer afford it. On a per capita basis, the country is far wealthier than it was forty years ago. The difference now is that we have bought into a global crap game that drives down wages, exports jobs and concentrates wealth in fewer and fewer hands. To suggest that we have to sacrifice our own people to play in the new economy is self-serving nonsense. If Canada can't afford an equitable society, no one can. Yet, in this country ranked by the United Nations as the best place in the world to live, three million of our citizens now depend on food banks and soup kitchens.

Like most of the people on their island, Jim and Sara have chosen to withdraw from an economy they feel offers nothing to them or the planet. Sustainability and living lightly on the land are the priorities here. "Over the years," Jim says, "this has been a very close-knit, co-operative community. Most people are apolitical, pro–life force, live and let live, anti–obscene development, pro–appropriate technology, pro–sharing the wealth of the planet, the knowledge that there is plenty to go round if it is redistributed, the capacity for wonder at the delicate mystery of the cosmos. They've worked very well together to get rid of activity that didn't measure up to this standard."

Jim believes that pot played a part in evolving the island's ethos. "From the way people act, conduct themselves in their relationships with one another, right through to the energy-efficient technology of their homes—so much of that grew out of the sixties and seventies, and now it's just part of the popular culture. The environmental movement. Go to any elementary school and interview the kids about what's important in their lives, and it's environmental concerns. Drugs, marijuana opened the door to all that, but once it started, this kind of consciousness is not drug-dependent and seems to drift all over the planet."

When it's time to take my leave I bring my boat around from the wharf, and the three of us stand talking on the beach for a long time. One of the questions I'd forgotten to ask Jim was about his parents, whether they had ever become reconciled to his marijuana growing. "I've never told them," he says, "and I don't think I ever will. They got hurt so much when I dropped out and moved here. Am I trying to protect them? I don't know. Am I afraid of their rejection? I don't know."

I give Sara the hug I've been wanting to give her and push off. From the top of the bank, Jim yells, "Spread the herb, brother," and goes off to water his gardens.

Running home, I take a roundabout route, north to the mainland coast, then southeast down Malaspina Strait. It is one of those high-summer evenings when the tide is full, the sea calm, and all the coast, from heat-hazy peaks far inland to the hammered brass of the open Pacific, breathes a slow sigh of peace. After sundown, beach fires wink on in front of widely scattered cabins, and a katabatic breeze draws an opalescent sheen of smoke across the water.

Evenings at the water's edge were a summer ritual when I was young. At dusk someone kindled a driftwood fire, and my parents, perhaps with a friend or two and a thermos of cocoa, made their way down to the beach to sit quietly talking. All around the curve of the bay, there were other fires and other people doing the same thing. New Brunswick television, my father called it, gently mocking my mother's down-east origins. Occasionally someone might leave and others arrive out of the dark, bearing a joke or a bit of news or resuming some discussion from an earlier evening. There was something comforting and familiar about those evenings, a primordial memory perhaps of other fires in other ages and stories told slowly in the shadows.

Often my younger brother, Wayne, and I were late arrivals. Fishing salmon out in Georgia Strait with assorted friends until past sundown, we'd run the two or three miles back to Granthams Landing in the afterglow. Our boat, a twenty-seven-foot Skeena River skiff rebuilt by my brother, Noel, at age fourteen, was entirely open and powered by a thudding one-lung Vivian gas engine that made so much noise we had to shout to hear one another. By the quiet of their fires, the summer people—polite folk from the wealthy west side of Vancouver—could hear us even better as we stretched a string of profanity, dirty jokes and juvenilia from one end of the beach to the other. Refined as she was by a Toronto finishing school, my mother bore this mortification before the community like a cross. And although she addressed us repeatedly and forcefully on the subject, we were incorrigible. Year after year she endured a summertime siege, which was lifted only when the city people had quenched the year's last fires and returned for the winter to more decorous neighbourhoods.

Coming up on Nelson Island with six or eight miles still to go, it is getting too dark to see driftwood and logs that could punch a hole in the boat, clipping along as I am at more than twenty knots. But off the left bow, a fingernail moon is rising over the Caren Range. Swinging right, I run until it hangs above the flashing beacon far ahead on the reef outside Secret Cove, where I launched yesterday. Then, with my way lit better than any searchlight could do, I ride the silvery road all the way home.

CHAPTER 9

RIDING
THE
BOXCARS

First you play and then you pay. Or so I found when I went up the mountain after an absence of more than a week, gadding about in the boat and in Vancouver. It has been hot and dry as a popcorn fart, and my plants were badly wilted. Hightailing for home, I started pumping.

After four days of hauling water I'm pretty well caught up, and the garbage cans, two dozen in all, are full at every garden. But there'll be no respite as long as temperatures stay where they are, in the mid-eighties, and my plants are sucking up two buckets of water every five days. In any case, they seem none the worse for my neglect. Within an hour after watering, a plant with its leaves drooping straight down will perk up as if it were made of inflatable rubber. Still, it's bad farming to let them dry out; they don't grow when thirsty, and there may yet be some residual stunting effect.

My labours seem like a lark compared to Ned's. In addition to his plots on Nelson Island, he has two gardens on rock bluffs way to hell and gone up the mountain above his place. When the ponds where he was getting water dried up, he and his son Jon, an elder brother of Danny's, dug three holes six feet down into a swamp to find a new supply. They pack it in buckets on their backs, a hundred or so feet up onto the bluffs—two hours to water twelve plants. There's a saying among dope farmers that their arms grow longer in the summer. But Ned's toil goes well beyond the norm. He has located his gardens so far from home partly to foil thieves but also because he's "scared shitless" of getting caught by the police, thanks to a nine-month jail term he served years ago for selling LSD to a narc.

By mid-August, the worst of the watering is over because I've reduced the number of plants by half in weeding out the males. Now, feeling like a traitor to my gender, I slaughter the last of them and replace them with females from the smaller pots. These transplants are only about half the size of their siblings in the big containers, though they may catch up in the six weeks left to harvest. As encouragement, I give them all a shot of 20-20-20 fertilizer and cut the bottoms out of the pots, allowing the roots to go down into the native soil. It's meager as moon rock but still capable of holding water and nutrient leached from the pots.

As I work through each plot, I keep a tally: Hillside Garden—31 females, Number Three—33, Skid Road—15, and 9 females in a new garden I made north of the swamp, using pots salvaged from the abandoned Pocket Garden. In all, 88 females, about what I expected in the spring. What I didn't expect was that I would grow more than 200 plants to get this many keepers.

These aren't just marijuana plants, of course. They're also chickens that no dope grower can resist counting before they hatch. *Clickety-clickety-click*—the mind totes up the profits: 88×4 ounces per plant = 352 ounces $\div$ 16 = 22 pounds $\times$ \$3,000 = \$66,000. Simple. Money in the bank, or at least under the mattress.

It's a mug's game, like mortgaging your home to buy lottery tickets, but irresistible nonetheless. From first seedlings to harvest, the anticipation builds, despite your earnest resolve against it. As the plants reach five feet, then six, visions of fat, sticky buds, bags and bags of them, dance before your eyes like the promise of the motherlode. You know it's crazy. So many things can still go wrong. You know the higher the expectations, the harder the fall. You know you are cranking up the anxiety—but you just can't help it. After all, even the best gamblers must sometimes indulge themselves in daydreams.

Within a year or two after clearcut logging, red alder springs up, thick as grass on the roads, making them look from a distance like green caterpillars crawling over the ravaged land. There is a short stretch of road like this above the Hillside Garden, a brushy tunnel on the open slash. Walking through it the other night just before dark, I found the air vibrating like a fiddle string with the high-voltage whine of insects. It was too dark to see, though I could tell they were big and fast, for bugs kept banging into my bare arms and legs and smacking against my face. This afternoon, when I come to the same place, I am horrified to find it alive with black-and-white hornets.

I'm allergic to hornets, especially this kind, and have been getting more so for at least twenty years. Ten years ago I was stung on the temple and looked as if I'd walked into a Mike Tyson left hook. I saw nothing out of my right eye for four days. Later, a sting on the calf bloated my leg like a duffel bag full of rubber boots. Ever since, I've been scared half to death of getting stung on the throat and suffocating as my pipes closed under pressure from the swelling.

Drawing closer, I can see that the hornets are eating something on the alder leaves, possibly aphids. Where I had lunch today in the deep shade of a mature alder grove, the leaves were alive with green aphids and ladybugs grazing on them like spotted cows.

There are aphids here too, and ladybugs—properly, ladybird beetles, named for the belief in the Middle Ages that they were sent by the Virgin Mary to help farmers—but there is something else that may be attracting the hornets. Saplings of only ten or twelve feet, these alders are open to the full blast of the sun, and their leaves have turned dark and sticky with sap sweated out by the heat. I've tasted this excretion, and it's mildly sweet. The ground beneath the trees is soaked with it, like spilled oil, and crawling with hornets and bumblebees licking up the sugar, if that's what it is.

After a few minutes it becomes apparent that the hornets have no interest in me, and I walk slowly through the roaring tunnel. I can't see whether they are eating aphids or sap or both, and I'm not about to stick my face close enough to find out.

On the open slash beyond the alders I stop to watch a pair of turkey vultures gliding down from the ridge above me, rocking on their wings like high-wire artists balancing with poles. The wind is against them, buoying them up on a stream of hot air and fireweed cotton. Passing directly overhead at a speed no faster than a jog, they peer down at me from such close range I can see every detail of their bald heads, red and wrinkled as sunburned foreskins. They make no sound, no raven's swish of feathers nor any cry, for all seven New World species of vultures are voiceless. For long minutes I watch them diminish to motes over the last ridge before the strait, and not once do they flap their wings.

As eaters of road kill and other carrion, turkey vultures may be one of the few species to benefit from the automobile. They have become ubiquitous as robins. Just the other day, six of them gathered around a dead fish on the shore below the cabin, paying little heed when I came down to watch them. And here on the mountain I see them often, wheeling over the slash or riding the updrafts, and I wonder whether they are testing the wind for a whiff of something dead. Experiments have shown that turkey vultures hunt, in part, by smell, and this seems to be confirmed by disproportionately large olfactory lobes in their brains. And yet, unlike bears, they don't seem attracted by the slaughterhouse stench of bonemeal. At least, I've never seen them near the gardens.

I run the hornet gauntlet again (actually, I walk it *very* carefully) and return near dark with the truck to finish watering the Hillside Garden. In recent days, kids have been razzing their dirt bikes on the powerline right-of-way a half mile below the slash, and I am wary of being seen. Nothing, not even the dope-sniffing dogs at airports, has a better nose for marijuana than a fourteen-year-old boy, especially if the pot belongs to someone else.

At the old log landing, nighthawks rise from the ground and circle me on velvet wings, like giant moths against the afterglow. They seem to have their quotidian round reversed; all day I hear them booming down the sky, and at night they are at rest. Do they come here, I wonder, for dust baths or to soak up the warmth of the ground?

The mosquitoes, as I am watering, are the worst I've ever seen on the coast. Sweating in the heat, I shed insect repellent faster than I can smear it on. Finally, I'm too busy with buckets, hose and flashlight to even bother swatting them. They're annoying but not threatening like the mosquitoes I remember on the Mackenzie River delta in July, where any exposed skin was covered within seconds. When we went ashore for gas, our Inuit guide's red mackinaw changed colour as if consumed by sudden mould. Mosquitoes swarmed in our noses, eyes and mouths, and you knew they could drive you mad if ever you were marooned there without repellent or fire to make a smudge.

At eleven when I climb wearily back to the truck, the first cool air is dropping like a benediction down the mountain. It comes in streaks of hot and cold, reminiscent of sea water on a rising tide, bearing scents of elderberry and creek ravines mixed with the resinous tang of scorched firs. The breeze fans the mosquitoes away, and I sit on the tailgate, drinking water from a jug and pouring the dregs over my head. Out in the strait, wind lanes wander aimlessly in search of a direction, cobbled silver under a half-moon. Other than crickets and small stirrings of the wind, I hear only the hoot of an owl from the ridge and once, far off, the keening of a siren, followed by red and blue pinpricks from the highway next to Davis Bay.

By the light of the silvery moon—who made that song famous forty or fifty years ago?—I drive the half mile of open slash with the headlights out, wary of attracting attention. If I can see Sechelt, Sechelt can see me. Tomorrow, a day of lard-assed self-indulgence, swimming and reading. And the day after, if the weather holds? Watering—what else?

Marijuana is one of those issues that seems never to go away. Just the other day, it was the subject of a radio phone-in show, and I was surprised by the number of complaints about addiction. These calls didn't accord with my own experience or with the science as I understand it, though they did echo my time in psychotherapy. All through my crash and recovery I smoked marijuana occasionally, even though my shrink advised against it. It's a mask, he said. Covers what you want to uncover. Since hearing this show, I've gone back to my notes (I taped every session), not for any therapeutic reason but to review his take on marijuana and addiction.

Finding the right psychotherapist is like buying boots—if the fit isn't right, you're going nowhere together. Neil Tubb was right for me. On my first visit I did most of the talking for more than an hour, then in twenty astounding minutes he showed me my inner workings, as starkly as an oracle spreading goat guts on an altar. As I left, he said it would take five to seven years of intensive work for me to straighten myself out. The cure, as it turned out, required just nine months of concentrated effort, and I came through my time with Neil convinced that he had, quite literally, saved my life.

I used to enjoy my visits to Neil. He lives—or did then—near the Victoria waterfront, overlooking Juan de Fuca Strait. I'd often find him sitting outside smoking—psychotherapists have addictions too. He's large and rumpled with grey hair and beard, an ex–RCMP narc, though seemingly free of any reefer madness fantasies about marijuana. "I never found that it had much effect on me at all," he told me at our first session. "It sure as hell didn't raise my consciousness. If I'm going to do anything mind-altering, I'd much rather have a belt of rum." But mind-altering, at least with drugs or alcohol, is not a harmless diversion in Neil's view. Toking would only delay my recovery, he said, and if I kept at it long enough it could do me in.

"Because the quality of the high diminishes over time," he warned, "the quantity has to increase. For some people who have a powerful need to repress things, it turns into a boxcar train that keeps getting longer ... because I smoke marijuana, I smoke marijuana, I smoke marijuana. It doesn't give it to me any more, so I smoke marijuana and do alcohol. Marijuana and alcohol. Then I do cocaine, and it just builds."

Neil's point was that as long as patients can hide behind booze or drugs, they'll avoid facing the psychological cause of their illness. But I was certain that didn't apply to me. My addiction was self-redeeming work, not dope, and I never believed that smoking masked my inner scars. In fact, opening old wounds was not difficult for me. My collapse had been so complete, so torturous, my ego defences were knocked flat, and facing even the most fearsome dragons in my psyche was preferable to living with the twin tigers of suicide and insanity. I guess that's why I was able to straighten myself out in a fraction of the time that Neil had predicted. I was ready.

At first I was uneasy about ignoring Neil's warnings, because he was so right about everything else. He knew exactly what ailed me and how to treat it. My family doctor agreed, prescribing Luvox, one of the refinements of Prozac. "You are so steeply in crash mode," Neil said, "nothing can be done until we get you back on the level with this drug so you can function." When the change first hit, after about six days on Luvox, I was filming herons on the Fraser River delta. Preoccupied with what I was doing, I didn't notice at first that I was feeling strangely and wonderfully different. My mood turned optimistic, free of cares and responsibilities, happy. My surroundings—tide pools, eelgrass, the flat calm sea and distant green of the Gulf Islands—all looked abnormally vivid, the colours brighter. I stopped work (it no longer seemed very important) and lay on the beach for the rest of the afternoon, just watching the puffy June clouds drift past. Driving home, I floated serenely through the rush-hour traffic, utterly without the usual frustrations. Over the next few days, as the chemical changes in my brain took hold, this new lightness of being became fixed. I began to sleep better, and my sense of humour returned. (Carole had been complaining for months that I wasn't much fun any more.) And not only did my crippling depressions vanish; I realized that I had been living for years under a cloud of constant low-grade depression, as if I were seeing the world darkly through an X-ray plate. That, too, was gone.

Although Luvox was truly a wonder drug for me, it dealt only with symptoms, not the causes of my malaise. Those I pursued with the same single-minded dedication I had been putting into my work. I kept a journal, read, meditated and carried out the assignments Neil gave me, strange and difficult things like writing a letter to my dead mother about my childhood with my left hand although I'm right-handed. Healing became my full-time job. Out of all this grew an understanding that I wasn't born with a dependent personality; no one is. I had learned my addictive behaviour from my family, and only when I could see how and why that happened was I able to make my escape.

The first step was redefining my notion of addiction. You can only get hooked, I thought, on things you swallow, inhale, put up your nose or into your veins. But as Neil peeled my psyche like an onion, I saw that people can become addicted to anything that helps paper over the cracks in their souls. Even good, ennobling things like hard work. Not that I overdosed on work as a kid. Except for cutting wood and helping a bit around the house, my time was my own. I sloughed off schoolwork and never took very seriously the few paying jobs that came my way in Granthams Landing. As a paperboy, for instance, I was known to throw the papers off the end of the wharf on Friday nights rather than miss the one movie of the week. Mind you, with only three customers in the winter months (four on Saturdays) spread over five miles, the financial incentives were not great. I have a snapshot of myself from those years, taken on the day of the launching of a tugboat my father and his brothers built on the beach where the Langdale ferry docks today. I was eleven or twelve. With a bowl-cut thatch of red hair, baggy corduroy pants rolled halfway to the knees, mud-caked shoes and a grin a yard wide, I looked as whole and happy as a kid can be. But even then the demons of a traumatic infancy and a troubled family were lurking within, and by the time I was into my teens they had a grip on me that I wouldn't break for nearly forty years.

Puberty was the first crack in my world. I don't know whether it's the same for all boys, but for me there was a period when my penis grew suddenly to adult proportions, while I was in every other respect still a scrawny kid. For a horrid year or so, I believed I was grotesquely deformed and saw myself doomed to follow in the sordid footsteps of Roger Ducharme, a sexual deviate who was hanged, according to the mythology of the day, for killing a woman with his immense sex organ. As kids, we strutted about raising forearm and fist and yelling, "Left arm, right arm, Ducharme," but suddenly the joke wasn't funny any more. Soon enough, however, I would discover that I was merely normal, and in time, relief would turn to regret.

While puberty was only a passing shadow, darker clouds were building on my horizon. By my early teens, the carefree nonchalance I'd known only a few years earlier gave way to shame: for my unconventional family (my father spoke like a wild-eyed anarchist at public meetings and my brother was studying ballet), for the hick town where I grew up, and most of all for what I perceived to be my weakness, shallowness and stupidity. Fumbling about for a way to redeem myself, I settled on hard work, the one thing I knew I could do. So at age sixteen I took myself off to an Alberta farm for the summer.

And work I did, for twelve, sometimes fourteen hours a day, six days a week, with chores morning and night on Sundays. There was nothing exceptional about this; farm people expected to work hard. Those who didn't (and many who did) had lost their farms in the Depression and gone elsewhere. The year was 1953, and the old people I worked for, Arnold and Ruby Golley, were free and clear of the desperate scratching that got them through the 1930s. They had a thousand acres in grain and pasture, a pure-bred beef herd, the best of machinery and no debts. And yet, like millions of Canadians, they were so deeply scarred by the lean years they could not let down their guard. A tiny terrier in rubber boots, Ruby raised chickens, turkeys and hogs, tended an enormous vegetable garden and hand-milked fourteen cows for the monthly cream cheque. These were her hedges against hard times, mostly unprofitable but hugely productive of labour. The Golleys were both in their seventies by this time, and Arnold was dying of stomach cancer, yet they still didn't feel they could afford a bathroom. We took our baths on Saturday nights, crouching in a tin washtub, and catalogue pages served as toilet paper in the outhouse.

The real running of the farm (and the bossing of me) fell to the Golleys' son, Jimmy, who had returned from a wartime stint in the air force. He was not an easy task master. Having toiled on the farm almost from infancy, Jimmy couldn't understand why I didn't know how to do even the most basic things like harness a team of horses. He suffered from headaches that made him morose and taciturn, the aftermath of a kick from a draught horse that fractured his skull and damaged the frontal lobe of his brain. Never the tyrannical boss, he was just remote and unhelpful at a time when I needed a companion and mentor.

After milking on Sundays I used to wander the fields, lonely and desperately homesick. At the time, farms in that part of Alberta were still separated by miles of bush, and if there were other teenagers around I never met them. Though I ached to quit and go home I stuck it out to the end of August, secure in the knowledge that although I was miserable much of the time, I was doing the right thing.

Many kids my age had summer jobs. They built trails for the Parks Branch, gutted salmon on their fathers' fishboats, waited tables or set chokers in the bush. But life went on. They played ball, pitched woo and came back in the fall to talk about their wonderful summers. Alone of all my classmates, I had cut myself off from friends and family and sentenced myself to two months of isolation and unremitting toil. It was an exercise in masochism: through suffering ye shall be redeemed.

After that summer on the farm, my course was set. I developed a full-blown dependency, an addiction to the only narcotic that could ease my anxieties and give me self-esteem. Though I knew I was obsessive about work, I'd have bridled at any suggestion that I was addicted. This was simply my nature, I told myself, something I was born with. And in a sense, I was right. The kinks in my personality were part of my heritage, but they came from my family, not from my genes.

My paternal grandfather grew up on an Ontario dairy farm before the turn of the century. Work was never-ending. On many farms sons were seen as an asset to be exploited, like draught animals, until they rebelled and left home. Although he never talked about it, I suspect my grandfather left the farm under similar circumstances. He took a divinity degree and became a prairie preacher, though he was never ordained because he could not accept the doctrinal and hierarchical rigidity of the Baptist Church. After only a few years, he left the ministry and worked hard and unceasingly at a variety of occupations for the rest of his life. At the age of eighty, he lay down and died after a full day on the job. To the end, I'm sure he believed that hard work was life's only reliable currency.

My grandfather had a mania for neatness and order. Every morning after he'd shaved, he immediately lathered up and shaved a second time, just to be sure. He dressed immaculately, and you could slice a finger on the creases in his pants. In old age he had a bad hip. I remember him hobbling around painfully, stooping to pick lint from the carpet and, I swear, bits of grit off the asphalt driveway. We were close, and I liked him very much, not least for his admiration of Tommy Douglas and contempt for Old Wattle-jowls, John Diefenbaker. But it would be years before I under-stood that he was a role model for my own addiction.

My father, Ted, inherited his father's dependencies, though they took a different form for him. Ted set out to make of himself an artist and a thinker. It was a worthy undertaking and not with-out success, but his efforts made me feel stupid as a kid because I hadn't the least inkling of what he was talking about. In fact, he never really discussed or explained his ideas to us. Rather, he lectured from on high as a wise man. He tells me today that he was aware of his distance from us at the time and regretted it deeply, though he was powerless to do anything about it. I remember an incident from my teens that characterized our relationship. I had expressed an interest in writing, perhaps as a career, and he replied, "Well, before you can write, you have to have something to say." It was true enough but ruinous to what little confidence I had. After listening uncomprehendingly to his talk of cosmic con-sciousness, psyche and ego, I believed I had nothing to say and never would. For years I could not write a simple letter without a terrible struggle with writer's block.

When I was finally ready to unravel my past, it was Ted who told me about the first two years of my life. I was born in Saint John, New Brunswick, where we lived for a time in the same house as my maternal grandparents, pillars of the local establish-ment. My grandfather was president and controlling stockholder of T. S. Simms & Co., the self-proclaimed "largest manufacturer of brushes, brooms and mops in the British Empire." By the stan-dards of the day, he was a tycoon—wealthy, well-connected to government and holder of high-profile national offices. He was also an extremely stiff-necked Baptist who forbade music and dancing on Sundays and cards at any time. So rigid was his teeto-talling, he poured the bottle of scotch given to him as retiring president of the Canadian Chamber of Commerce down the hotel toilet. Against this background, imagine the uproar when my mother announced, sometime early in 1934, that she and Ted were going to have a child out of wedlock.

That child was my elder brother, Noel. He was born into a climate of moral outrage, and there was still plenty of it around by the time I arrived two years later. Noel and I were taken in hand by my grandmother, a tall woman with the imperious bearing of the registered nurse she was. Without fear or favour she applied the child-rearing theories of the day, which consisted essentially of civilizing little savages. Almost from birth we were fed, put to sleep, awakened, picked up and laid down according to a rigid schedule. To this day, Noel has a profound antipathy to being on time for anything. The regimen had the opposite effect on me; being late still makes me break into a sweat.

Early in the war, my father moved the family west to escape a lifelong sentence of working off his moral debt in the offices of T. S. Simms & Co. Every second summer beginning in 1946, my mother, my two brothers and I journeyed east to spend July and August with my grandparents. Those were wonderful, unforget-table trips, crossing the Rockies on steam trains with open-air observation cars and bucketing through prairie thunderstorms in the Lockheed Lodestars of Trans-Canada Airlines. But in New Brunswick we were still savages. Although my grandparents were generous and kind, they were obsessed with appearances, espe-cially ours. Wherever we went out in public, to visit relatives in Maine or business associates in Montreal, or simply to the stuffy dining rooms of the CPR hotels where my grandparents invariably stayed, my brothers and I were subjected to nit-picking criticism of our manners, dress and deportment. We weren't barbarians; we'd been taught how to hold a fork and which way to tip the soup bowl. But no matter, we were made to *feel* like uncouth clods. The eastern visits ended in 1952, and I returned primed for redemption on the farm the following summer.

Of course, I understood none of this at the time—the bittersweet summers in New Brunswick, the sweat and anguish of my teens, the decades of running ever faster to elude my demons. But looking back now, I can understand why my maniacal drive was such a divisive force in my life. On the one hand, it nearly killed me; in the months before my collapse I was certain I would never live to see sixty. But on the other, it propelled me to do things in film and television that I wouldn't have missed for the world.

Utterly without experience in broadcasting, I was hired in 1965 to host the B.C. edition of *Country Calendar*, a weekly television show for farmers and fishermen. The CBC at that time, well before it was gutted by budget cuts, was a remarkable organization. Staffed by world-class technical and creative talent, it recognized an obligation to train people, to give the country eloquent and perceptive voices through which Canadians could speak to one another. With an unselfishness I'll never forget, I was taken in hand by staffers and carried until I could stand on my own feet. Within a year, I had escaped the merciless lens and was producing and directing on my own. Two more years, and I had my own documentary series. If you had ambition, CBC would give you all the rope you needed to hang yourself. In the fall of 1969 I had nine half-hour films in production at the same time, and I was producer, director, writer and researcher of them all. Without even a script assistant to answer the phone, I was working with four different film editors at the same time, dashing between them, babbling "cut here" or "dissolve there." The pace was insane. My guts were burning up, and the family doctor told me I was a bleeding ulcer waiting to happen. I was going up fast—and it was destroying me.

Before the end of the sixties, I was looking for a way out. Whenever I made a film about something that seemed to offer a more sane and healthy lifestyle, it became the escape hatch of the moment. A portrait of a crab fisherman led to inquiries about boats and experiments with traps. A film about Christmas-tree farming mushroomed into an abortive enterprise on two miles of Sechelt Peninsula powerline right-of-way. Of course, I had time for none of this. My few free weekends should have been spent with my wife and three kids, instead of bashing trees and falling asleep exhausted on the Sunday night ferry. I was saved from my ambivalence by a film series that kept me in the South Pacific for nearly a year. By the time I returned, much had changed. I had left the CBC and cashed in my tiny pension in order to move my family to Fiji. And a film I had made on the Fraser River before leaving had won CBC's top documentary award, clearing the way for me to produce for the national network, the National Film Board or anyone else.

Freed from the grind of local television, I made fewer films, mostly hour-long productions. But the monkey was still on my back, whipping me to work like a madman. And while the pressures were of a different kind, they were getting worse. To survive as a freelancer, I had to keep three films going at all times: one in the proposal stage, another in development and a third in production. On average, two of every three proposals failed to win production approval—a fairly typical ratio in the trade—often after weeks or months of unpaid work. The films themselves were becoming more ambitious, tougher to pull off. *Tankerbomb*, an investigative documentary on supertankers, took months of dodging obstacles thrown up by secretive oil and shipping companies. *Promised Land*, on the Mackenzie River Valley, entailed a ten-day snowmobile trip on Great Bear Lake in forty-below weather. I loved staring down the odds, proving to myself that I could beat the oil companies at their own game or get a rare caribou-hunting sequence on film. I loved the adventure, the ever-changing scene and, above all, the craft of filmmaking. Even the spin-offs were wonderful. On my travels in Nova Scotia, Ontario, New York state and Virginia I took apple tree cuttings to plant in an orchard of ninety heirloom varieties on my Sechelt farm, where I now lived alone. Winter evenings, I carved masks and rattles from curved knives of my own manufacture, an outgrowth of films on West Coast Native art. By day I was riding high, but I was waking every night with anxiety attacks, which by the early eighties had become so severe I dreaded going to bed.

At the time, I would have said that my apprehensions were purely financial; freelancing was a scramble, and my income was always modest. In truth, it was not money but my identity that was on the line. I had become Mike Poole, producer and director, and to stumble would mean the loss not just of my livelihood but of my legitimacy as a person. I would be nothing, a nobody. Haunted by such specters (though it would be years before I recognized them), I began for the first time to do work purely for the bucks. It began with *The Beachcombers*, the long-running CBC TV drama series set in Gibsons, just twenty minutes down the road from home. As a director, I could make three to four thousand dollars for a five-day shoot plus a few days of prep time and editing. It was good money, but I should never have done it. While the standards of production and acting (with some exceptions) were high, I thought the series concept was crap, relying on scenery and phony situations to hide its lack of any real roots. In the mid-eighties I turned back to documentaries, many of them natural history films for David Suzuki's television series *The Nature of Things*. But the die was cast; no matter what sort of work I did, nothing could stave off the bust-up that was coming.

Although my demons are now banished and I sleep in sweet peace, I haven't been able to cut the last link to the bad old days. First thing every morning I still swallow ten milligrams of Paxil, a successor to Luvox. I spent nearly a year trying to wean myself off it, gradually reducing the dosage by minute amounts. But at about three milligrams I bottomed out and the clouds rolled in. Why? I'm healthy and happy, satisfied that I've healed my emotional wounds. Could it be the effect of old scars, dead spots in the soul that never go away? Or is it purely physical, some chemical deficit that my body is unable to make up, as my doctor suggests, adding quickly that neither he nor anyone else really knows. "Anyway, why should you beat yourself up about this?" he asked me. "Diabetics don't blame themselves for needing insulin. For all we know, this is nothing more than some malfunction in your body."

Maybe so. But there is a larger picture I can't dismiss so easily. Depression has become a worldwide pandemic in the past two or three decades, increasing tenfold by some estimates. That makes it the psychological equivalent to the soaring rates of breast and prostate cancer. I believe those cancers will someday be traced to an environmental cause, a global contamination of air, water or food. So I wonder if there is a parallel epidemic loose in the human mind, touched off by some pathological shift in human consciousness—perhaps the loss of spirituality or our lonely isolation from the natural world.

Popping my daily pill, I worry about that. I'm also bothered by the thought that Paxil is a "disassociator," to borrow Neil Tubb's word. Talking about marijuana, he said some people smoke to duck their problems, to be something or someone else. I'm confident I don't use dope that way; the person I'm getting in touch with when I'm stoned is me, my unconscious mind. But I'm not so sure about Paxil. Except for a dent in my wallet every month, I'm oblivious to my dependence on it. No symptoms, no side effects. Addictions are supposed to be harmful, so does this mean that I haven't got one, or can I only get off the hook by going back to that solemn landscape under the clouds? I wish I knew.

Addiction is a slippery concept, I've discovered. The word's original Latin meaning was "bound to" or "surrendered to," as in the case of slaves legally tied to their master under Roman law. By Shakespeare's time, the word had also come to mean "devoted to," displaying highly focussed, concentrated effort and commitment. The nineteenth-century anti-opium and temperance movements linked addiction to drugs and alcohol, defining it as a vice or illness characterized by tolerance and withdrawal symptoms, and before long, the medical profession had claimed addiction as their own turf by declaring it to be a disease. More recently, anti-drug warriors and academics looking for their next research grant have attributed addiction to drugs rather than to persons, as if narcotics were demons that take possession of their victims. Today addiction is a debased word, co-opted for so many special agendas it no longer has any clear meaning. Many authorities, including the World Health Organization and the American Psychiatric Association, would like to see it struck from the professional lexicon.

Behind the confusion is a fundamental disagreement about what actually happens when a person gets hooked. One school of thought holds that addictions are purely psychological. A cell cannot crave, they argue, meaning that physical dependency is impossible without a psychological predisposition. Others maintain that some drugs, notably tobacco, can addict anyone exposed to them. I suspect that both mind and matter are usually involved, though exceptions abound, beginning with my own work dependency, where chemicals weren't a factor. Mired in uncertainty, I sometimes think fondly of the Victorians who dismissed the whole issue as a matter of breeding. Those who gave way to spirits or opiates simply lacked character. They were, it was said, "addicted to intemperance."

Bear trouble. For weeks my friend at the Hillside Garden has been dropping by every day or so for a drink of water, rather than amble down the hill to the creek. Fine. Glad to be of service. I've even been leaving water outside the patch so that he needn't trouble himself with tearing down the fence (rebuilt because of deer at this one garden). But he prefers the water *inside* and, just to let me know he isn't beholden, he swats the garbage cans about before he leaves, puncturing half of them. Okay. I can accept that; he was here first. But today the ingrate has gone too far.

Coming down the hill, I pass garbage cans scattered on the open slash (a dead giveaway for airplanes) and see ahead that one entire side of the fence is flat on the ground. The real wallop is waiting inside: the bear has gone through my plants like a DEA wrecking squad. At first glance it looks as if he's just been entertaining himself by raking down branches. But a closer look reveals the awful truth: the bear is a dope fiend.

About a dozen plants are damaged, a few only slightly, many half gone and one stripped bare to the stalk, save for a single ragged cola at the top. The buds have been nipped off and eaten, as neatly as if I had cut them myself with shears. Though far from mature, they would likely have enough THC to give the bear a rise. He must have downed at least a couple of pounds—a six-thousand-dollar lunch. Who knows, he may already be hooked and craving his next fix.

Reefer, as I have dubbed him, will be back. To discourage him, I've decided to assault his most delicate organ—his nose. What is offensive to me, I reason, should be far more repugnant to him, given that a bear's sense of smell is thought to be a thousand times keener than ours. Sniffing around the cabin, I come up with bleach and ammonia and mix them together, fortunately outside in the driveway. On contact, they erupt in a spout of foam and noxious gas like a high-school chemistry experiment gone awry.

Back on the mountain, I dip into buckets of ammonia and bleach with a large paint brush and sprinkle the ground around every plant, like a priest scattering holy water. If I knew some appropriate snatch of liturgy, some incantation to lend efficacy to the ritual, I'd repeat it. But I don't, so I settle later for an evening of reading about how animals use drugs.

Many species have, somewhere in their varied diet, a substance that satisfies an innate urge to get high. So ubiquitous is this need, it has been called "the fourth drive," after sex, thirst and hunger. And although there is no proof, it seems likely that humankind discovered intoxicating plants by watching animals. Abyssinian herders are said to have taken up coffee drinking after seeing their goats get a buzz from eating the wild berries we now call coffee beans. Yemeni goats got frisky after nibbling the leaves of a non-descript bush, turning their owners on to khat, a popular Middle Eastern stimulant chemically similar to amphetamine. Animals in tropical Asia were observed to be unusually calm after eating from the snakeroot plant, since found to contain resperine, a tranquillizer that would revolutionize the treatment of mental illness. Aboriginal people in the American Southwest may have learned about the hallucinogenic qualities of the datura plant from watching hawk moths flop about crazily after they drank its nectar. Siberian tribesmen were perhaps alerted to the psychedelic powers of mushrooms by the appetite of their reindeer for *Amanita muscaria*. Birds crash, cows waltz and elephants turn morose on fermented fruit, though our ancestors probably didn't need any help in learning how to get looped on alcohol.

As for Reefer the Bear, the most omnivorous creature in the western forest, I doubt that he needs my dope to get stoned. He must know about some mind-bending native plant, somewhere high in the alpines or deep in the fungal damp of a cave or canyon, that will give him his jollies whenever he wants.

While perhaps not Reefer's favourite odours, bleach and ammonia are apparently not offensive enough to put him off his grass. In the Hillside Garden this morning, I find one big plant eaten right down to the stalk and another badly roughed up. For good measure, he trashed a plant in Number Three Garden and carted one of my garbage cans away into the woods, perhaps as a memento of high times.

So, what next? I suspect that my noxious substances didn't work because they're water-soluble, and it has rained hard since I spread them; there's no trace of odour around the plants. It will take something more lasting to do the job. Back at the cabin, I go through the paint shelf and come up with creosote. It stinks, won't wash off and will burn your skin. This I paint on the rim of every pot. Around the outside of every plant, I tie cords dipped in the oily goo, taking care to keep them away from the buds, lest the dope become tainted. Short of deadfalls or land mines, what more can I do?

Reefer's depredations are not quite as bad as they seemed at first. Some of the hundred-dollar branches he knocked down were not eaten, and I've been able to resurrect them with string ties to the central stalk. Even without Reefer, I'd be doing a lot of this. As the colas thicken and add weight, the longer, lower branches are prone to split away from the stalk, especially in heavy rain. This may be a weakness of a particular variety, or the result of too much nitrogen. Usually the fallen branch is still joined to the stalk by a hinge of skin, so it can be tied up again and patched at the split with tape or grafting wax, if the crack is large. With practice, you can spot the branches most likely to break and tie them up before they let go. For many growers, myself included, this is a never-ending job in August.

Had I been brooding about my losses to Reefer, a phone call that came last night would have restored perspective. It seems that a grower friend has lost his entire crop to ... not thieves, not the police, but moose. "Moose?" I said, incredulous. "Moose ate his dope? In the Okanagan?" And then I laughed, for what else can you do with an image of a stoned moose? Needless to say, my caller was not this particular friend; marijuana growers love to gossip about one another's misfortunes.

My friend had drawn a *very* short straw. Even twenty or thirty years ago, moose were so rare in the southern interior that the chances of finding one in your marijuana patch were next to zero. For at least a century moose have been spreading slowly into British Columbia from the north, and so recent is this shift, there is no word for moose in many of the Indian languages in the southern half of the province.

After a few days to put my latest treatment to the test, I make a quick tour of all four gardens, and the good news is in: Reefer does not like creosote up his delicate snoot. Other than a little desultory pawing, the plants are undisturbed. But just to let me know that he's not pleased, Reefer has chewed or clawed holes in virtually every one of the two dozen garbage cans I have—had—on the mountain. Apparently he has a sense of play, as well as revenge. In three places on the road to the upper gardens I've had to cut alder trees that were bent low across the road. All had been raked by bear claws for at least ten feet above the ground. Reefer, it seems, has been swinging down saplings like Robert Frost in his birches.

My plants have pretty well stopped growing, the largest at about six and a half feet, and their energy is now flowing into flower heads. They are lovely to behold, bristling with pistils, vivid mauve against the emerging purple of the topmost leaves. Backlit in the late-day sun, the flowers sparkle with resin. The swelling flowerheads now crowd against one another, turning each cola into a solid, sticky mass of bloom up to three inches in diameter.

This is one drawback of my variety. If the weather turns wet— it's been clear now for nearly a week, despite ominous forecasts —dense colas invite mould that can gallop through an entire garden in a few days, making it worthless. Many growers have bred *ruderalis* or *sativa* genes into their plants to get a more open cola. The usual trade-off is reduced production—a fair exchange in wet years.

Some days I would welcome a little rain, just to damp down the fireweed. With August nearly behind us, the seed pods are mostly broken now and the flight of the seed cotton has swelled to a torrent of glinting silver motes, rushing uphill on the wind and tumbling over the ridges. A glorious sight. But pushing through a fireweed thicket unleashes choking clouds of cotton that get into any orifice not covered or clenched. (I've had to stop wearing contact lenses.) The other day I wore a fuzzy flannel shirt on a foray into the bush and emerged looking like something found in the lint trap at the laundromat. In sheltered places out of the wind, fireweed will hold on to its seed tufts for a long time, swelling to six-foot columns as thick as a fist and silvery as hoarfrost before they finally fly apart.

· The air is so full of this stuff, it is sticking to the resin on my plants. There's no getting it off, and I worry that it will look like mould to the buyers. But they must be used to it; most outdoor dope in B.C. is grown near fireweed. Besides, the mould that attacks marijuana in outdoor gardens is brown, though I have seen both green and white mould on marijuana that spoiled in storage.

As I leave the slash just before sundown, a stab of scarlet brings me to a stop at the edge of the woods, where a pileated woodpecker is feeding in a chokecherry tree. A formidable driller of snags, the bird is not cut out for this work. Its problem is one of physics. The cherries are all far out at the ends of branches much too limber to carry the bird's weight, which is considerable, given that pileated woodpeckers are as large as crows. It goes out headfirst, inching forward and craning its neck but never quite reaching the forbidden fruit. Lower and lower sags the branch, until the woodpecker flips over and hangs upside down like a monkey, flapping and calling its addled *yuk-yuk-yuk-yuk*. Three, four times the performance is replayed. Once it somersaults and lands in a crutch, leaning back on its tail like a red-hatted cardinal in a Vatican easy chair. Finally it falls, flips neatly in the air and swoops away into the timber, trailing lunatic cries.

CHAPTER 10

ALL IN
THE LINE
OF DUTY

On the first days of September, the nail biting begins. I was over at Ned's place a few days ago, expecting the usual horse laugh or two, and he lumbered me with the news that the RCMP helicopter has been in the area, scooping a hundred-plant garden from the mountain directly across Sechelt Inlet from my patches.

"Phew! Close call," I said. "I guess they've moved on by now."

"Yeah, they've gone up around Powell River and Cortes Island," Ned said. "But they'll be back."

Always a ray of sunshine, Ned threw in the added good news that some kids had been snooping around his gardens on the mountain, and he is now sleeping every night with his plants. At his side he keeps an Alsatian so fierce even its growl can draw blood.

The final broadside into my foundering confidence came on the radio news. The RCMP—again that remorseless eye-in-the-sky—have scored a million dollars' worth of dope from a garden in the marshlands of Burnaby, a Vancouver suburb. Even allowing for the inflated claims of the police and the stupidity of growing in an urban area, the report was not uplifting.

It was time for a hard look at my own situation. For at least a month I'd been ducking the obvious: my plants had become the most conspicuous thing on the slash. As the leaves turned dark purple, almost black, they contrasted ever more starkly with the fading autumnal colours all around them. Number Three Garden, in particular, stood out like hot pants on the Queen. To camouflage the plants with bracken or saplings, I'd have to drape them so heavily they wouldn't get enough sun to ripen. Something more drastic was called for.

Now, after three gruelling days, I've made the big move, relocating every plant in Number Three Garden to better-hidden sites. Naturally, it poured for two days before I began, adding several tons to the pots. Naturally, it then turned searing hot, opening my spigots so wide I had to carry a towel to keep the sweat out of my eyes.

Pray God for a little foresight. The new location is among stunted cedars on the slope above the old site—exactly the kind of cover my brother and I laboured for a whole day to clear last March. It's obvious now that I should have chosen my garden sites not to suit the young plants in spring but in anticipation of the mature six-footers of September. I should also have paid more heed to the location of last year's dead bracken and fireweed. Those sites, which looked bald and exposed in spring, are now jungles of head-high growth, ideal camouflage.

When I began lifting them, I found that the plants had sent roots through the drain holes at the bottom of the pots into the ground beneath. They snapped with an ugly tearing sound as the containers came away. To give the plants a fresh start, I cut out the bottom of each pot, unraveled the tangled white root mass within, and set it into a shallow hole lined with new soil. Thirty buckets, lugged up the bank from the truck.

The job done, Number Three is disguised as well as it can be. The plants are scattered in groups of four or five among the cedars, though the purple is as obvious as ever against the yellowish evergreen. As for the other gardens, they seem pretty well hidden between the undergrowth. Hidden, at least from my earthbound perspective. But from the air? If only I knew.

Since mid-July a plant in the Hillside Garden has been acting like one of those mutant superplants every grower hopes will descend like manna from heaven into his plots. Its flowers began to develop weeks ahead of any other plant and, by early August, were already forming dense colas. Now, when I come to pollinate it, the colas are huge, roughly five inches in diameter, and the flowers are exceptionally resinous, frosted white all over the pistils and calyxes and well out onto the narrow bud leaves. Under a twenty-power magnifying glass, the resin glands (capitate-stalked glandular trichomes, to give them the full grandeur of their scientific name) stand up like leggy mushrooms with round heads of purest crystal. Best of all, the plant matures early; the first pistils are already brown and withering, a sign that harvest is only days away, at least two weeks ahead of any of its mates.

Although growers debate the matter endlessly, I believe the optimal moment for harvest is when a third to a half of the pistils have turned brown. At this point, the taste and aroma of the dope is less resinous and tarlike and the high is lighter and more cerebral than marijuana left until all the pistils have died. The resin glands also change if picked too late, turning cloudy and losing some of their potency.

For pollen, I have kept two male plants far from any of my gardens, one in partial shade and the other in a hot spot on the slash. As in love and war, timing is everything here. Males mature two or three weeks before females, and the trick is to contrive an overlap, so you have viable pollen when the females are receptive.

Though the literature is vague on this point, it seems that pollen remains viable for only a few days after it is shed. My male in the sun has long since cast his pollen to the winds—billows of yellowish grains as fine as flour. But the shaded plant is just hitting its peak.

This morning, when the dew was off, I slipped plastic bags over two of its branches and cut them off close to the stalk. Now, taking care not to spill pollen, I slip the bags over branches on my precocious female and twist-tie them tightly closed. A brisk slapping about spreads the pollen to the flower pistils, and the bags come off again. Some breeders leave them on for a day or two, though I can't imagine getting better pollination than I did last year, using this same method. Between them, two branches produced between five hundred and a thousand seeds, far too many to bother counting.

Earlier, Ned had given me a useful bit of advice: avoid pollinating on a windy day. If a puff of wind catches the bag when you have it open, you may find your entire plant and half its neighbours bearing unwanted seeds.

Going the rounds today, I've been doing another pre-harvest task, though with some ambivalence. Marijuana, especially strains like mine with a lot of *indica* characteristics, has big leaves, a handspan or more across, which create a lot of shade. Some growers remove them from the upper part of the plant late in the season to expose the buds to sunlight and speed maturity. Others, some of them very knowledgeable, are dead against the practice on the grounds that these leaves are essential to a normal cycle of growth and maturity. After trying both ways, I've settled for removing leaves only in the last weeks before harvest. No question the extra light ripens the buds, though I wonder whether they fill out as much as they might otherwise do.

The weather is holding, bright and hot, while I count the days and watch the sky. Perhaps in part to break the tension, I do something today I vowed never to do: bring someone to see my gardens. Marijuana growers are notorious for bragging about their product and opening the door to trouble. But my motives, I would like to think, are different.

Bill Nicholls, an old friend, has been fighting a losing battle for the past three years with non-Hodgkin's lymphoma, a slow but incurable cancer. A tumour the size of a grapefruit is wrapped around his aorta. It is inoperable. After two courses of chemotherapy and one radiation treatment, his cancer has been checked but not stopped.

The time will come when Bill will have to endure another round of chemotherapy or radiation. To combat the accompanying nausea and vomiting, I would like him to try marijuana, probably the most effective known remedy for these side effects. I gave him a few joints for his earlier treatments, but I know he didn't smoke them. Although he has never said anything about it, I'm sure he's been infected by drug war propaganda with fears of addiction or hallucinations. Now, I am hoping that seeing the plants and talking about their properties will ease his apprehensions.

But it's not just fear. Bill is a little guy, constructed of whipcord and wire, and hard as the back of God's head. His way is to tough things out. He grew up in a mill town, Port Mellon, at a time before there were any roads to the outside world, and everyone lived in the shadow of the smokestacks, breathing the sulphite stench of papermaking (which Bill believes is the source of his cancer.) I met him first in the spring of 1948. The school at Gibson's Landing, as it was known then, hired a couple of fishboats to take two softball teams to play the kids at Port Mellon. I was the catcher on the grade eight team and pretty hot stuff,

I thought—until I saw Bill play. As the opposition shortstop, he speared grounders and line drives like fish in a barrel and threw with a howitzer arm. He hit and ran us to distraction, and when we were properly whipped he moved over to third base on the senior team and shone for another nine innings.

Wary of helicopters, I park the truck in the timber and we walk the half mile to the Hillside Garden. On the first steep pitch, Bill is slower than he used to be, though still pretty mobile for a guy with a tumour in his belly. At the garden, he strokes the feathery marijuana leaves and inhales their spicy essence. "So *that's* what it looks like," he says. "I didn't know it was such a beautiful plant." Bill has become a gardener in recent years and discovered in himself a feeling for such things.

I show him the buds, and he looks through the magnifying glass at the resin glands. I rhyme off the list of ills for which marijuana is an effective treatment—glaucoma (the only drug that works in advanced cases), epilepsy, multiple sclerosis, migraine, menstrual cramps, labour pain, asthma, paraplegia, quadriplegia, insomnia and a variety of other medical conditions. More recently, I tell Bill, thousands of AIDS victims have used it to relieve nausea and combat wasting syndrome. I run on like a snake-oil salesman, hoping that all this will demystify pot for him. But he is noncommittal.

For some time now, I've been passing on clippings and articles to Bill about cancer treatments. I gave him some literature on Essiac, an aboriginal herbal remedy, and he has been taking it faithfully. Whether it works or not doesn't matter; it's a life raft for Bill's hopes, something to buoy him up when conventional medicine lets him down. I've also been sifting through the marijuana literature. The irony is that a century ago, he could have bought pot—the drug he's now so wary of—at the local pharmacy. Cannabis extract was one of the most widely prescribed drugs in the Western pharmacopoeia before drug prohibitions pushed it off Canadian shelves in 1923 and after 1937 in the United States. Doctors had lost a valued tool, and they weren't happy about it; the American Medical Association made a formal complaint to Washington. But Congress was unmoved, and marijuana as medicine was gone for good. Or so it seemed.

Recently, the therapeutic use of marijuana has been making a comeback. It began with a false start in the seventies and early eighties when thirty-five U.S. states endorsed the medicinal use of pot, only to be blocked by federal government refusal to release any marijuana supplies. But a big crack in the bureaucratic wall opened in 1991 with the founding of the San Francisco Cannabis Buyers' Club, a group of patients who banded together to secure a reliable supply of marijuana. Despite police raids and harassment the club prospered spectacularly, growing within six years to more than eight thousand members, all certified by physicians as sufferers of conditions that will respond to marijuana.

Since California voters endorsed the therapeutic use of marijuana in November 1996, the number of patient-buyers' clubs in the state has grown to about twenty. In Arizona, the only other state to pass a medical marijuana initiative, buyers' clubs, if they exist at all, are small underground operations, in constant danger from the police. According the U.S. National Association for the Reform of Marijuana Laws (NORML), there are perhaps fifteen clandestine clubs in the U.S. outside of California, and all live a precarious existence. NORML sees an embryonic tolerance for medical marijuana, however, in a pattern of sentences and plea bargains that are somewhat more lenient for buyers' clubs than for ordinary pot infractions.

In Canada, after one failed attempt in Toronto, the country's first marijuana clinic, the Cannabis Compassion Club, was founded in Vancouver in April 1997. Despite evictions by unsympathetic landlords, a chronic money shortage and reluctant doctors, the club has grown beyond 150 members and gained the tacit co-operation of the police. Strangely, in Canada's marijuana Mecca, the club has a lot of trouble securing a reliable supply of clean and affordable pot. Clean because mouldy marijuana can give AIDS patients aspergillosis or salmonella, and affordable because the club's only income is the markup in charges on marijuana. American buyers take the cream of the local crop and keep prices high. With much of the club's clientele coming from Vancouver's impoverished Downtown Eastside, this is a serious obstacle.

Plans are afoot to establish cannabis buyers' clubs in Toronto, Montreal and probably elsewhere. Certainly, there is public support; 83 per cent of Canadians favour legalizing marijuana for medical use, according to a 1997 poll. But it's hard to see how any club can survive without access to Medicare money, and that's not likely to be forthcoming without research to document the efficacy of marijuana. Medical strains have to be standardized so that doctors and patients can depend on consistent strength and psychoactive properties. Optimal dosage and treatment regimes for particular illnesses have to be worked out. And comparative studies should be done to determine whether the synthetic form of THC, known as dronabinol (brand names: Marinol, Nabilone), is indeed a substitute for marijuana. (Anecdotal evidence suggests that it is much less effective, perhaps because it lacks the complex of chemicals in natural marijuana).

For a time in the 1970s the U.S. government funded research into therapeutic uses of marijuana, and it even supplied a handful of patients with marijuana for "compassionate use" from its cannabis research farm in Mississippi. But all that ended with the election of Ronald Reagan as president in 1980. Ever since, federal government agencies such as the DEA have stonewalled research, though holding the line is becoming more difficult. After two years of collecting testimony and reviewing research for one of the most comprehensive studies ever done on the medicinal value of cannabis, the DEA's own administrative law judge, Francis Young, concluded that "marijuana, in its natural form, is one of the safest therapeutically active substances known to man." The agency was profoundly embarrassed and hastily rejected Young's findings, ruling that marijuana would remain classified as a dangerous and utterly useless drug. Under U.S. law, proof of marijuana's efficacy would force the government to reclassify it from Schedule 1, the category of banned substances like heroin and cocaine, and make it available by prescription.

The irony here is that our everyday use of prescription drugs is creating dependencies fully as serious as those ascribed by the DEA to illicit drugs. And the excessive use of antibiotics has set in motion a deadly cycle of viral immunity and ever more powerful drugs, triggering the mutation of superviruses like the resurgent tuberculosis bacillus. When used therapeutically, marijuana and opiates *are* different from other drugs, though not in the way anti-drug warriors would have us believe. Unlike antibiotics, they do not create superviruses. Marijuana is an analgesic, an anti-convulsant, a sedative, an appetite stimulator, a mood elevator, a migraine remedy and many other things, but not a curative that sets off defensive reactions in other life forms.

I was never able to persuade Bill to try marijuana. His cancer spread to his brain and lungs, and he was in a coma when I saw him last, hovering in a limbo between life and death, where he stayed in my mind long after the end. For months, waiting for the ferry (Bill lived nearby) or hearing the phone ring at the cabin in the evening when he often called to talk sports or rage comically at the state of the world, I found myself brought up short by the stark reality of his absence. Time usually heals, but with Bill, the further his death recedes the more I miss him.

It's hard to understand why anyone would want to withhold marijuana from a patient like Bill; none of the usual arguments about addiction or crime or unhealthy side effects apply when someone has terminal cancer. A while ago, I came across a couple of novel explanations from Bruce Alexander, a psychology professor at Simon Fraser University, in his seminal book *Peaceful Measures: Canada's Way out of the 'War on Drugs.'* Alexander believes that the drug war is not fundamentally about drugs. He sees it, rather, as a device used by both anti-drug warriors and their opponents, whom he calls resisters, to cope with the same set of emotional problems. The two most important of these he identifies as the need to blame and the conflict between societal control and individual autonomy.

The need to deflect blame from ourselves, to find a scapegoat, Alexander argues, is driven by the frustration of living in a world that "provides a daily horror show of physical and emotional violence." This violence can manifest itself in ways as diverse as rage over a speeding ticket, assaults on the earth's biosphere, murder and suicide, or obscene consumerism on a planet where millions are starving. He writes:

> It seems to me that drugs serve as the current scapegoat because they so well symbolize the genuine chemical menace that faces modern society. Contemporary civilization threatens to toxify and corrupt itself and the earth with pesticides, nuclear waste, industrial chemicals, chemical and biological weapons, legal drugs, sewage, growth hormones, and so forth ... This deadly chemical dilemma is neatly exorcised by seeking to destroy a set of illicit drugs that are presumed to be highly toxic and also

cause people to lose control of themselves [both wrongly, Alexander maintains]. These illicit drugs become the poison that threatens civilization.

Anti-drug warriors engage in authoritarian repression, Alexander argues, not only because drugs have a real potential to increase the personal power of their users to resist societal control but also because "the impulses for personal autonomy that they seek to repress in others are ones they know well in themselves, but deny or subdue ... Drug warriors genuinely fear their own individual autonomy as well as that of the resisters." For their part, resisters are motivated only partially by a direct concern with drugs, Alexander believes. While their rhetoric "celebrates, and typically overstates the virtues of drugs in personal development and growth," their right to use them is "a symbolic affirmation of a long-lost ideal of complete personal freedom."

And then there are the more tangible rewards. As Alexander notes, the war on drugs is a very serviceable war. It serves the imperial interests of powerful nations, especially the United States, in getting their way with developing countries. It serves the globalization agenda of transnational pharmaceutical corporations. It serves the financial interests of drug traffickers and dealers, keeping supplies limited and prices high. It serves the aspirations for power and wealth of bureaucracies and police forces. It serves the lucrative moral crusades of the religious right. And everywhere it serves the insatiable appetite of governments for centralized power and control over their citizens.

If marijuana is a victim of Western industrial society, I wonder what other gifts of the natural world have succumbed to the same forces. Somewhere between 25 and 40 per cent of the modern pharmacopoeia consists of drugs derived directly from plants, or synthetic copies of natural substances. Many can be traced to the botanical knowledge of aboriginal peoples. As the plague of twentieth-century extinctions sweeps the planet, this chain of discovery is being broken everywhere. With only a fraction of the world's 700,000-plus plant species tested, who knows what miracle drugs are being lost before they were ever discovered?

Though I admit to an occasional fit of temper, I don't think of myself as a person with a need for vengeance. That said, I have just treated myself to a full measure of it. And oh, how good it feels!

Walking to my gardens near the old skid road this afternoon, I caught Reefer the Bear at his bath. From the logging road that skirts the swamp, I often peek through the screen of alders to see if there are any birds or animals at the little pond. The road is high there and less than a hundred feet from the water, a perfect vantage point.

Reefer was sitting upright on the bottom of the pond, or so it appeared, though the water was so roiled I could see neither his bottom nor the pond's. A strong westerly was rattling the leaves and whisking away my scent, leaving him utterly oblivious to my presence. The day was bright and hot—swimming weather—and he had immersed himself up to the neck. Languidly, he paddled the surface and scratched an ear. A stick drifted within reach on the wind. He pushed it about with a forepaw, like a kid in the tub with a rubber duck.

Reefer is smaller than I expected, three or maybe four years old. He has a ginger muzzle and lively ears that twitch away the flies buzzing around his head. He also has an advanced case of amotivational syndrome, the awful price of his thoughtless dalliance with marijuana. For five minutes I watched, and he could manage nothing more ambitious than a yawn.

My intention was to put a rocket under Reefer and send him hightailing for the hills. For a moment my resolve weakened; such a shame to break the tranquillity of this sylvan idyll. But then I thought of the thousands of dollars in lost dope, the smashed plants, punctured garbage cans, downed fences and hours and hours of work cleaning up after this vandal. Cupping my hands to make a loud pop, I smacked them together as hard as I could and hollered, "Hut, hut, hut, you fat bastard. Git on out of here."

There is only one word for Reefer's reaction: he levitated. One moment he was in the water, the next he was standing on the bank, raining water. He paused there for a second or two, trying to locate the source of the sound. I clapped and yelled again, and off he went on a tear through the slash, weaving like a halfback between stumps and bush and crashing away into the timber.

The pond, when I walked down to it, looked as if a depth charge had gone off. Rafted fragments were all that remained of the delicate water plants. The lush banks looked like a buffalo wallow. A few shell-shocked water striders were the only life in sight. Reefer had been on a romp here, doing cannonballs and belly flops like some fat plutocrat in his swimming pool.

Of course, the last laugh was his. Any contrition I might have felt was dispelled by the discovery of one of my tallest and best plants, toppled by the swipe of a paw and trampled flat.

A storm is brewing as I leave the slash in the gathering dusk. Strands of cloud, layered in darkening shades of grey, are hurrying up the strait ahead of the approaching blast from the Pacific. Smoke from the pulp mill south of Nanaimo is stretched flat along the east coast of Vancouver Island. Let it rain and rain hard, if it must. But let it clear again soon, for mould is the enemy now. Two weeks of good weather and the crop will be in the barn.

CHAPTER 11

DOING
THE
GAZELLE

The second week of September begins with heavy rain overnight, and I'm on the mountain early, looking for mould. Ugly brown crud, it first appears deep inside the cola, next to the stalk, where there is no light or air. I part the buds gently and look within. They are soaking wet—colas this dense need a day or more of sun to dry out—but so far, blessedly, no mould.

Susceptibility to mould is determined both by the conformation of the plant and by its inherent resistance, or lack of it. There's a trade-off to be made here. While thick bushy varieties with dense colas are problematic on the coast, they are more productive than sparser strains and, for many growers, worth the risk. Timewarp, for example, is currently the hot variety on the B.C. Gulf Islands. But Jim, the grower I visited a few months back, doesn't believe Timewarp can a survive a wet autumn. His strain, Larry, with its more widely spaced buds, has endured week-long October storms with no significant mould.

It is commonly believed, wrongly in my experience, that rain itself is damaging, knocking the resin glands off the leaves and buds. But as anyone who has ever manicured sticky green marijuana will know, the resin is highly resistant to water and can only be cleaned off your hands with gasoline, alcohol or some other solvent.

As for Dieter, my own variety, I don't know what to expect. The colas are dense, though the plant itself is not nearly as bushy as some I've seen. Developed as it was in an arid part of the B.C. Interior, its mould-resistant qualities have never been tested on the coast. Last year, my first with Dieter, was exceptional; September set records for heat and lack of rain.

So far my plants are clean, though the outlook today isn't promising. The strait is sealed under a lid of cloud, heavy as putty, and a big blow is forecast for tonight. It's with surprise and delight, then, that I see the skies tear open near noon and the sun beat down on my gardens. Making the most of it, I go round shaking water out of the colas and tying up any that were knocked down by the rain.

Emerging from the timber on the way to Number Three Garden, I'm brought up short by the sight of tire tracks in the mud at the edge of a big puddle on the road, made since last night's rain. There is only one set of tracks; someone has gone up the mountain but not come back. He's still here somewhere, and at this season, chances are good he's looking for dope to steal.

Where the road swings uphill to the open ridge, the gravel has been churned up by wheels slipping on the steep pitch. Halfway up the hill, a truck is rammed almost out of sight into a gap in the roadside alders. It's a green crewcab, with steel reinforcing welded around the box, the kind of vehicle favoured by people who work in the bush. There is a tangle of wire rope, torn raingear, plastic oil jugs and an axe with a broken handle in the back.

On the open top of the ridge, where I haven't been since April, I can see no footprints in the mud where seepage crosses the road. This is bad news. If my visitor hasn't come this way, there's only one other direction he could have gone—down the road towards Number Three and the gardens by the skid road.

Back on the main road, I go quietly, stopping every few steps to listen. The wind has fallen into one of those lulls that often precede a storm. I haven't gone more than a hundred yards when I hear footsteps—*think* I hear footsteps. Stepping into the roadside brush, I hold my breath and listen. Yes, now there's no doubt. I can hear the faint crunch of feet on the dry alder leaves that cover the road. And they are coming closer.

I wait until I can see the man through the bush, and when he is about thirty feet away, I step into the middle of the road. He stops dead, a big guy with a black plastic garbage bag in his hand, which he tries to hide behind his legs. It looks to be half full with something lumpy. He's about thirty, six-three or -four, wide in the shoulders, lank sandy hair, a long horsey face spotty with plukes.

"What have you got in the bag?" I demand.

"Oh, is that your truck I saw down the hill?" he says, shifting uneasily.

"What have you got in the bag?"

"You didn't see my partner, did you?" he asks. "I've been looking for him."

"What have you got in the bag?"

This time I don't wait for another evasion. "You've been stealing other people's dope, haven't you?" I manage to say, my voice so taut with rage I can barely speak. This frontal assault is not a calculated risk; I have the kind of boiling radiator temper that makes me stupidly oblivious to the consequences of even the most intemperate acts. This guy could drive me into the ground like a tent peg, but he does just the opposite. He melts, turns to mush.

"No, no, I-I-I found it," he stammers. "Just there, down the road. Come on, I'll show you." He is backing up, his face drained as if he's been gut-shot. "I'll show you, I'll show you."

He turns, walking fast the way he came, then breaking into a run when he's nearly out of sight. I hear him crash into the brush at the roadside and plow uphill through the timber, taking a hellish roundabout route back to his truck.

It's not me he's scared of; it's the knowledge of what can happen to people who are caught stealing dope. In California, pot thieves get shot. In B.C. they've been beaten to a pulp, hung up by their thumbs, forced to eat dogshit (an unfortunate case of wrongful conviction) and, rumour has it in one case, beaten to death, shot for good measure and thrown off a bridge into the Fraser River. If I've heard these stories, this thief has heard them too, and many more besides.

A quick survey confirms what I suspected: the contents of the garbage bag was a single plant growing in an ill-concealed spot on the way in to the skid road. The branches have all been snapped off at the stalk. He didn't find either the skid road garden or Number Three, though this was at best a pyrrhic victory. The discovery of that one plant would be enough to bring him back looking for more.

I hang around until I hear the truck start up and rattle away down the hill. I've been thinking hard about how to stop this guy, and I have a plan. But I will have to act fast; he will stay away for a few days, expecting me to be watching my patches. Two or three days, but no longer.

At the cabin I get on the phone, calling Ned first. The thief's truck is distinctive, and I'm hoping someone will know whose it is. Ned doesn't, but he suggests several people who might. One call leads to another and so on for an hour, and then I score! I get a name and, from the phone book, a street address on the outskirts of Gibsons. After a restless night, I drive by the address on the way to the 6:20 A.M. ferry and, sure enough, the truck I saw on the mountain is in the driveway.

In Vancouver, I'm first in the door when the public library opens. Within half an hour I've found what I'm looking for. From a fat file of newspaper clippings on the Hell's Angels motorcycle gang, there emerges a horrific image of a skull, embellished with wings and horns, topped by the legend: Hell's Angels Inc. It's creased and fading with age, but photocopied and touched up with pencil and felt pen, then photocopied again for maximum contrast, it looks real enough.

At home in North Vancouver, I get on the computer and type the following in large letters beneath the Hell's Angels insignia:

> WE ARE IN THE BUSINESS OF SELLING MARIJUANA. TO GUARANTEE OUR SUPPLIES, WE CONTRACT GROWERS. THEY LOOK AFTER THE CROP, WE TAKE CARE OF SECURITY. THIS IS WHERE ASSHOLES LIKE YOU COME IN.
>
> TWO OF OUR SECHELT GROWERS HAVE SEEN YOU STEALING THEIR DOPE. OUR POLICY IS STRAIGHTFOR-WARD. YOU GET ONE WARNING. REPEAT, ONE. RIP OFF ANY OF OUR GROWERS AGAIN AND WE WILL SEND SOME PEOPLE TO DEAL WITH YOU.

I drive to Surrey, a Vancouver suburb most often associated with the Hell's Angels, and mail my missive there to give it a cred-ible postmark. By tomorrow, or the next day at the latest, Mr. X. will find it in his mailbox. In all this, I am relying on the force of a stereotype that depicts the Hell's Angels as marijuana drug lords. Whether or not it's true in B.C., people believe it. I can only say that in all my pot dabbling, I have never encountered any connection with the motorcycle gang.

Though my little ruse worked—at least I never saw my thieving friend or his truck again on the mountain—the incident left a bad aftertaste. I had done no harm and certainly felt no sympathy for my victim; stealing marijuana, the plant of pleasure, enlightenment and benign goodwill, strikes me as something close to sacrilege. And I could have done much worse. I'd toyed with the idea of posting a notice to marijuana growers in pub washrooms all over the Peninsula, advising them to have a talk with Mr. X (whom I would have named) if they'd had pot stolen from their gardens. I rejected this as too dangerous. There are scores, if not hundreds, of growers in this area, and all of them have likely been ripped off at one time or other. I could have been the cause of real violence.

No, it wasn't contrition that made me feel bad. It was anger and its aftermath. Anger, I believe, is a fire that burns the crucible that holds it, not its intended target. Sometimes, if the circumstances are right, anger can be cathartic, a welcome release and highly effective. But for me, it is almost always a toxic indulgence that poisons the mind and spirit. For weeks after my encounter on the mountain, I was haunted by fantasies of dynamiting the thief's truck, breaking his legs, even shooting him and dumping his body into Malaspina Strait. Ugly, ugly thoughts.

I knew the lesson well enough: you can't play with shit without getting it on your hands. But I had no idea what to do about it. There's no way to grow marijuana, at least not outdoors, without confronting thievery, and I was not about to abandon my gardens. That left only one alternative: control my anger. But I've been working at that for years. Now, instead of just getting mad, I get mad at myself for getting mad. That's not exactly progress, but it's at least a change.

These last weeks before harvest may be the toughest of all for the dope grower, even though there's next to nothing to do, other than checking for mould and maturity. All watering has stopped, to lower the moisture content of the buds. Fertilizer is withdrawn so that the smoke won't have a chemical taste. Weak branches are long since tied up. The main task is waiting—and trying not to worry.

For the last third of the season, big growers like my friend Dieter camp out with their plants full time. Which explains why lone wolves like me have become an endangered species. Partnerships of two or three growers make it possible to have someone constantly on watch. A week on duty, a week or two off, just like a regular job. But for all the partners to make a living, the output has to double or treble. Last year, Dieter and two friends harvested fifty pounds of buds, which sounds pretty bountiful for eight or nine months' work—until it's divided by three.

Since the early 1980s, the hazards of autumn have been made much worse by the passion of the Asian market for wild pine mushrooms (*Armillaria ponderosa*) that grow in the forests of British Columbia and sell in Tokyo for as much as a thousand dollars a pound. Just as the marijuana gardens are ripening, thousands of mushroom pickers swarm into the hills all over the province, lured by the chance of more money from one lucky afternoon than they could make in a month bagging groceries in town. Though they pose no problem for me—mushrooms are not happy on logging slash—the pickers are hell on two feet for growers like Dieter. His gardens are miles from any road, way back in a mountain bowl ringed by bluffs that only the most masochistic hiker would tackle. And yet, almost every fall, mushroom pickers blunder onto his turf. With diplomacy, or bluff and bluster if necessary, he steers them aside. Most are no trouble, but some, if they see the garden, will go to almost any lengths to come back and rip it off.

Confrontations, busts, raids—the consequences of illegality— are a big part of what makes marijuana culture more interesting than potato farming or raising hogs. I think sometimes that everyone who ever put a pot seed in the ground has a hair-raising tale to tell, stories of narrow scrapes, chases, wild rides by night, rapids run, chasms leaped, forest fires escaped, cops and criminals eluded—melodrama without end, all in the name of saving the precious stash. Whenever they get together, dope farmers trot out their stories, and I love to listen. Some of them are true (some of the best stories, actually), and many of course are bullshit, or an artful blend of the two. And that's fine. Every trade needs its mythic dimension.

There are, of course, dope growers who have no need to expand on the truth; their real careers are outrageous enough without embellishment. Richard Fears is a charter member of this fraternity. Hoot, as he is known to all except the police, has an unblemished record of growing marijuana every year for more than three decades and never making any money. At least, not real money. Five, maybe ten thousand dollars in a big year. All the rest, hundreds of pounds of buds and untold thousands of potential dollars, have succumbed to a scourge of calamities that would have driven a less resilient soul to seek a legal occupation.

But not Hoot. He is sustained through life's rebuffs by a philosophy of peace and gentle acceptance, which I suspect has been with him since he was kicked out of a New Westminster high school in his teens and took to the gypsy life. "I could write a book on how to lose your crop," he says, "so that's why I've become a philosopher."

Stoned or straight, you laugh a lot in Hoot's company. He was one of those itinerant figures who drifted in and out of the Kettle River Valley, a hippie haven in the southern interior where my folks lived in the 1970s and '80s. Summers he could usually be found tending his dope garden. Winters, when I asked after him on my occasional visits home, people would say he was off in India or the high Andes, talking with God.

Hoot got an early start on the drug scene. By the mid-1950s he had had his first toke in Greenwich Village and sat on New York sidewalks with his lips stained purple by Benzedrine sucked from cotton balls. He wandered the South Pacific, Europe, Asia, Central and South America, and every spring he was back in British Columbia, ready to put in another crop. Today, in his early sixties, his pattern is unchanged. He travels by winter if he can afford it— "Give me a plane ticket and five thousand dollars and I'm good for six months"—and rumbles around B.C. in an old pickup, growing dope and making charming birdhouses from salvaged materials, which might generate some income if he didn't give most of them away.

When we meet in an Okanagan farmhouse, Hoot looks healthier and happier than I've seen him in years. He could still use a good dentist, but gone is the half-starved raggedness of the brown-rice hippie. Lean and fit, he sports a flowing beard and patriarchal mane of silvering hair. Though we haven't seen each other for some time, I've been hearing secondhand about his exploits, especially one involving a houseboat.

"Now, that was a wild scene," he says, unperturbed as usual by the contemplation of disaster. "We got into it because we'd had such an awful time with the cops the year before. The heat was just vicious. For a whole month the narcs were chasing us all over the territory, so by the time we got the crop off and sold, we were just worn out. I went to Mexico, and when I came back in the spring my partner, Pete, said let's try something different, and I said I'd like to do a trip on water.

"We bought an old homemade houseboat in Vernon, big thing with three pontoons down each side. We loaded it right to the roof with everything we'd need—tools, propane bottles, rolls of plastic, marijuana plants and seeds, fertilizer, food—everything you could jam into it. And just to top off the load, we rescued two half-crazy huskies from the local pound. Poor buggers had never seen a day's freedom."

Hoot is a sucker for dogs and probably kids, too, though he has never had any of his own. As we talk, the infant daughter of a friend is crawling about on the carpet. Occasionally, as she passes, Hoot extends a helping hand and she stands between his knees, listening with rapt, if uncomprehending, attention.

Hoot and Pete's plan was to cross the Monashee Mountains to the east of the Okanagan Valley and plant their garden somewhere away from roads on the shores of the Arrow Lakes, two stormy intermontane sheets of water, altogether more than a hundred miles long.

"Did either of you know the lakes, have an idea where you were going?" I ask.

"Oh hell, no. We'd figure that out when we got there. Preserve the element of surprise, you know. A bit of adventure."

They met their first surprise on the western slopes of the Monashees. Wheezing and threatening to expire, their old van refused to pull the immense weight of houseboat, huskies and an old lifeboat they'd loaded on top "in case of emergencies." They got their caravan off to the side of the narrow road, nearly rolling it down an embankment, and Pete limped back to Vernon in the van and "borrowed" another vehicle in the dark of the night from a used car lot.

"We just got started again," Hoot recalls, "and the fucking fuel pump packed it in. Not enough gas to pull the load. But it's one of those vans with the engine inside the cab, so we take the cover off, and all the rigging off the carburetor, and I start pouring gas out of this can straight into the engine. Well, no problem pulling that houseboat now. But God, what a hair-raising ride that was— fifty miles of winding mountain road and we don't know whether this thing is going to blow up in our faces. I'm standing there pouring in the gas all the way to Arrow Lake."

Hoot and Pete made their entrance at the Needles ferry landing just as the crew was preparing to embark on the first lake crossing of the day. The road down to the loading ramp was steep and, on this April morning, covered with loose gravel.

"The brakes had been okay on the highway," Hoot says, "but they couldn't handle the load on this last steep pitch. We started sliding sideways and the ferry crew scattered everywhere, running for cover. Oh, oh, I thought, this is going to look like a plane crash on an aircraft carrier. Pete's eyes were big as saucers. I jumped out and ran alongside, throwing rocks and chunks of driftwood under the wheels, but they rolled right over." Hoot is on his feet as he tells this, heaving imaginary logs like matchsticks. "The gas can had dumped over in the cab and Pete was choking on fumes and scared shitless he'd be incinerated. At the last second, the whole rig slewed around straight and onto the ferry."

Across the lake, they launched the houseboat. Bubbles surfaced ominously around the pontoons, which were leaking and threatening to sink the whole enterprise. Working in frigid water—thick shelves of ice still ringed the lakeshore—they patched the leaks with chewing gum. But the motors wouldn't work. Undaunted, they pulled the whole circus back on the road and had them fixed in Nakusp, the nearest town, while RCMP officers sniffed suspiciously around their rig. They drove on to the north for another ten miles, launched again and made a perilous crossing of the lake in a storm. Finally they came ashore in a lovely, isolated bay and made themselves at home in driftwood camp.

"But you weren't on a camping trip," I remind Hoot. "Was this country any good for growing dope?"

"Well, we looked around and we found some magic—a broad sort of bench with sunny open places between the trees and light, sandy soil that you could shovel just like a garden. All we'd have to do was add fertilizer. It was just beautiful. But there was one little problem: it was almost five hundred feet above the lake, up these bluffs so steep you could hardly claw your way. So here's these two old geezers packing hundred-pound tanks of propane for heating the greenhouse straight up these cliffs."

Setting to work, they finished the hothouse, rigged water lines and prepared beds of soil where seedlings would grow until they were large enough to plant out. Then, just as they were ready to sprout their first seeds, a helicopter appeared from west of the mountains and circled low over the fledgling plantation. It landed on the beach two miles down the lake, and the occupants sat around on logs for the afternoon, having what appeared from a distance to be a picnic.

"We watched them and decided they were only some government workers buggering off from the office for the day. But we weren't going to take any chances, so we moved the whole show."

Greenhouse, soil, watering system—everything had to be taken up, carted away to a new, more secure location and set up all over again. Work went ahead quickly now, and within a few weeks hundreds of seedlings had sprouted. But all was not well with the happy dope growers.

"Things were falling apart for us," Hoot remembers. "We were both worn out, really tired, and out of money. We got to nattering at each other and Pete decided to pull out, at least for a while. I took the houseboat and the huskies, who were now wilder than ever, down Arrow Lake to Castlegar to sell it and raise some money. I nearly lost it in a storm and had to stand half the night up to my chest in that icy water to keep it off the rocks."

To get back to their gardens, Hoot had to drive to Needles in the stolen van—"siphoning gas all the way"—cross the lake on the ferry and then walk fifteen or twenty miles over mountains that were "swampy as hell and loaded with bears." He had "no gun, no food, no money. All I had was blueberries and water." But Hoot remembers that trip as just another episode in a summer of wonders. "It was so beautiful. Geese and loons and a deep bed of moss on top of this cliff where I used to lie overhanging the bay. The houseboat had sold, and once I had some supplies I didn't want to leave. Walk along the shore at night and everything would sparkle with phosphorous. It was just magic."

I hear a yearning for days of sun and wind in Hoot's voice. Here in the Okanagan, a blizzard has swept in from the north and snow is hissing softly against the windows. Hoot has no money to travel this year.

And so the summer slipped past. The gardens flourished wonderfully, and Hoot's golden idyll went on and on. On, that is, until Labour Day weekend, when the world came barging in. I can imagine the moment: Hoot sitting by his campfire, contentedly sipping his morning coffee, and then specks appearing on the water across the lake, then more specks, expanding and spreading rapidly into a flotilla of boats heading right for the camp.

"It was like being an aboriginal somewhere," he tells me, "watching the ocean when the Europeans arrived. I'd had all this quiet, nothing but nature all summer, and all of a sudden I see this armada of boats coming. I just couldn't believe it. I didn't know it yet, but they weren't coming for any picnic on the beach. They were mushroom pickers and they'd be going right up the hill, right towards the gardens."

The gardens were scattered in four separate openings in the forest. Without Pete, who had still not returned, Hoot couldn't possibly intercept the pickers heading for all of them.

"I was trying to dash from patch to patch, and I just couldn't do it all," Hoot recalls. "I'm madly picking mushrooms and stuffing them under the pine needles to throw the pickers off the track. I'm pulling up water lines, running back and forth, wondering who to cut off and who to let go. And all the time these people are coming up the hill, spread out like a military skirmishing line." At least two pickers stumbled right into the gardens, though they left the plants alone. But this was just the beginning.

For the next several weeks mushroom harvesters came in waves, like assault troops on a beachhead. Pete had returned, but even with his help they could not fend off the invaders. Reluctantly, they decided to pick early, to sacrifice quality rather than risk losing everything.

"Even then we didn't get a break," Hoot says. "We only needed a few days to get everything cut and hung up to dry. But the mushroom pickers just kept coming. I remember running through the bush with huge bundles of heavy, green dope over my head, and I see mushroom pickers coming in a line. I'd drop down in a hole and wait until they'd gone by and jump up and get going again." Hoot lurches around the living room like a gangly Atlas struggling with a badly balanced globe. "Luckily they had their heads down hunting mushrooms, or they'd have seen this crazy man galloping through the forest with a haystack on his head."

Pete had brought back *Scurvy,* their long-lost lifeboat, which had spent most of the summer sunk on the far side of the lake, but it was in no condition to transport even the small crop they had managed to salvage. From a marina at Nakusp they rented a small motorboat and, loaded to the gunwales with bundles of wet dope wrapped in clear plastic, two crazy huskies and their few possessions, Hoot and Pete crossed the lake for the last time.

"We were so pissed off and burnt-out with the season," Hoot says, "we just motored right up to the ramp in front of the marina, where two cops were sitting having coffee with the marina owners. Pete backed the van down and we threw all these fat green bundles into the back, right in front of them. They watched us the whole time but never made the connection. There's a lot of fern picking in that area. They must have thought no one would be stupid enough to unload dope there."

Hoot sold his share of the crop in October, taking a lower price for a quick turnaround. By November he was on the plane to India. "I usually try to go somewhere spiritual," he says. Come spring, he was back, psychic batteries charged and ready for another summer in the dope wars.

Not once since we began talking has Hoot shown any anger or bitterness; the worse things get, at least in retrospect, the more he laughs. "But surely," I ask him, "taking the kind of risks you do, you must have come a cropper with the police?"

"Yes and no. I've never been convicted of anything. But I have had a few squeakers," he says. "I guess after a while you just don't give a shit. Three or four years ago we rented this lovely farm—a nice cabin, the Kettle River running through the back, beautiful country, hot dry climate, perfect for marijuana. Only trouble was that a busy highway ran right past the front. We could see the cop cars going by about two hundred feet away."

"Well, what was the idea? Did you figure on being so obvious that no one would bother taking a second look?"

"No, we were just having a good time. We'd sit on the porch and laugh like hell. You hit a certain point, a certain age, where you don't care any more. We said to ourselves, here we are, this is what we're doing and we're going to have a hell of a lot of fun doing it."

"Well, at least you must have hidden the dope out back."

"Nope. We planted it right beside the cabin, almost an acre of it in one huge patch in openings around the pine trees. We built a huge greenhouse and started eleven hundred plants. By the time we weeded out the males we still had six to seven hundred. There were too many to bother counting."

It was a risky, crazy venture, and they came very close to pulling it off. "We got right through to the last week of the season," Hoot tells me. "Two choppers had been buzzing us regularly, but we weren't going to cut and run. We had all these maps of the Caribbean laid out on the floor, and books on sailing. We were going sailing, going to have our own sailboat in the tropics. At the end of August, the plants were small and I said to Pete that we weren't going to get much. Then all of a sudden they just exploded. It was so beautiful. I said, hell, we can buy two boats and stay down there ten years."

One of the helicopters had been especially persistent, circling low over the farm. Hoot remembers it as an instrument of psychological warfare. "The motor was out of sync, somehow, so you could hear it coming and coming forever, this irritating thrashing that went right into your brain." He mimes a helicopter swooping down over the couch and across the floor, drawing a burble of laughter from the baby. "The Japanese used to do that during the Second World War. They used to have motors out of sync, and the guys on the ground would say, 'Here comes washing-machine Charlie.' It was psychological."

But Hoot and Pete refused to be spooked. They held off harvesting until the first colas were mature. Then, on the very day Hoot brought in the first buds and began pruning, their luck ran out. Hoot still laughs when he thinks of it.

"It was the last day of September. Pete was away on the coast, visiting his girlfriend. I'm sitting out on the porch, bare balls in the sun, pruning these big beautiful buds. All of a sudden I hear this screech of tires turning in our driveway. I stand up, pick up my pants, and I see this guy in a blue uniform pounding up the driveway towards the cabin. So I jump off the porch and hide behind this little pine tree, only about ten feet away. This guy hasn't seen me, and he comes up and knocks on the door."

"Did you have time to get the buds off the table?"

"No, there was no time. There's scissors, bags, buds all over the table. I know the jig is up."

"But what's with the blue uniform? Only city police wear them."

"It was an Environment Canada uniform. I'd heard those guys had been seen down at the RCMP office, so they were narcs. Just about then I hear dog claws scratching, getting out of the back of the truck. So I start to tippy-toe away. The guy looks up and sees me. We make eye contact, and the chase is on. Now, I'm an old geezer, pushing sixty, and I'm barefoot, and here's this young guy in good shape with shoes on. Anyway, I'm doing the gazelle, clearing four-foot bushes at a bound, going through the berries and buckbrush. I'm still hanging onto my pants, but I haven't had time to put them on. I chance a look over my shoulder and I can't believe it: I'm leaving this guy behind. He's hollering at me, 'Stop or I'll shoot,' and I can hear the dog barking. The other guy is running with it on a leash. The river's about five hundred feet behind the cabin. By the time I get to it, the closest guy has fallen at least a hundred feet behind. I'm into that river and across like stink. Scrambling ashore, I look behind and they've both landed up on the riverbank and the guy hasn't let the dog off the leash. I just scurried into the bush."

"How big is the river there? Did you have to swim?"

"It was deep in just one spot, and I think I must have run across the surface with Jesus boots. I'm not a swimmer, but I knew I could swim at that moment." Hoot may not have enjoyed himself at the time, though he's rocking with laughter now.

"So you made a getaway, but had to leave everything behind. What about your i.d., your driver's licence, wouldn't they nail you anyway with that?"

"No, no. Years ago I learned to hide everything outside the house, in case of a raid. Pete had the truck and there was nothing in the place to identify either of us, or so we thought. But that was the least of my problems."

"How do you mean?"

"Suddenly I realize, boy, you've really hit the jackpot here. It's the end of September and it'll freeze overnight, and I've got a wet pair of pants. Period. No shoes, no socks, no shirt. Then I hear this dog barking and I know they've crossed the river. So I make a long circle, way up on the rocky bluffs, across some cliffs and down through the bush to the river again. By this time the chase has been going on for three or four hours, but I've got the edge because I know my way around these woods. I cross the river to throw off the dog—I can still hear him way off—and then walk nine or ten miles down the riverbank, almost to Westbridge, where I know some people."

"So what kind of shape are your feet in by this time?"

"Unreal. I was an inch taller, my feet are so puffed up, so cut, so swollen from being in and out of ice water. About this time I hit upon an abandoned cabin, and I scrounge some old rotten curtains for a cape and a pair of felt boot liners that were full of holes." As he tells this, Hoot shuffles from kitchen to living room with a mug of tea in his hand, hunched like a ragged crone. "After dark I'm limping down the road, looking like somebody out of *One Day in the Life of Ivan Denisovich*, and this truck passes me, then slams on the brakes and backs up. 'Hoot,' this friend says, 'I've never seen you looking better. Hop in.'"

Hoot was able to head off Pete before he returned and blundered unwittingly into the trap. The police did find some identification, though, and Pete had to disappear for a time onto boats working the more remote regions of the coast. Hoot was identified by his fingerprints, and friends who have since tapped into police computers say he is still "wanted for questioning." After a month to let things cool out, some friends of Hoot's recovered his passport and other i.d. from under a stump near the cabin.

"What about the bud?" I ask. "Did you have any hidden?"

"No, nothing. We were both fugitives on the road, broke, hiding. We just stayed loose, kept moving around. But nothing changed. That was three or four years ago, and I've grown every year since—though not on the highway. Drug laws in North America mean whatever the cops say they mean. It's madness, you've got no rights. I haven't been charged with anything, and Pete can't find out what the score is. They're doing the smoke game on us, but I don't care. I just carry on as I always have."

When I leave Hoot we stand outside on the porch, watching the driving snow draw curtains across the orchards and timbered hills across the valley. "I haven't had any good money years," he tells me, without complaint, "but I've had other things: good friends, comradeship, adventures along the way and, best of all, all those wonderful summer days with my plants. No matter what happens, I'll grow every year, just for mental health."

Hoot and I are much of an age, both shaped by the 1940s and '50s, both from this part of the country. And yet we have led such different lives; Hoot turned inward to his spiritual being, while I took the outward path, looking always for the main chance. We are content in our different ways, though I envy his philosopher's cool. I can't imagine that Hoot would ever poison his mind over a little confrontation with a dope thief.

Hoot gave me one of his birdhouses when I left. I haven't hung it in a tree because its doorway is too big; starlings would get in, and I'm not about to provide housing for European riff-raff. It sits on a shelf in the cabin, and whenever I look at it I see in its quirky construction and artful blending of weathered cedar, driftwood, stones, shells, moss and tufts of lichen the expression of a peaceful and whimsical soul.

CHAPTER 12

UNDER
THE
LIGHTS

September 15. Another date for the diary—first harvest!

Humming snatches of "Bringing in the Sheaves" (I believe God would approve, if not the Methodists), I clip all the upper colas from my superplant and lay them reverentially in a plastic tote box. They are thick as a man's fist and lovely beyond my fondest hopes. The bract leaves are almost black, the dead pistils rusty-brown and the living ones mauve, the calyxes apple-green. From top to bottom, the colas sparkle with resin like a silver thaw in the morning sun. Straight off the plant, this variety stinks like dead cow, much too funky for my nose. But cured slowly over the next couple of weeks, it will turn sweet as June hay.

The two branches I pollinated earlier will be left until the end of September for the seeds to ripen. Already, the calyxes are beginning to swell.

Fitting the lid loosely on the box (green marijuana will "sweat" and deteriorate rapidly in a closed space), I hide it in the underbrush. Late this evening I'll come back for it, when all danger of police roadblocks has passed. I must be infected by Ned's paranoia; he was stopped recently on the highway (without any contraband aboard) for a routine vehicle check, and now says he will only transport dope late at night.

Hanging in the cabin loft, my eleven fat colas are so rank I sleep on the deck down by the water. It is a wild and beautiful night—waves running white under a hunter's moon, stars drawn close and buffed bright by a cold blue wind from the North Pacific. The radio this morning tells of a giant ridge of high pressure shunting storms north into Alaska and Yukon, a potent augury of fine weather.

With the mould patrol suspended and nothing to harvest for at least ten days, I have no desire to stay here and play warder to my plants. I didn't get into this game for confrontation; if helicopters are going do an *Apocalypse Now* on my gardens, I want to be elsewhere. So I've decided to accept an invitation from a friend of a friend to visit his indoor grow room on Vancouver Island, a gesture of remarkable trust, considering that we've never met. I've seen grow rooms before, but this one, I'm told, is unusually sophisticated.

Brett lives on a stump ranch he bought for a song twenty years ago, before land prices took off. When I turn in at the driveway the place seems familiar, though I've never been here before. Familiar, I realize, because it contains the archetypal elements of the abandoned coastal homestead: a gap-toothed orchard of ancient apple trees, waist-high hay uncut all summer, tired fences and buildings of split cedar, weathered silver. Before their revival as hobby farms, every back road on the island had one of these relics, survivors from the early years of the century when families scratched out a living with a few cows and chickens and part-time work cutting shakes or gillnetting salmon.

Out back, behind its derelict façade, the place has been transformed. There are raised beds of vegetables, clumps of dahlias and mums with heads big as saucers, a young orchard heavy with Gravensteins, Bramleys and Spys, and a lordly broadleaf maple towering over a swing and a cool expanse of lawn. Farther back, the revival peters out in a sway-backed barn and straggle of sheds, all made of cedar shakes worn thin by lifetimes of wind and rain. The house is deceptive. Outside, it is finished in cedar like the barn, though better maintained. But inside it is entirely rebuilt— teak floors, massive split-stone fireplace, space-age kitchen with pricey German appliances, Persian rugs, big-name watercolours, a Steinway baby grand and a Mexican bronze sculpture I'd die for. There's money here, plenty of it, but it's not put out front on public display.

Brett and I talk for a while at the kitchen table. Speaking slowly, earnestly, he explains that he has been involved in civil liberties issues since burning his U.S. draft card in the 1970s, and is more concerned than ever about the erosion of personal freedoms, particularly by "corporatism, globalization and the collusion of government." Our mutual friend had said that Brett was "pretty idealistic," and I'm wary of raising his expectations too high. "I'm not a marijuana activist," I tell him. "I'm just trying to do my bit by writing openly about something that's illicit and shouldn't be. That's all." But Brett has made his decision. Abruptly, after half an hour and fewer probing questions than I expected, he pushes back his chair and announces: "Everything seems cool to me. Let's go have a look. We've got two hours before the kids get home from school."

Instead of going down to the basement, he leads me out the back door. This is a surprise; all the grow rooms I've seen before have been in basements, hidden behind false walls or moveable cupboards or under trapdoors covered by carpet. I mention this to Brett. "If the police ever search your house," he says, "or a dope thief breaks in, those are the first places they look. Those tricks are old hat."

He lets us into one of the sagging sheds out by the barn and hooks the door from the inside. Scraps of lumber, cordwood and boxes of dusty jars cover most of the broken floor. Brett moves a cardboard carton aside, reaches through one of many holes in the planking and pulls out an iron rod about eighteen inches long.

"This is the lock. Nothing moves unless it's out," he says, leaving me none the wiser. But then he gives a push on the junk in front of us and—abracadabra!—a section of floor about four feet square rolls smoothly aside. "It's not as fancy as it looks," he says, "just a square of three-quarter ply on wheels, with some two-by-four for track."

Beneath the floor is a plywood disk about three feet in diameter. When Brett lifts it aside I am looking down a round hole in the ground, ten or twelve feet deep, with a blaze of white light at the far end. Brett asks me to remove my shoes and dust off the cuffs of my pants "in case we've picked up any bugs from the lawn." Then he tells me to climb into the hole, feet first. "Just slide down," he says. "You won't go fast."

The shaft is formed by a length of steel drain culvert, two feet in diameter, set into the ground at an angle of about forty-five degrees. A plank, waxed and polished smooth, lines the lower side of the culvert, and overhead, as I slide down, are wooden hand-holds every foot or so. Brett launches himself much more nimbly into the chute and reaches back to close the rolling section of floor behind him, shutting us in like nuclear warriors in their bunker.

When my feet touch the floor I stand up in another world. Everything is white—walls, ceiling, floor—except for ranks of intensely green marijuana plants, trembling in the constantly moving air. Six painfully bright lights, each a thousand watts, Brett tells me, crawl slowly back and forth across the ceiling on motorized carriages suspended from tracks. The purr of fans and gurgle of trickling water fills the air. A jungle reek of green pot assails the nostrils.

"The whole thing is a balancing act," Brett explains. "The trick is to keep everything adjusted—balance the pH and ratio of nutrient to water, watch the temperature and humidity, and keep a close eye on the plants. They'll tell you right away if they're not happy. Brown leaf tips if the mix is too rich, that sort of thing."

Except for starting new plants and harvesting, the system almost runs itself. Timers and switches turn the lights on or off every twelve hours, circulate nutrient and water to the plants—the system is hydroponic, without soil—and control the fans that regulate humidity and temperature. A carbon dioxide generator raises CO_2 levels in the room, which Brett tells me has boosted production by about 25 per cent.

The plants are smaller than I expected, none more than three feet tall and some barely half that size. "That's because I don't grow batches all of the same age," Brett says. "There's five to six pounds of bud coming out of this room every month. If that all matured at once, I could never keep up with the manicuring. It has to be done green, right off the plant, because I don't have space here to hang plants up to dry and prune later." A mound of untrimmed buds awaits his attention on a silkscreen, stretched taut in a wooden frame. "I do all my manicuring there," he says. "The screen lets any loose resin fall through but catches the leaves and stems. The resin collects on glass underneath, and I scrape it off and sell it for hash. It's strong as hell but, to my taste, the buzz isn't as nice as grass."

"Where do you dry?" I ask. "It seems pretty humid in here."

He opens a narrow cupboard, stacked floor to head-height with trays of fat buds, spectacular dope glinting with crystal. "An intake fan down there in the bottom pulls air from outside, and it goes up through the trays—see, they're screened on the bottom—and an exhaust fan on the top blows it back outside."

"But what about the smell?" I wonder. "I didn't smell anything up there in the shed."

Brett grins. He's proud of this little wrinkle. "All the exhaust air from the room goes into a buried duct that runs over to the barn. The outlet is up in the loft, under a mountain of loose hay. By the time it gets to the surface it smells just like old wet hay."

Water, air, electricity and gas for the CO_2 generator all come to the room through buried lines. Occasionally Brett brings bottles of concentrated fertilizer and a few chemicals down the chute. Otherwise, the room is entirely self-contained. Since he started up seven years ago, he has introduced no new plants or seeds. All that time, Brett has been cloning the same variety, a cross of Northern Lights and a Hawaiian *indica*, from descendants of the original plants. He shows me a cupboard jammed full of cuttings he is rooting in little blocks of rockwool under fluorescent lights. Once rooted, they are "vegged" under four 400-watt halide lights left on eighteen hours a day in another cupboard. At about eighteen inches in height, they are moved into the open grow room and quickly flipped into budding under the twelve-hour light rotation. From veg to harvest, the cycle takes eight to nine weeks.

There's a feeling down here of total isolation and security, similar to the sensation I've had in deep, warm mines, which hardrock miners believe is the world's best place to work because "the weather is always the same." "It's pretty snug," Brett acknowledges, "especially on a rainy winter night. But it's not foolproof. I do a lot of graveyard shift because I can't risk coming down here when the kids and their friends are around. And I guess the biggest danger is the power. Our bill runs about two hundred and fifty dollars a month."

Escaped odours and suspiciously large electricity bills are the Achilles' heel of the indoor grower. A former building contractor, Brett provides himself with a ready excuse for using a lot of electricity by maintaining a large shop equipped with heavy-duty machinery in the old barn.

"The thing is to avoid suspicion of any kind," he says. "If the police start sniffing around, they can get B.C. Hydro to put a gizmo on your meter that shows the pattern of electricity use over twenty-four hours. If it jumps way up and down every twelve hours, they've got you. I could eliminate even that risk if I divided the room in half and ran two sets of lights on opposite rotations. But that's a pain in the ass for a lot of reasons. And the room's too small, anyway. It's only ten by twenty feet."

"Even so," I point out, "they'd have a hard time finding it. How did you ever build it without being seen?"

"We did it all in a three-day weekend. Me and two friends I used to do construction with—which is still my storefront. My wife took the kids away, we rented a backhoe, dug the hole, buried the services, threw in prefab forms, poured the cement and buried the whole thing, all in three killer days. We drank a lot of beer and prayed like hell nobody'd come around." When Brett's room was up and running, they built two more almost identical rooms, one each for the two friends.

I ask him if he'd ever considered growing in sterilized soil, which some growers believe produces a more natural-tasting indoor marijuana than hydroponics. "No," Brett says. "It wouldn't work here. You have to change the soil after every crop, and that would mean a lot of packing up and down the chute. Too much work and too risky. Besides, it's a phony issue. Soil growers use chemical fertilizers just like I do because compost and manure cause too many problems indoors. I withdraw all fertilizer for the last week or two before harvest, and that gets rid of any chemical taste."

Leaving the bunker—much riskier than entering because he never knows if a visitor might be outside—Brett opens the sliding cover a crack and listens before sticking his head up and looking carefully around. Later in the afternoon when Brett's wife, Carrie, comes home from her nursing shift at the local hospital, he sends the kids, a boy of seven and a girl of nine, out to play, and we sit talking again at the kitchen table. "What you've got going here," I say, "is a money factory. It just keeps running forever."

"That's true," Brett says. "You get used to always having cash in your ass pocket and ten to twenty thousand stashed under a brick somewhere. You have to be a bit discreet, buy things on credit, make payments on the car over several years, don't flash your cash. But within those limits, anything you want, you just go and buy it. That's what's really addictive about marijuana."

"Addictive?"

"Well, the longer you're on the cash fix, the more you seem to need it. It's like the yuppies who get married and put off having children year after year because they want to be more secure in their careers, have more money in the bank, more expensive toys, before they take the plunge. They get so hooked on security and comfort, they never do have kids."

"Why would you want to quit growing dope?" I ask. "It doesn't seem like an onerous way to make a living."

"Two reasons. First, it's like having a cow. You've got to milk the damned thing every day. Sure, I can leave the room to take care of itself for three, four days, even a week without any trouble. But that's about the limit. And when I come back, I've got hours of catch-up to do. Sometimes I'm out there all night. Second, there's the whole paranoia trip, especially for Carrie."

Carrie has been strangely quiet all this time. "You're not comfortable with it?" I ask her.

"I won't deny that I like the money," she says. "And it's great having Brett home all the time; he used to be away so much working. I never go near the room—that's the bargain Brett and I made. But it's like having a pit full of poisonous snakes out there. There's always this feeling that someday they'll break out and cause something terrible to happen."

Every indoor dope-growing family I've ever known has had this rift between husband and wife. Except for manicuring, it's the man's thing. He does the work, develops the special knowledge and derives the satisfaction when his efforts pay off. Shut out of the process, the woman worries about detection. Whenever they get together with other growers, the men natter on about their plants while the women pray for the day some other topic will enter their lives. And then, of course, there are the kids.

"Carrie and I disagree about the kids," Brett says. "When they're old enough, say twelve or fourteen, I think we should tell them how we make our living. Give them a choice, even let them help out if they want to work with me. How many kids have a chance to do real work with their fathers any more? I think that's important. But Carrie doesn't want them involved."

Carrie shakes her head. "No, I don't. It's a secret I have to keep hidden all the time, gnawing away inside, and I don't think the kids should have to feel that way too."

"What really drives all this," Brett says, "is that Carrie and I disagree about the law. Because it's illegal, she feels guilty. I don't. It's the law that's guilty of interfering with my private . . ."

"That's not fair," Carrie cuts him off. "I don't feel guilty at all. The law is wrong and it should be changed. But I recognize how the community feels, and I know what it would do to our life here if Brett were ever caught. He doesn't care about that. I do."

"Okay," Brett concedes. "But it's not that I don't care about the community. It's just that I believe pressure from the community to conform is a kind of tyranny. If you don't resist that sort of thing, it just gets worse. Today it's what we grow and smoke, tomorrow it's what we say or read or believe. I know that sounds paranoid, but living in the States in Vietnam time taught me about community pressure. I disagreed with the war, but my community had no respect for my right to dissent. I had to get out of town, out of the country."

Carrie and Brett are profoundly in agreement about one thing: they loath the dealing part of the marijuana trade. "That's where you're really exposed, and there's no way you can avoid it," Brett says. "When you've got ten pounds of bud in the car, twenty-five thousand dollars on the line, anything can happen. The dealer may be under surveillance by the cops, and you get nailed with him. Or he's been ripped off himself and he wants you to front him."

"Front him?"

"Give him the stuff on credit. Or at least part of it."

"Every time Brett gets on the ferry for Vancouver to see the dealer," Carrie says, "I just hold my breath until he gets back. I'm really afraid he'll get shot or something like that."

"Actually, I've been pretty lucky," Brett says. "I've lost some money fronting, but there's never been any violence. No threats or guns, although I've heard stories about that sort of thing. And I've only had to change dealers once in seven years. But loyalties mean nothing in this business. Soon as someone hits town with bud that's a little better or cheaper than yours, your dealer is not your friend any more."

"So where is all this headed?" I ask them.

"I'd like to get out, but I'm not ready yet," Brett says. "People have been saying for years the market was getting oversupplied, and now I think it's happening. Everybody's got a grow room. I even know a doctor who's got one. So the price is dropping; it's down about five hundred dollars a pound in the past three years. And with money the only reason for doing it, the time may be coming when it's no longer worth it."

"As far as I'm concerned," Carrie says, "the sooner we get out of the business, the better."

The family discord is relieved by the kids tumbling in the door and hollering for dinner. We head into town for a Chinese meal, and I catch the early evening ferry from Nanaimo. As I sit on the top deck, watching the sun bowling down the long alley of the northern strait, it occurs to me that indoor pot growers strike a kind of Faustian bargain, selling their peace of mind for cash beyond most peoples' dreams. Unlike outdoor gardeners, who make themselves nearly immune from prosecution by growing on public lands a safe distance from home, indoor growers live literally on top of their darkest secret.

The majority of indoor grow rooms are located in cities. There are seven hundred in Vancouver alone, according to a recent police estimate ("guesstimate" would be more accurate). At the time of their statement, police said they had about seventy premises under surveillance, mostly because of reports of suspicious odours on nearby streets. Authorities are also alerted to the location of grow rooms by electrical fires; growers turn on too many lights, over-heating the circuits, or they botch an attempt to wire directly into incoming powerlines, bypassing the electrical meter. In either case, the fire department turns up and calls in the police.

These scenarios are avoidable. Grow shops sell negative-ion generators that will deodorize the air before it is vented. And it takes only the most rudimentary electrical knowledge to calculate the load that can be carried by wire of a given gauge. These things happen because marijuana growers are human: some are very good at what they do, some very bad, and all the rest, the great mediocrity, are just average. But average isn't good enough. Surviving in a criminal activity, especially one as risky as cultivating pot in a densely populated urban area, requires a shrewd and suspicious mind. Marijuana growers are more likely to be naive, docile and incurably amateurish.

Nothing illustrates this better than Black Thursday. That was the day—October 26, 1989—when the Bush administration in the U.S. launched a national assault on indoor growers, code-named Green Merchant. Law enforcement officers in forty-six states raided hundreds of grow rooms and dozens of retail garden stores, seizing equipment and customer lists. Nearly all the stores had been advertising in two marijuana magazines, *High Times* and *Sinsemilla Tips*, and for years growers had been mail-ordering equipment and supplies, leaving a trail of credit card receipts and delivery slips that led drug agents right to their doors. The records of United Parcel Service alone gave drug agents more than twenty thousand leads. The busts continued for months, and thousands were jailed. Garden store owners lost their businesses and some were given long prison terms for complicity, even though they had no certain knowledge that the supplies they were selling were being used to grow pot. (Hothouse growers of everything from African violets to tomatoes use the same supplies, and were nonplussed to find federal drug agents at their doors.) Even *Sinsemilla*

Tips, the bible of marijuana cultivation, succumbed to the heat, losing so many advertisers that the magazine folded.

If Canadian growers are aware of the American calamity, the lesson hasn't sunk in. Many routinely park their cars in front of the grow shops where they buy their supplies, even though police may be across the street writing down their licence numbers. I know a Vancouver Island grower who was nabbed in this way. Recently, a lawyer who specializes in drug cases told me that armed criminal gangs are now beating police to the punch, following growers home from the stores and stripping rooms of equipment and pot crops. Such unpleasantness could be avoided if growers paid cash and took a taxi to their cars when they have too much to carry.

In the United States, computer geeks have come up with the ultimate protection for the indoor grower—the cybergarden. Sensors monitor light, water, humidity, carbon dioxide levels and temperature and feed the information into a personal computer. Using customized programming and solenoid switching, the computer tracks and adjusts all variables. By attaching a modem and remote access program, the gardener can tend a crop from anywhere in the world. The system comes with a motion detector and a "Mayday" program that will dial a beeper number if security is breached, warning the gardener never to return. By routing all data through a remailer—an untraceable e-mail address on the Internet—the grower can thwart any attempt by the police to track him down. And, for good measure, by incorporating a computer virus into the system, the computer can be programmed to self-destruct after it detects a security breach and alerts the grower. In theory, the gardener would only have to visit the grow room twice, to plant and to harvest. In practice, according to experienced growers, the cybergarden is pure cyberfantasy and will never replace the eyes and hands of a skilled gardener. Marijuana culture, they insist, is too unpredictable to be programmed weeks or months in advance.

Naysayers aside, such systems already exist. According to a 1995 *New York Times* article, a New Hampshire company sells a cyber-garden complete with equipment, software and step-by-step instructions. Just add water, fertilizer and plants, and return in ten weeks for the harvest. I have never met or even read an account by anyone who has actually seen a cybergarden up and running. But that's hardly surprising. Growers so obsessed with security are not likely to be offering guided tours.

No matter how elaborate the precautions, urban marijuana gardening remains a precarious business conducted in basements, closets and attics. Yet there seems to be an indoor grower on every block. In these times of chronic unemployment, I suspect many just drifted into the trade for want of other prospects. Steve, for example, whom I met with surprising ease by making inquiries through a Vancouver hemp store. He arrived in Vancouver in the early nineties with a wife, a young son, a degree in German literature and no chance of finding work in his field of expertise. Then one day a friend gave him some marijuana clones. Other than smoking pot in his native Ontario, Steve knew nothing about marijuana. But he brought the plants home anyway, announcing to his wife that he would try growing them in the spare bedroom of their basement apartment.

"She thought I was nuts," he recalls. "I didn't seem to have any feel for plants. I mean, once when my wife went away for a couple of weeks, all her house plants died."

Steve set out to educate himself, reading grow guides, consulting garden shops, experimenting, observing. Three months later he took off a successful crop and invested the earnings in more lights and plants. Two or three more crops financed a move into a rented house in a ritzy neighbourhood, with a state-of-the-art grow room in the basement and a tax-free annual income well above $100,000. Steve had come up fast, and he'd been lucky.

"When we were in the apartment," he tells me, "the lights were pulling so much power the wires caught fire outside the house. I blasted them with a fire extinguisher. The fire department and B.C. Hydro came but fortunately didn't come inside. Our grow room was right in the center of the apartment; you had to walk around it to go to the bathroom. Just a blanket over the door. Then the owner said she was having Hydro come and check the wiring, so we got the fuck out of there. It was pretty scary."

This is the ever-present threat in urban growing: you don't control your space. Even if you own your house, one chance visit by a plumbing inspector, fire marshall or tax assessor and the jig is up. Danger hovers like a spectral bird over Steve and his family.

He claims not to be worried about such things, though I wonder. Sitting in his truck overlooking the sandflats at Locarno Beach he is tense, and his hands shake. He tells me he smokes more than an ounce of high-octane dope a week, beginning first thing every morning. The volatility beneath the surface boils over when I ask him how he feels growers might fare if the government ever legalized marijuana.

"Well, I'm sure as hell not about to lie down and let them take control so they can tax it," he says. "Fuck that! For years it was the people who stood firm for what they believed in who kept the marijuana culture alive. I'm not going to let anybody step in now and tell me what I've got to do with my thing. Forget it. Have my stuff tested, have the government regulate maximum THC, turn it into something bland and homogeneous? No way, no way. Fuck that!"

"Couldn't you just ignore the government?" I ask. "That's what growers are doing now."

But Steve is adamant. "If the government gets involved, big tobacco companies would shift into marijuana, cut the price, break the market and just smash the small growers. The government would back the big companies all the way because the bureaucrats can't keep an eye on all the small growers, make them pay taxes. Thousands of growers would be put out of work, growers who are now supporting the communities they live in, rather than giving their money to the government to squander."

Not everyone in the trade foresees such a bleak future for growers should the government ever legalize marijuana. Marc Emery, for example, believes that big companies will never be able to produce the range and quality of pot demanded by the market. "Rothmans and people like that will supply the mass market," he says, "but connoisseurs will still pay higher prices for specialty marijuana, just like people going into Starbucks to choose between several expensive coffees."

A former Ontario bookstore owner and veteran of censorship wars with Canada Customs, Emery is easily the most vociferous and effective marijuana activist in Canada. He also knows something about marketing. Starting from scratch in 1994, he built a spectacularly successful Vancouver hemp store, grow shop, cannabis legal aid storefront, marijuana seed company and café where customers could smoke but not buy pot. His entrepreneurial skills put him on the front page of the *Wall Street Journal* in a story about the B.C. marijuana industry, which also featured Steve and his grow room. But by early 1998, exhausted by legal battles with the Vancouver police (more than a dozen charges) and with city council, Emery sold most of the business to his employees. Perhaps the final blow was the end of smoking in his Cannabis Café, stubbed out not by marijuana laws but by a ban on smoking in city restaurants.

When he was riding high, Marc Emery had twenty-eight employees and was paying taxes on more than $2 million in sales. The offices of his company, HempBC, located in an old downtown warehouse, were a madhouse of frenetic activity, with Emery at the center calmly answering phone calls, writing payroll cheques and offering off-the-cuff prognostications to anyone who dropped by. On one of my visits we talked about legalization and the harm I thought it might do to pot growers, who were an important part of his clientele.

"Look, there's no problem," he insisted. "The price won't come down nearly as much as people think. It's currently about two hundred dollars an ounce in B.C. When it's legal, top quality will still sell for fifty to seventy-five dollars. What could destroy the small grower is government interference. That's why I've always said in our five points for legislation that we want legalization without regulation."

The quality I've always admired most in Marc Emery is his brass. Nothing displays it better than his five "Conditions for Peace," the terms he has offered the federal government for a truce in the war on drugs, at least as it applies to marijuana: legalization of cannabis; no regulations on growing or sale; a pardon for all past pot offenders, with all criminal records to be wiped from the books; restitution of all legal fees and confiscated money or property, plus payment of a per diem for each day spent in jail, all to come from taxes on cannabis sales; and finally, an official apology to the nation from the prime minister for the war on marijuana.

"Since marijuana is not harmful," he told me, "there is no need for regulation. Anybody should be allowed to grow it, consume it, sell it, buy it, trade it in whatever fashion. Besides, the government will never be able to regulate it, even if they try. You've already got probably 100,000 independent growers, and they're not going to give up just because it's legal."

Much as I found Emery's peace terms right and just and enormously cathartic, they ignored the most basic rule of conciliation: when dealing with a grizzly bear, always leave it an avenue for graceful retreat. It seemed to me there was nothing to be gained by demanding restitution and an apology that no government will make, if only to avoid legal liability. But Emery was defiant. "We're not interested in compromise," he said. "The government is wrong. With a hundred million people worldwide buying marijuana, it will be legalized within a decade. As soon as one or two countries change the law, all the rest will too, because they'll be losing too much revenue if they don't. Greed motivates governments as much as anybody else."

Marc Emery and Steve do some business together. In addition to producing bud, Steve is breeding plants and selling high-grade marijuana seed, partly through ads in *Cannabis Canada*, which Emery still owns. Among Emery's many legal battles is a court challenge of laws forbidding seed sales. The crux of the case is whether pot seeds, which are not psychoactive, should be covered by drug laws.

Steve's ambition as a seed producer is to replicate the pioneering work in marijuana breeding done by the Dutch. "There are guys here in B.C. who have twenty, thirty years' experience breeding a particular strain, but no one else has access to it," he tells me. "I want to get those strains out there so people can use them, real B.C. bud, not Amsterdam bud." He would also like to form an association of growers dedicated to the improvement of marijuana. "When we sell people high-priced crap," he says, "we are opening the door for the government to step in and regulate.

People here don't complain because they are not very well informed, as compared with Holland, where the sale of varieties is organized. You ask for Haze there, you get Haze; ask for Skunk, you get Skunk. Here, it's rare that a dealer can tell you what sort of pot he's selling."

Whatever its merits, Steve's plan for an association of pot farmers is a long shot in a trade that has thrived for three decades on the stubborn independence of its growers—growers like Ned, who scoffed when I told him that Steve was offering twenty-five cents a seed for new varieties.

"Who's he kidding?" Ned said. "If I sold him Rasta, he'd cross it with his own varieties, call it some kind of wonder plant and sell the seeds for five or ten bucks each. Fuck that."

Back on the Peninsula, I make a quick tour of the gardens, keeping a sharp eye out for helicopters and RCMP support crews on the ground. If I'm ever to be caught green-handed, this is the most likely time. The plants are very close to ready, a few of the top colas already showing brown pistils. Some growers I know would harvest right now. Mule-headed I may be, but I haven't compromised quality yet, and I don't intend to start now.

Waiting for the big day when the crop comes in, I've been picking away at a pet project. One of the few concerns I've had about living here again is the lack of attractive places to walk. The Peninsula trails are all too distant or too enclosed in bush to appeal to me as places for my daily hike. And walking every day for at least an hour is important to me; it's the legs that let you down as you get old. The muscles, if you keep them hard, activate valves in the veins of the legs, helping to lift blood to the heart. For this, and for the sheer pleasure of it, I am making my own trail.

Inland, about ten minutes' walk from the cabin, an old skid

road loops for a mile or two through the burn where I had my marijuana garden last year. It's an attractive stroll, though one that affords only an occasional glimpse of the strait. Immediately behind it, however, a mile-long ridge rises perhaps six hundred feet, and I have cleared a path up the slope at one end. The prospect from the top is glorious—from the green mirrors of Secret Cove and Buccaneer Bay in the southwest to the humped spine of Texada Island in the far northwest, the view opens onto a majestic sweep of strait and islands and sky. Too high and too difficult to log, the ridge looks exactly as it must have when Capt. George Vancouver passed below in 1793. Glades of arbutus and virgin fir are interspersed with sheets of lichen-flecked granite and beds of ankle-deep moss. Eventually, my trail will descend the opposite end of the ridge from where I started and lead back to the skid road. It will be a walk for all seasons—wild in winter gales, a place of shade and birdsong on summer mornings, the resort of Easter lilies, crimson currant and the sweet scent of arbutus bloom in spring and, on days of autumn westerlies, the lair of tumbling ravens, black against the sun-crinkled sea. I hope to be walking it still in my nineties, even if I'm drooling and being fed with a spoon.

The only thing missing from this picture is a dog. It must be a dozen years since I had one, and I've felt the lack every day, especially when walking in places like the ridge. I'd have gotten another dog years ago, except that I like big, active animals that have no life in the city.

My last dog, a corgi named Megan, was not big, though she was certainly active. Unlike many corgis, she was neither fat nor lazy, and she spent most of her fourteen years running flat out after balls, squirrels, cats or anything else that moved. She was actually my youngest son's dog, given to him as a Christmas present when she was the size and shape of a loaf of hovis bread.

In time, I inherited her, and she became my constant companion when I lived alone on the farm, greeting me when I came down the ladder from the loft in the morning, hiking, swimming and canoeing with me and dozing, tired and content, by the heater in the evening. Putting her down, when the end came, was one of the hardest things I've ever had to do.

In her last six months, Megan's hindquarters broke down, so I had to help her up stairs. As she became less active, a chronic skin condition worsened to raw, weeping patches that resisted every treatment. Finally one morning she suffered what appeared to be a stroke, falling repeatedly and whining in apparent pain. Her time had come, but I couldn't bear the thought of taking her to the vet; she was terrified of them, and just the antiseptic smell of the office would make her tremble with fear. I didn't want her life to end in terror and abandonment.

I dug a grave in the orchard, in the shade of an apple tree where Megan used to lie and watch me work when she was worn out after chasing a ball or stick. Carrying her down from the house, I laid her on the grass, patted her for a few minutes and then, before I lost my nerve, put a bullet into her brain. She died instantly, painlessly, and I buried her quickly, as if that would somehow ease my sense of loss. It didn't, of course. Hiking that day with friends on Mount Elphinstone, I felt the constant ache of grief, and when I came home that night the house was an emptier, lonelier place. For weeks, months I suppose, I missed her sorely.

The remedy for the loss of a dog is to get another one immediately, preferably a pup, foolish and full of energy. That wasn't an option after Megan; a move back to the city was already in sight. Next time, though, there will be two dogs, a wise and seasoned companion and a younger dog to ease the pain of parting when it comes.

CHAPTER 13

DEALING
IN
PARANOIA

Occasionally over the months I've been labouring on the mountain, Carole has asked me an annoyingly pertinent question: how do you plan to sell all this stuff? With a wave of the hand, I airily dismiss the matter. "No problem," I say. "Dealers need dope to make their living, too. They'll be there when I need them."

Now that I'm looking down the barrel at a harvest of eighteen to twenty pounds, I'm not so sure. Last year's crop was less than five pounds, and some of it is still unsold. No dope-starved dealer has flung himself on my neck, begging me to sell. I've got a few regular customers who take an ounce here, an ounce there, and a branch office manager for a national investment firm who buys a pound and supplies his friends. But that's about it. No market in sight that will even begin to soak up this year's harvest.

For some reason I can't fathom, I've never asked Ned if he has a reliable dealer. I'd always assumed he didn't, because he's chronically short of money and always seems to have marijuana to sell. Asking a grower about his dealer, even if he's a friend, feels a bit nosy, like inquiring into someone's bank balance or sexual preferences.

But today, on a trip with Ned to Nelson Island, I pop the question. "Jesus, I wish I did have someone," he says. "The few good dealers I've had keep going out of business on me, or buggering off to Costa Rica or something like that. Now all I can find are flakes who never have any money. I didn't get rid of last year's stuff until August, and that was only a lousy seven pounds." No help there, I tell myself.

We've come to the island to see what we can salvage from the extensive damage done to Ned's plants by deer, despite fences. "The buggers are starving," he'd told me when he called last night. "They'd climb Everest if there was dope growing on top." Now, as we are crossing an open bluff, a plane appears high overhead, and Ned dives for cover. Still standing in the open, I tell him he's nuts; from that height the pilot couldn't see an elephant.

"Well, I'm not taking any chances," he says. "You never know."

This is more of Ned's paranoia, the long hangover from his nine months in jail. He did his time in Oakalla, a notorious hell-hole of murderers, junkies and rapists, long-since closed as a festering sore in the Canadian prison system. Later, when we are taking a break from fence mending, I ask him what it was like inside.

He ponders for a long moment, then laughs and asks me: "What's the worst thing you can imagine?" Before I can answer, he continues: "How about a night in bed with Margaret Thatcher? Well, it was worse, a lot worse."

He tells me about the constant fear of violence, disgusting food and unceasing, maddening noise in the cell blocks. And about his wife kissing him when she came to visit, slipping a balloon containing hash and LSD into his mouth.

"I swallowed it, and when it came through the other end I washed it off and hid it in my cell. We didn't have to work Sundays, so I planned a trip for the next Saturday night. The guards would smell the hash if I smoked it, so I swallowed it, a great big chunk. About half an hour later I started to feel pretty weird, and realized that the hash had got damp in the balloon and soaked up some of the LSD. Jesus, what a ride! I was high all the next day."

Though Ned manages now to find the lighter side of prison, there was nothing diverting about the manner in which he was busted.

"Back in the sixties I used to sell a few lids of dope around English Bay in Vancouver," he tells me when we are sitting on the beach logs, sipping tea before heading home. "Just small-time stuff, like a lot of kids did so they could hang out for the summer. But then I got married and moved back to the Peninsula. With three young kids and regular work, I quit dealing altogether. About that time, a guy who was hanging around the Wakefield pub started pestering me for LSD. Sometimes I had a few tabs for my own trips, although I wasn't in the business and didn't want to sell him anything. I hardly knew the guy. But he kept after me, pestering and pestering me to get him just one tab so he could try it. So finally I did, and the bastard turned out to be a narc."

In a clear case of entrapment, Ned was locked up for selling $12 worth of LSD, and his wife and three young kids were forced into a mean hand-to-mouth existence on welfare. I'd like to think that kind of judicial abuse can't happen today. But there are still hard-assed cops and zealot judges around, and when it comes to conflicting testimony in court about how a bust was made, it's the police who have credibility, whether they deserve it or not.

As we are running back across Agamemnon Channel, it comes to me why Ned, a thirty-year veteran of the dope game, still has trouble finding a dealer: his hitch in jail has made him too wary to reach out. Everyone in the marijuana culture lives in a little bubble of security with other pot people they know and trust. There are millions of these bubbles, all more or less independent and mutually suspicious. (The force of these barriers was brought home to me in Amsterdam by a man I saw at the marijuana seed store wearing a team jacket from Nova Scotia. When I spoke to him as a fellow Canadian, he turned away without a word, as if I had the ebola virus.) If your bubble doesn't contain a reliable dealer, you have to venture into the danger zone to find one. That means asking awkward questions and meeting strangers, a risk that Ned is loath to take.

In truth, my position is even more tenuous than Ned's. Sentences for pot crimes have diminished so much that his chances of going to jail for a second offence are nil. And if he chooses to activate them, he has many dormant contacts in the marijuana trade. The best I can come up with are a few minnows I got to know in the hard times when I bought dope on the street. But to sell a crop the size of mine I need a big fish, one of the dealers who buy hundreds of pounds and move it across the country and into the U.S.

It's not that I haven't been trying. Last winter, when I was still making inquiries about going into commercial production, I met just such a person. Wanting to sniff out the prospects before I took the plunge, I asked an old friend, a hippie pot-grower–turned–lawyer, if he could arrange an information-only meeting with a big dealer. After months of waiting, the phone rang one day and I was given a terse set of instructions: "Martin" will talk with you at such-and-such a time and place.

Our meeting was in a deserted Vancouver park, under a cold January drizzle. Martin appeared from a mist-shrouded grove of trees like a figure out of a gothic novel. He was dressed in an enormous coat of dark-brown oilskin, reaching almost to the ground, and wore a broad-brimmed hat of the same material. We squelched down on a park bench, Martin impervious to the rain and me soaking my backside through the newspaper I'd brought along to sit on.

Marijuana dealers, Martin explained right at the outset, fall into two distinct categories. Big dealers like him are wholesalers, he said. They deal in pounds and sell to distributors or smaller dealers, whom he called retailers. Retailers may buy from wholesalers or directly from growers, but they normally sell only ounces or fractions of ounces to the public. Martin wanted it understood that he wasn't a retailer.

"They are different businesses with different standards and risks," he said. "Retailing is messy, people coming to your door day and night, dozens, maybe hundreds of different customers. That can lead to trouble, which is why retailing is a kind of catch-all for all sorts of people. Most of the retailers are straight shooters, but you also get some of the refuse of the marijuana business, sleazy, sloppy people who give short weight and poor quality. Wholesaling is a lot cleaner, but there's a lot more money on the line, and that brings its own kind of problems."

Like many big dealers, Martin began in a small way, growing outdoor dope on a commune in the 1970s, then selling small quantities on the street in Vancouver and Toronto. He graduated to a telephone pager and home deliveries, but had to run for cover when the police nearly caught him in a sting operation. He got his start in the wholesale trade through cronies from the commune who had set up their own indoor grow rooms. Unhappy with their dealer, they fronted Martin nearly fifty pounds, which he took to Toronto in an old van and sold for top dollar. A couple more deals and he had the cash to pay good prices up front. As word got around, Martin's roster of growers grew and, in more than a decade, he had never looked back.

Martin works out of "a very ordinary house on a very ordinary street" in suburban Surrey. The house's only concession to dealing is a sophisticated burglar alarm system and a hidden vault that Martin said "rivals Fort Knox." He meets clients elsewhere and does his loading and unloading out of sight in a closed garage. His wife comes and goes to a regular job, managing a gas station and convenience store, which they own.

He has two partners, one living elsewhere in Surrey and another in a town just across the border in Washington state. The Surrey partner is on the road most of time, travelling the Interior and Vancouver Island with a van and a briefcase full of cash. He meets each grower about once a month, picking up eight-ounce Ziploc bags of marijuana and paying with a mix of small and large bills. No matter how reliable the grower, he checks at least one bag for moisture content, manicuring and odour, and he eyeballs all the rest. If the dope is new to him or suspect in any way, he smokes some of it before he buys.

Martin does the same job in the Vancouver area, though a lot of his time is spent down in his basement, sorting and packing marijuana for shipment, about 275 pounds a month. The best dope goes to the U.S. market because it pays the most, and whatever can't be sold there is shipped east, the bulk of it to Toronto. Although Martin wouldn't tell me how much he gets on American markets, there's an indication in current retail prices: about $5,000 U.S. a pound in San Francisco, more than double the going rate in Canada.

"We don't even try to sell in the Vancouver area," Martin told me. "There are just too many growers and small-time dealers, too much of it around."

A courier drives the shipments east, making drops in Edmonton, Regina or wherever they're needed on the way to Toronto.

Sometimes in the winter, if the roads are really bad, he goes by train. But flying is out; too many sniffing dogs and a risk that luggage will be opened if there is a bomb scare. He never goes east of Ontario. "Quebec is a hash market," Martin said, "always has been. All that stuff comes in from offshore. Whatever market there is for grass is all tied up by the biker gangs."

But it's the shipments south of the border that interested me. U.S. Customs is vigilant, and the penalties for getting caught are not pleasant to contemplate.

"That's where my partner in Washington state comes in," Martin said.

The American partner (he's actually a Canadian) runs a small business on the Canadian side of the line and drives across twice a day, five days a week. He uses a small border post where everyone knows him, so they just wave him through, no questions asked. Even so, except for a few pounds in emergencies, he doesn't carry marijuana through the border crossing.

"Why not?" I asked Martin.

"Look at a map," he said. "The B.C. border with the U.S. is about four hundred miles long, most of it wilderness. There are literally hundreds of unpatrolled places where you can just walk across. That's how we get big shipments into the States. Having a partner in Washington gives us a safe place to store the stuff until it's picked up. If there's a fuck-up, he can make the delivery himself. And he brings large sums of American cash back into Canada. The customs guys are his friends, he stops and bullshits with them, even golfs with a couple of guys on the American side. They're not going to look in his wallet or search his car."

Wouldn't it be simpler, I wondered, to use one of the professional drug couriers who take millions of dollars worth of marijuana across the border south of Vancouver each year? Equipped with fast cars and boats, police scanners, two-way radios and night vision goggles, they cross even the most heavily guarded sections of border like smoke through a sieve.

"There's a rule in this business that I call 'need to know,'" Martin said. "Nobody—your wife, kids, friends, even your dog—should know what you're doing if they don't absolutely have to. If you can do it yourself, a courier is just one more person who doesn't need to know that you're dealing marijuana. One less risk you have to take."

"So, what are those risks?" I asked.

"Everything depends on good will and trust, which means you have to know the people you're dealing with. But growers and retailers come and go, so sometimes you have to deal with new people, people you don't know. That's always dangerous. The guy could be a narc. Or he could just be stupid or sloppy. He's like a guy who can't swim—you try to help him and he takes you down with him. So I won't touch a new grower or retailer unless they come recommended by someone I've dealt with for a long time. The other danger, and I think a much worse one, is routine. You do the same thing, month in, month out, year after year, and you get careless. You lose your edge, start cutting corners, and then one day you make a fatal mistake and you're finished. Legally, I could be extradited to the U.S. and jailed for life under American law."

Routine, as he calls it, is the source of Martin's most persistent difficulty with the growers who supply him. Bored with endlessly cranking out bud, some dry their dope too quickly, so that it feels right on the outside but remains damp at the center. Later, when the moisture comes out, mould will make it worthless. Or growers become slack in their manicuring, leaving large buds undivided, which speeds up a tedious job but increases the weight of stems in the dope. Or, to boost production, they may switch to a high-yield, low-buzz variety without telling their buyer. Unless he happens to smoke it, the difference may not be apparent—until the complaints come in from the customers.

"But handling the kind of bucks you do, there have got to be other risks—violence, rough stuff, guns," I said.

"You know, that's a really bum rap laid on marijuana dealers by the cops. They like to tar us with the same brush as heroin and coke dealers—as hardened criminals, as parasites who prey on defenceless people and get them hooked. That's bullshit; marijuana dealers aren't drug pushers and never were. Sure, there's a few scumbags in every trade, a few morons peddling grams to school kids, biker gangs who don't give a shit who they hurt. But real dope dealers won't touch the hard drugs. If a guy's a bad actor, word gets around and no one will deal with him, except maybe other bad actors. Other than a few bad debts, I've never had any real trouble in more than ten years. I've never been threatened, never even seen a gun."

By this point in my conversation with Martin, my pants and shoes were soaked. I was getting so cold, I had trouble speaking without my teeth chattering. But there was something else I wanted to know: how did he launder all that cash, that embarrassment of riches?

"That's where the gas station comes in," he said. "If a small dealer is careful not to be too flashy, he can spend his cash without attracting attention. But on my scale, you've got to have some way to launder your money. The gas pumps and the store generate a lot of cash. When we take that to the bank, there's no way they can tell, or even suspect, that some of it's dope money."

Federal law requires banks and other financial institutions to record all cash deposits of more than ten thousand dollars. If there is a suspicion of criminal activity (which may also involve smaller cash transactions considered to be abnormal for any particular account), the bank's security staff alert the RCMP. If they can get a search warrant, the police then have access to confidential information in any account—contrary to the widely held belief that bank accounts are private.

Finking on their clients is a touchy subject with financial institutions. They insist they report to the police only on the basis of "strong" suspicion. But, as a discretionary action taken unilaterally without outside review, reporting on clients is subject to abuse. Many hundreds of such reports are made to police in Canada each year. "Suspicious" transactions extend to any suspected criminal activity, not just the laundering of drug money. Someone could be nailed for tax evasion, for example, by making unusually large cash deposits. And even if the financial institution is dead wrong in its suspicions, federal law protects it from any legal action by the account holder for breach of client confidentiality.

Despite these considerable powers, money laundering laws are widely thwarted in Canada, perhaps most commonly by the use of bank drafts. A number of individuals, called smurfs by the police, buy drafts from many different banks, credit unions and trust companies, in amounts under ten thousand dollars. The drafts are then collected by a middleman and deposited in the dealer's domestic or foreign account. "Interac" computerized bank tellers are used in a similar way, with marijuana retailers instead of smurfs making cash deposits at a number of different branches and crediting the money to the wholesaler's account. If these transactions are done on a regular basis in roughly similar amounts, they are unlikely to attract attention.

The legal net is at least as porous in the U.S., even though regulations may actually be tougher. For example, all cash deposits exceeding ten thousand dollars must be reported to the FBI, not just recorded, as in Canada. But the sheer volume of financial activity overwhelms the system, and the FBI cannot begin to investigate the reports it gets.

I asked Martin if this explained how he laundered the large quantities of American cash generated by U.S. sales.

"No, we're never had to make large deposits down there," he told me. "There's no problem getting rid of it. The Yankee dollar is still the best currency to take anywhere in the world. We pay cash wherever we go, and believe me, we've had some great holidays. Two of us own a house in Palm Springs—we do a lot of golfing. We invest some of it in businesses in the States. A restaurant in Oregon, among other things. My partner here in Surrey has put two of his kids through American universities. One's a surgeon, for Christ's sake. Imagine what that cost! In the summer, when there's lots of tourists, we get rid of quite a bit of it through the gas station. One way or another it goes. Spending it is always easier than making it."

Although I certainly wasn't going to try to sell Martin my piddling few pounds, I was interested in how he treats outdoor marijuana.

"We'll take it," he told me, "but frankly, it's a pain in the ass because it's less consistent than indoor. You've got to check it out pretty carefully, smoke it and look through the whole lot. And that's a shame, because many people prefer it to the indoor. It smells and tastes better and, for my money, it's often a better smoke. Some dealers are discounting it now, paying about twenty-two hundred dollars, compared with twenty-five hundred for indoor. I don't discount it, but I don't go looking for it, either."

A new element in the market, Martin said, is locally made hashish, extracted from resinous bud leaves that would otherwise be thrown away or sold cheaply as shake. For want of a regular supply, a substantial hash market everywhere west of Toronto has gone begging for years.

"Someone has worked out the formula for making it, and the product is pretty good, almost as good as Afghani or Lebanese," he said. "I'm seeing more of it all the time. I buy a bit, just to encourage the guys who are trying to improve it. I'm only paying two hundred dollars an ounce, but that'll go way up once the product and the market are established. An ounce of hash goes a hell of a lot farther than an ounce of grass."

I asked, finally, about Martin's plans, curious about his take on the future of the local marijuana trade.

"Oh hell, it's endless," he said. "The States is not going to decriminalize, and we're going to just keep pumping it over the border. I've made my pile and I'll be out of the trade within five years, but the business will outlive me. Although I like dealing, I'm tired of having to live the way I do to cover my tracks. What would you choose, if you had the choice—a crappy house and a crappy gas station in crappy Surrey, or a pad on the beach in the Caribbean?"

A week after Martin walked off into the rain, an envelope arrived in the mail. No return address and nothing within except a small square of cardboard, doubled over and taped shut around the edges. Inside was a wad of black hashish, wrapped in aluminum foil and squashed flat as a dime. It was, as he attested, pretty damned good.

I never had an address or phone number for Martin and didn't want one; if he were ever to be busted, I sure as hell didn't want to be even remotely suspect. In any case, contacting him now that I needed a dealer was not an option. Our understanding was that he would talk to me purely as a favour to a mutual friend. Talk, and that was all. No dealing, and I could hardly go back on the arrangement now.

As a rule in the dope trade, the larger the sale the lower the price. Grams right now are going for $15, ounces for about $200 and pounds for around $2,500. If I sold my marijuana a gram at a time, I'd get the equivalent of $426 an ounce or $6,816 a pound. But I'd also be pretty long in the tooth by the time I got rid of it all. And yet there are dealers who move a lot of marijuana this way, usually by servicing large markets in a low-income part of town.

I know a dealer like this and actually sold him a few ounces, though his small orders and low prices rule him out as a solution to my problem. Still, I drop in now and then on Floyd just to watch how he operates. He's a supremely talented Native artist, working in gold and silver, which he shapes into jewellery and engraves with the mythic iconography of the Northwest Coast. He is also a heavy dope smoker and father of a brood of young children, both expensive habits. To supplement his income, he deals on the side.

Floyd's jewellery is much in demand, and he is often back-ordered for months. To keep his dealing from interfering with his real work, he has arranged his studio on the east side of Vancouver to facilitate both. Wearing a telephone headset, with an earphone and tiny microphone, he takes a stream of calls, while leaving his hands free to do his engraving. His goldsmithing bench, an old writing desk with many small drawers and pigeon-holes, is located just inside the front door, within easy reach of the customers who keep popping in and out.

Most of Floyd's sales are small, fractions of an ounce or single grams, which he (or someone in his family) has weighed ahead of time and sealed in tiny Ziploc bags. From a supply of loose marijuana in one of his small drawers, he can quickly measure out other amounts on a digital scale. Many of these transactions take less than a minute—a rap at the door, a hand extended with fifteen dollars, a word or two of greeting and thanks, and Floyd returns to work. Anyone who wants to sample the product simply takes a seat and joins the people who always seem to be hanging out in the studio. Most are friends from Haida Gwaii, the Queen Charlotte Islands, or villages on the Skeena River. Every half hour or so, a joint goes round, and you get to try the stuff that Floyd is currently selling.

As dealing, all this seems like pretty small potatoes. But it's fortunate some people are willing to do it; many dealers balk if asked to sell less than half an ounce. For fifteen dollars, Floyd sells enough marijuana for a couple joints and a few hours of happiness. His quality is always tops—he's a discriminating buyer—and the weight honest. Not a bad deal, especially when you factor in the sickness, hangover and possible violence that could result if the same money were to be spent on a crock of rotgut wine. The undertow from Vancouver's skid road, only a few blocks to the west, runs strong through this neighbourhood.

After some enjoyable evenings at Floyd's, I was pleased to reciprocate by giving him a photograph I found years ago at the Public Archives in Ottawa. Taken at Massett in the Queen Charlottes in the 1890s, it's a portrait of his ancestral family, Haida aristocrats standing tall and strikingly handsome in formal Victorian dress. Floyd was delighted and hung it over his desk. But I didn't for a moment take this as an invitation to ask his help in finding a dealer. That would be pricking his bubble and bad form to boot. So I'm still out there looking, albeit with diminishing confidence that something will turn up.

Strange and disturbing how time accelerates as you get older. The summers of my childhood, endless careless days of gold and blue, have turned intense and fleeting, like quicksilver glimpsed and lost between the fingers. Here on the mountain, summer has slipped away almost unseen. The woods, ringing only yesterday with spring birdsong, are suddenly gravid and nearly silent.

Eating lunch today on a stump above the Hillside Garden, I see only two vultures wheeling over the creek ravine. No eagle has appeared in a month. The red-tails have gone elsewhere. My summer choristers, the thrushes, are mute or flown south, and even the olive-sided flycatcher's cheery whistle is missing for the first time since April. Other than a chattering flock of pine siskins heading east over the slash, all is still.

Later, walking to the upper gardens, I hear a clatter of wings ahead. Keeping close to the roadside screen of alders, I steal within sight of a big dogwood at the edge of the timber next to the marsh. Branches are tossing about and a flash of grey shows between the leaves—wild band-tailed pigeons feeding on dogwood seed clusters. I haven't seen this in years.

Band-tails were probably my first encounter with hunting, with killing things to eat. When I was eight or nine we moved to a ramshackle cottage in Granthams Landing, where band-tails roosted in the tops of lofty firs behind the house. It was wartime and lean times for the family; anything edible was fair game for the pot. One day my father, an ardent duck hunter before we left New Brunswick, loaded his double-barrelled 12-gauge and brought down one of the pigeons. I remember it lying in the salal at my feet, soft pearl grey with a white bar across the back of its neck and a lovely yoke of iridescent bronze and purple. The tail feathers, pale-tipped with a dark bar, I kept for fletching the arrows we were making at the time. (Ted was reading us the story of Robin Hood, and we would have died for shirts of Lincoln green.) He split the skin of the bird's breast and took out the meat in a single piece, hot and rank with a wild, alien smell. My mother stewed it for hours with several others my father shot, and yet they still came to the table so tough—as the saying goes—you couldn't get a fork in the gravy. The meat was dark brown and oily, gamy but good, I thought.

Later, in my early teens, I hunted band-tails on my own, gunning for the high-roosting birds with a .22 or creeping up on feeding flocks with a double 20-gauge. Success came rarely. The flocks were big—twenty, thirty, perhaps fifty pigeons weighing down the dogwoods, making a racket you could hear a hundred yards off. There were always one or two perched high on sentry duty, ready to lead the flock rocketing away before I could get off a shot.

Here on the edge of the marsh, only three band-tails erupt from the tree as I draw closer. My ornithology books say nothing about a population crash of the sort that is decimating songbirds east of the Rockies. Loss of both nesting and wintering habitat are a big factor there, and poisons in the environment still take their toll. The decline is rapid and severe. Texas radar stations that track the songbird flocks crossing the Gulf of Mexico say their numbers have dropped 50 per cent since 1960. Are band-tails affected by any of this? Or have they merely changed their habits, joining perhaps with the multitudes of city pigeons that scrounge a living around the grain terminals? I watch for them there as I pass, look for their distinctive banded tail and the white slash behind the neck, but I've seen none.

On days like this, it's hard to imagine a better life than growing marijuana. My spirits are buoyant, the weather sharp and clear, the crop heavy and oh so close to ready. As I walk back to Henry the Ford just after sundown—I'm parking now at the bottom of the mountain, taking extra care—the sky is lit by fiery herring-bone clouds that cast an ethereal glow over the hills. Choirs of angels would not be out of place. This used to be called a butter-milk sky, after the pattern that buttermilk left on the inside of the glass. There was even a song in the forties that began "Oh buttermilk sky . . ." But who drinks buttermilk any more? Even if they did, it's now made with a culture and leaves a different pattern on the glass. Is nothing sacred?

CHAPTER 14

A HARVEST
OF
TROUBLES

September 21. First day of autumn, and the long-anticipated first day of harvest. Real harvest this time, not just the few colas I snipped from my superplant a week ago.

No parent ever awaited the arrival of an offspring more eagerly or monitored its progress more closely. Almost daily I've been bustling from garden to garden, calculating the percentage of dead pistils on the flowers and peering through my twenty-power magnifying glass at the resin glands. Clear, fully formed mushrooms are what I'm looking for. Any cloudiness in the resin means I've waited too long, and it's losing potency.

Listening for helicopters and scanning the sky, I park Henry on the powerline and climb the steep pitch through the timber to the turnoff onto the branch road to the Hillside Garden. The foghorn at Merry Island light is baying faint and far off, and when I break onto the open slash Georgia Strait is plugged. Killing time until the dew is off my plants, I plunk down for a half hour on my overturned tote boxes to watch the fog bank shunting east before the morning westerly. Along the near shore, it rolls in dirty billows up the windward slopes of points and bluffs. Farther out across the strait, islands are stranded like a ragged fleet of battleships, plowing through seas of clotted grey. Before noon, the sun will lick the waters shining blue.

The harvest, when I finally get to it, does not go as quickly as expected. My intention is to take only the top colas, leaving all the lower branches—at least two thirds of the plant—to ripen a few more days in full sun. Shaded as they are, these buds are slower to mature. And for no apparent reason, there are always a few laggard plants that ripen up to a week behind their mates. All of which mires me in a lot of dithering about what to cut and what to leave.

In the end I'm pretty selective, taking only colas of perfect maturity, often only one from a plant and never more than three or four. But when the patch is done, I look back—always a fatal mistake—and see others that appear ready, or so close to ready that maybe they should go too. I'm torn between the desire to produce the very best smoke possible and the apprehension that police or thieves could scoop the crop at any time. A bird in the hand, etc. So, round I go once more, eyeballing buds and crystal and finally clipping another half-dozen colas. Repeating the process in Number Three Garden, I stash the tote boxes in the bush, where I'll retrieve them after dark.

My hands, by this time, are so coated with resin I look as if I'm wearing black gloves. Until I get home and clean up with gasoline, the best I can do is rub them with dust to keep my fingers from sticking together. Meantime, if the cops were to stop me on the highway, I'd be carrying so much hashish I wonder if I could be charged with trafficking.

Altogether I've picked nearly a hundred colas, way too many to dry in the cabin loft, where my superplant has been hanging. That leaves the space beneath the cabin rafters, in full view of anyone passing outside. Radical measures are called for: the cabin will have to be converted to a darkroom. With battens and sheets of black poly I blank out all the windows, working from the inside so that no one can poke holes and peek through. I hang a sign on the front door: *Darkroom Work in Progress—Please Knock before Entering.* Under the rafters I staple fishing line, stretched taut in rows a foot apart, the length of the cabin.

At sundown I return for the hidden tote boxes, driving through a landscape tinted orange again, this evening under a sky full of mares' tails. Back at the cabin I begin the long job of hanging the colas, first trimming off all the big leaves, which would droop over the buds and slow their drying. Some growers say these leaves also give the smoke a rank flavour, though I can't vouch for that. The colas are hung close together but not touching, leaving space for air to pass between. Too far apart and I'll run out of room; there will be three twenty-foot rows by the time I'm done, and most of the crop is still to come. The final act is setting up a slowly oscillating fan in the corner farthest from the dope. A gentle breeze is best, just enough to keep the air moving without knocking the colas together and dislodging resin. High in the loft, at the peak of the rear gable end, an exhaust fan draws off the damp air, maintaining a negative pressure so that no odour escapes around the front door.

Well past midnight I linger, tired but contented, over tea and toast, beholding my swaying ranks of marijuana and feeling as if I'd just hung up a deeply satisfying work of art. My dope is, after all, a creation of sorts, or a dream at least, come alive after six hard months in the making.

September 24. Late yesterday afternoon, just as I was starting up the hill to my gardens, I met a late-model pickup coming down. Backing out to the main road to let him pass, I saw that he was loaded with cedar boughs and salal, evergreens to be sold for floral displays. An evergreen picker! God spare me, I thought, the last thing I need right now. Roaming as they do far from the roads, evergreen pickers on the mountain would be a real threat to my gardens.

Another jolt awaited me on the way to Number Three Garden. Trimmings from cedar boughs were strewn on the road below the bank where my plants are hidden. Further on, past the pond and all the way to the landing above my skid-road gardens, alder branches that were blocking the road had been freshly cut with shears.

Oh no, I thought, what was under that load of evergreens? A truckload of my marijuana? But a quick check of the gardens dispelled my fears. Nothing had been disturbed, no footprints, no trampled bracken. The picker was just on a scouting trip, nipping alder branches out of his way as he walked. Finding nothing except a couple of roadside cedars, he went on up the mountain. Or so it appeared.

Nonetheless, I had a bad night. I lay awake for hours, fantasizing the loss of my crop and contriving elaborate plots to get it back. When I slept, I dreamed of ugly confrontations with men in red pickups and awoke sweating, tension cutting like piano wire through my chest. This morning I'm tired and furious with myself. Where is the guy who said dope farming is a game? The guy who said you shouldn't do it unless you can take your losses with a grin? Where are your balls, I ask myself? What happened to your cool?

But enough of this masochism. I've decided to pick everything the day after tomorrow.

September 26. Overcast last night, so there's no dew this morning. I start with the Hillside Garden, leaving the truck at its usual place on the powerline and hiking across the slash with three tote boxes. If they're not enough, I'll stow the surplus in garbage cans. God knows, Reefer has punched them so full of holes they are useless for anything else.

The Hillside Garden is about a hundred yards below the landing at the end of the road. The slope is covered with young firs a few feet higher than my head. From the logs that I walk on to hide my tracks, I can see between the treetops and into the garden from some distance away.

About halfway down the hill, I have an uneasy feeling that something is wrong, something has changed. Although I don't realize it until later, what's missing is the glimpse of purple marijuana tops between the evergreens. I carry on, jumping from log to log, watching carefully where I put my feet. Pushing between the last trees at the edge of the garden, I raise my eyes to—nothing. Every one of my thirty-three plants is gone.

A quick look around tells all. Every stalk has been cut just above the ground and the entire plant taken away. This is the work of the police; thieves take only colas and leave the rest. But unlike thieves, the police don't wander around in the bush looking for dope. The garden could only have been spotted from the air. So what else did the helicopter find?

Damping down my fears, I leg it fast across the slash and up the long hill through the timber. Hope fades when I see that a vehicle has crushed the alder branches snipped by the evergreen picker on the road to Number Three (police helicopters work with support crews on the ground), and it dies altogether at the sight of bootprints on the sandbank below the garden. For a fleeting instant as I crest the rise, a reprieve seems possible. A flash of purple shows amongst the bracken. But it's only an oversight, two plants missed by the police. Everything else has been cut and carted away.

Hurrying on to the skid road I find that my gardens there are untouched, as is another small patch across the road above the pond. This seems a minor miracle, for the helicopter must have passed right overhead to get to Number Three.

But the post-mortems will have to wait. Fetching the tote boxes from the road, I start clipping colas whether they are dead ripe or not, determined to salvage what I can from the wreckage of my crop. Within an hour everything is stowed away, three boxes plus a bit extra in a garbage can. All that remains are a few immature buds that were hidden away from the light close to the stalk and bottom of the plants. These I will leave to ripen for another week or so.

Gradually over the past hour I've been calming down, regaining perspective. Pouring tea and laying out my lunch on the boulder overlooking the valley and mountains to the east, I take stock. In all, twenty-four plants survived the blitz and sixty-four perished. But it's pounds not plants that matter, and they tell a different story. All but two of the twenty-four were surplus plants, confined too long in small pots, which stunted their growth and cut the yield to less than half what the big plants would have produced. Together with the colas I'd taken two days ago, the return for my labours would be five to six pounds of bud, no more than a third of the crop I was counting on. And the quality of about half of that would be inferior, for the buds on the surplus plants were not as fat and resinous as the lovely colas in my lost gardens.

And so, after months of apprehension, the dreaded sword of the law has descended. I am angry at first, and disgusted. The sight of all those severed stalks, still bleeding sap, just makes me want to walk away from it all. Away from all those weeks and months of wasted toil, away from an idiot's folly. I should have known the helicopters were unbeatable.

But then, returning past the pond and down through the woods, I begin to feel a wonderful lightness, as if a long siege has lifted. The morning overcast has broken open, and a fresh wind from the Pacific is soughing through the treetops. My stride lengthens and I swing along, face upturned to the sun shafting down through forest shade. I'm tanned and fit and fifteen pounds lighter than when I first came here in March. I've heard the voices of the mountain, glimpsed the hidden lives of its birds and animals, revelled in its shifting moods and colours. No one can take these things away.

I find myself thinking of next year. My gardens were found because they were too big, too concentrated. I'll go to small plots, five or seven plants at the most, scattered in openings in older slash. I know just the spot! I'll plant in the ground rather than in containers, so there'll be less watering, bigger plants. I'll get clones, all females, avoiding half the work I did this year. I can cash in on my experience, the mistakes I won't have to make again. I'll know better now than to build fences, for instance. The watering system is ready to go. I've got the soil mix down pat. It'll be a snap. Yes, you bet, I'll give it another try.

By the time I get home I'm almost buoyant. I phone Carole with the bad news and manage some small jokes. As the day unfolds I'm pleased with myself; no black dogs of depression lurk in the shadows. True to my resolve, I'm taking my lumps with a shrug and even a grin, albeit a little strained.

My only lasting regret is for my plants. It's like being absent when someone close to you dies. If you never see the person's body, there is no sense of parting, no clean end to the relationship. Like any gardener, I had a real relationship with my plants, and I would like to think they had one with me. I looked after them as well as I knew how, and they responded. I knew many of them as individuals—the three giants in Number Three Garden; plants in the Hillside Garden I helped to their feet and nursed back to health after the ravages of Reefer the Bear; my superplant, whose seeds were all lost to the raid.

Of course, I too would have cut them down, though not to squander their powers in some righteous conflagration. Preserved as valued friends, their incandescent magic would have rippled on and on, like the mysterious calls of the great whales, through the boundless deeps of human consciousness.

CHAPTER 15

AUTUMN
DREAMS

In the second week of October the geese return. And what a morning to be heading south! Autumn's first real snorter slammed into the coast overnight, bringing branches, cones and Niagaras of rain hammering down on the tin roof of the cabin. Lying awake at first light, I can hardly believe my ears when I hear the cackle of snow geese cutting thinly through a lull in the storm. They are most likely migrants returning from Wrangel Island, beyond the Bering Strait. And here, near the end of their 2,500-mile journey, they are flying straight into the teeth of a forty-knot gale. This I have to see.

It is still half dark when I come down the path to the deck, buttoning my slicker against the driving rain. At first it seems that I've missed them. The grey expanse of Malaspina Strait is empty, save for dark rollers and flecks of lighter grey where seas are breaking. No bird or boat is moving. But then I hear cackling, faint and lost for long moments under the rage of wind in the firs on the point. Finally I see them, a half mile out and low down, scattered in small flocks of thirty, maybe fifty birds. Making heavy work of it, they change height or direction erratically, as if groping for soft spots in the wall of rushing air. Snow geese are sometimes called wavies after these fitful patterns in flight. They are flying as hard as geese can fly, shouting encouragement back and forth, yet they seem to take forever to fade away into the rain, vanishing well short of the sheltering hills across the bay. The last to pass is a lone straggler, dropping farther and farther behind its flock.

After breakfast, with the rain easing but the wind still howling, three more Vs labour past, strung out like surf scoters, right down next to the water. Riding the surface layer of air slowed by friction with the waves, they are making better headway than the earlier flocks. With binoculars, I can follow the white winking of wings almost into Welcome Pass. Then at the last moment the geese wheel left into Smuggler Cove for a pit stop, avoiding the blast of wind and waves piling into the far end of the pass from Georgia Strait.

Near noon, with the storm breaking up, I park Henry the Ford in the timber next to the marsh and set to work snipping the last buds from my gardens by the old skid road. Standing alone as individual nodules rather than colas, they are free of mould, despite heavy rains over the past ten days. Two weeks ago, when the harvest first exposed them to the light, these understorey buds were pale, insubstantial things, dismissed by growers as "fluff." Now they are surprisingly solid, and though still small, they will add a welcome half pound to the crop.

By the time I've finished the wind has swung smartly into the west, peeling cloud like a dirty bandage from the weeping underbelly of the sky. The peaks across Sechelt Inlet, bare as the mountains of the moon just days ago, emerge stark white against the blue. Lower down the trees at timberline are groaning with snow, awaiting the afternoon sun to unload their burden.

The snow in the mountains will melt and come again several times before it stays for the winter. But down here, closer to sea level, winter's wet regime is already in place, and the country is the better for it. Extended too long, summer heat stretches this coastal rainforest taut. Alders sweat, moss shatters underfoot, and the parched air twangs with a tension that builds right through September some years and then lets go in the first prolonged rain of October with a sigh that is almost audible.

In the edge of the timber beside the marsh, steam is rising from mossy logs and rock outcrops, fired by sunshafts with a luminous green energy they haven't had since spring. From the ground to the crowns of the tallest firs, the glint of sun-shot silk radiates from a thousand spider webs. And way up there in the canopy, golden-crowned kinglets keep up a steady peeping so high and thin, it hovers at the upper limit of my hearing. From deeper in the forest come the sounds of a squirrel cutting fir cones for its winter larder and dropping them *tap-tap-tap* down through the limbs. A varied thrush—swamp robins, we used to call them—back from wherever it passed the summer, trills from willows bordering the marsh. All these things are portents of the coastal winter, sights and sounds animated by the fall rains, like the mushrooms I find thrusting sulphur-yellow, white and brown through the hard-packed gravel of the skid road.

The pond has risen a foot above its September low, flooding its banks and drowning the floating plants, or at least the few that remained after Reefer had left off bathing for the year. Free now of its summer algae, the water is clear to the bottom, though tinted still, like the varnish on an old master's painting. But there is little to see. Gone already are the creatures of summer, hidden away in burrows, egg sacs and chrysalises, dreaming the winter-long dreams of transformation. Nothing moves other than a few water boatmen, sculling slowly to the surface for air and diving again to their watery haunts.

On the way back to the truck I hear geese again and climb to the crest of the open ridge to watch them pass. The flocks are bigger now and way up high, two or three thousand feet overhead, riding a wind out of the northwest that will sweep them down to the Fraser River delta in less than an hour. There, they'll circle and set down among thousands of their kind, all cackling greetings and mutual congratulations on their triumphal return.

After supper (goop again, day three), I head over to Ned's with half a dozen beer for what is supposed to be an evening watching the World Series. But our interest soon flags—too many booted grounders and cornball commentators—and we turn instead to mutual commiseration over our ravaged marijuana crops. Ned got hit the same day by the same helicopter that hammered me.

"Dickheads," he fumes. "What kind of asshole goes around destroying a harmless plant grown by harmless, hard-working people? Why don't they find something useful to do, like fighting candy theft at corner stores?"

All summer Ned had been telling me about the spectacular performance of a new strain he was growing on the bluffs, way up the mountain. In September he said some of these plants were so broad, he and his son together could barely reach around them. These were the plants they had hand-watered so laboriously. "The cops got them all," he moans now, "every goddamned one of them. They missed a second patch I had on another bluff, but naturally that garden was a lot more shaded and the plants were scrawny, reaching for the light."

"How did they land?" I ask. "I thought you said it was too steep, or there were too many trees for a chopper to set down."

"That's what I thought," Ned says. "They must have one of those cable arrangements, so they can hover and let a guy down. Christ almighty, what next?"

Ned is at the end of his tether. The bluffs were a garden of last resort for him, after fighting losing battles with dope thieves closer to home and salvaging next to nothing from his deer-infested Nelson Island plots. "What's a guy to do, for God's sake?" he asks. "Move indoors?" Ever the purist, Ned finds the idea repugnant. "That's not gardening, it's chemistry. Marijuana wants its feet in the shit and its head in the sun. I'll be fucked if I'll smoke weed that grows like rats in somebody's basement."

I try to lead Ned to the bigger, brighter picture. "Look, for every guy who got burned like you and me, there are a thousand growers who took off a full crop. The cops are in retreat. Almost every day some police officer, politician or coroner is in the papers, calling for an end to the war on drugs."

"That's great," Ned says, without enthusiasm. "These guys are finally admitting what everybody else has known since Christ was a cowboy. But that sure as hell won't buy any groceries for me this winter."

Ned is not to be consoled. He sends me home, nonetheless, with an interesting tidbit of information. It seems that his eldest son picked up some pub talk about the rip-off of my Pocket Garden last spring. Young punks, not the police, did the deed, and they were mightily pissed off to discover in July that what they had stolen were not female clones but unsexed seedlings, almost two thirds of which opted to be males.

Leaving Ned's, I open the back door a crack, nip out and slam it quickly behind me to prevent a tide of puppies from flooding into the kitchen. There are nine of them on the back porch, a parting gift from a stray mongrel that seduced Ned's female Alsatian. Now he can't give them away and hasn't the heart to knock them on the head. As I navigate the shit-slick steps, Ned hollers from a crack in the door: "Do you know any Korean restaurants? Tell them I've got puppies for sale. Real cheap, guaranteed organic."

The next morning I'm back at it, manicuring buds as I have been every day for the past week. Snip, snip, snip, boring, boring, boring. One of life's most tedious jobs, it's made worse by the tendency of the leaves to lie flat against the bud as it dries. Taking care not to dislodge the resin, you have to work your scissors under the leaves in order to trim them short. (Like many growers, rather than scissors I prefer trimming with the short-bladed spring-loaded shears used by fishermen for mending nets.) I remove the larger leaves entirely, cutting them close to the bud stem with the points of the blades. It's slow work that soon palls, unless you have someone to talk with (Carole, thank God, helps every weekend) or a distraction such as the radio. Once they're trimmed, I dry the buds in a layer about four inches deep at the bottom of open paper bags from the supermarket. Very gently, I stir them morning and night. When they are dry almost to the point of getting crackly—usually after about three days in a cool, dark place—I store the buds in quart sealers and check them over the next few weeks for any sign of mould.

Snipping here, hour after hour, I've decided that I shouldn't get so exercised about marijuana as an issue. It's not that I feel any less passionate about the law stomping on my civil liberties. But there's nothing to be gained by anger or impatience; time is on the side of marijuana. Every year, as the reefer madness crowd ages and dies off, the number of people who know the truth about pot grows. One day, we'll raise our heads and look around and find that the silliness has faded away, just as Prohibition did. It's inevitable. As someone said, most of the AIDS epidemic could be eliminated tomorrow if we outlawed sex. Marijuana could be eliminated, too, if we outlawed mind-altering. Short of eliminating the human species, neither is going to happen.

I've been in touch with Jim and Sara recently, to find out how their season went. Once again Jim's elaborate precautions have protected them from the law, despite an unusually thorough combing of their island by police helicopters. They are worried, though, about the market. When his summer Mighty Mite harvest came in, Jim told me, the market was flooded as never before, and the price had dropped right out the bottom. They were saved by an angel, a local buyer who took all their crop at a very good price. But they feel they've had a warning of tougher times to come, and Jim is hedging his bets by opening up a new vocation for himself as a mountain guide.

It's the same for Dieter, my friend in the Interior, though there was no angel for him. He and his partners harvested another huge crop, which they have no prospect of selling anytime soon. They took a big price cut on last year's harvest, and some of it is still unsold. As for Hoot, I haven't heard a word in months. Last spring he was planning another mad adventure to some mountain Valhalla, and who knows, maybe he finally got off a big crop. If so, with his luck, this would have to be the year when the market crashes. But no misfortune will change Hoot; when I next see him he'll be full as ever with droll stories and healthy vibes from his summer in the sun.

As for my own prospects, I'm picking up a few more customers as word gets around that my dope is good stuff. No big sales, just an ounce here, an ounce there, though I'm getting top dollar. At this rate, I'll probably still have some of it when next year's crop comes in—a bumper harvest of course, twenty pounds at least. And how will I sell it? Well, as I tell Carole whenever she raises the subject, it's much too soon to worry about details like that.

October 17. Under the high blue sky of a fall afternoon, I go back through all my gardens for a last time, packing out garbage cans and buckets and making a final, futile search for the two cans highjacked by Reefer. He's gone elsewhere now, likely to fatten up on spawners at a salmon stream before climbing into the Caren Range to snooze away the winter, dreaming no doubt of stony days under the summer sun.

I won't be here when Reefer shows up in the spring. Much as I've come to know and love the mountain, I'll be growing my marijuana elsewhere next year. Having scored here once, thieves and the police are sure to be back. I'll miss this place—the high, wide prospect of the strait, my little discoveries of life in the marsh and pond, the many voices of the wind and the rustle of the creek below the Hillside Garden, swelling even now in autumn freshet. But my only real regret is leaving behind three truckloads of soil with the potential to produce quality marijuana for years to come. My consolation is the knowledge that it won't be wasted, even though I haven't the energy to pack it out. Already, the peat pots are disintegrating under the assault of roots from surrounding trees. Within a couple of years, three at most, rampant growth will surge over my gardens, drowning all trace of my puny struggles, dreams and disappointments under the inexorable tide of the rainforest.

AFTERWORD

It seems I was not cut out for a life of crime. I grew marijuana for two more years, losing 90 per cent of it to thieves in the first year and nearly as much in the second before giving it up as a bad job. Moving indoors, the usual remedy for such troubles, had no appeal; I couldn't see spending half my waking hours in a bunker where the sun never shines.

As time permits, I still grow half a dozen plants for our own use in a spot on the slash that seems to be immune to police or thieves. And when time does not permit, there is always Ned and the latest wonder variety he has coaxed into existence.

The following summary of cannabis facts and fables is drawn largely from Lynn Zimmer and John Morgan's *Marijuana Myths, Marijuana Facts* (New York: Lindesmith Center, 1997).

MYTH: *Marijuana is much stronger than it used to be.*
FACT: It all depends on which marijuana you are referring to. The baseline for potency was established by DEA tests on a small number of low-THC marijuana samples in the early 1970s. Even at that time, the best marijuana was much stronger than the DEA samples, and it has probably increased in potency since then, though it is nowhere near the 30 to 40 per cent THC levels claimed by anti-marijuana propaganda. What has gone up is the average potency of marijuana available on the street, largely through the replacement of low-grade Mexican "bunk" by much better domestic marijuana. Even if THC levels had increased significantly, marijuana would not necessarily have more punch, as pot of widely varying potency has been shown to deliver much the same psychoactive effect. Moreover, stronger is probably healthier, because smokers take much less tar into their lungs if they need only a few tokes instead of several joints to get high. Weak or strong, overdosing on marijuana is unheard of, and no fatality resulting from an overdose has ever

been recorded. Animal tests indicate that you would have to smoke at least forty thousand times the effective dose—what it takes to get high—to kill yourself. The ratio for alcohol intoxication ranges between four and ten to one, depending on the individual, and thousands of North Americans die every year of alcohol overdoses.

MYTH: *Marijuana damages the reproductive system.*
FACT: This assertion rests largely on the claims of Dr. Gabriel Nahas, an author of anti-marijuana books and articles, whose research in the 1970s is still widely cited despite its repeated condemnation by reputable scientists. Nahas subjected tissue in Petri dishes to marijuana derivatives and generalized the results to humans, without validating his findings in actual human populations. Other scientists claim to have found declines in testosterone levels and negative effects on the sperm of pot smokers. This research has been shown to be inconsistent, inconclusive and unrepeatable. As for prenatal exposure to marijuana, some American researchers claim that the fetus or the child following birth may be negatively affected. But studies in Jamaica have found no effect on the fetus and, in some respects, a positive calming influence on infants whose mothers smoked marijuana.

MYTH: *Marijuana damages the brain and causes permanent loss of memory and cognitive function.*
FACT: Although marijuana impairs short-term memory while the smoker is high, there is no evidence that the effects persist when the intoxication has passed, normally within two to three hours after cannabis is smoked (six to eight hours if eaten). The allegation of brain damage comes mainly from a notorious study done in the late 1970s that subjected rhesus monkeys to enormous doses of marijuana for six months. Its author was rebuked for bad science by the American National Academy of Science. The American Medical Association commissioned its own

study of especially heavy marijuana users in 1977 and found no evidence of brain damage. Of course, marijuana does act on the brain—that's why we get high. But no study has ever demonstrated cellular damage, mental impairment or insanity.

M Y T H : *Marijuana damages the immune system.*
F A C T : Again, this assertion is based on experiments that used extremely high doses of marijuana on animals. The results were never duplicated in humans. No clinical or epidemiological study has shown an increase in viral, bacterial or parasitic infection in human pot smokers. And, persistent rumour to the contrary, there is no evidence that marijuana increases the risk of HIV infection or advances the onset or intensity of AIDS symptoms. In fact, it is probably the most effective treatment for the AIDS wasting syndrome.

M Y T H : *Marijuana causes lung cancer and other respiratory damage.*
F A C T : This is the one well-established physical risk associated with marijuana use by otherwise healthy adults: heavy pot smoking can aggravate chronic respiratory disease. If used in moderation, however, the dangers from marijuana smoke appear to be slight. Although it contains roughly the same quantity of carcinogens as tobacco, when used on its own, without tobacco, marijuana has never been known to cause lung cancer. Whether this is due to its chemical makeup or to the fact that most tokers smoke a great deal less than tobacco addicts is unknown. Research has found no link between marijuana and chronic bronchitis or emphysema.

M Y T H : *Marijuana is addictive.*
F A C T : Fewer than 1 per cent of marijuana users smoke pot daily, and even fewer become dependent on it. A very few tokers develop a tolerance, requiring larger doses to produce the same effect, and some report inverse tolerance, smoking less to get high over time. The majority of

cannabis users take up the habit in their teens and either abandon it in their thirties or cut back to occasional use through a process known as "maturing out." Withdrawal symptoms are generally mild to nonexistent, though some users do require professional help to lay down the habit. Marijuana does not cause physical dependence.

MYTH: *Marijuana leads to the use of hard drugs like cocaine and heroin.*
FACT: The so-called "gateway effect" is a classic case in which correlation does not equal causation. Since marijuana is the most popular illegal drug in North America, people who have used LSD, cocaine and heroin are likely to have also used marijuana. But that does not demonstrate cause and effect. In fact, most marijuana users never use any other illegal drug. For them, marijuana is a terminus, not a gateway.

MYTH: *Marijuana impairs motivation and performance.*
FACT: Nothing has been found in the pharmacological properties of marijuana that alters the attitudes or abilities of its users to work or study. Obviously, people who are frequently intoxicated on any drug will not be productive members of society. But laboratory studies have found no lessening of work motivation or productivity in people given high doses of cannabis. Marijuana users tend to earn higher wages than nonusers, and the grades of college students who smoke are equal to the grades of those who don't. There is an association between heavy marijuana use and students who get low grades in high school, though the failing grades usually come first.

MYTH: *Legalizing marijuana would cause carnage on the roads.*
FACT: Driving studies have shown only slightly slower reaction time and minor impairment of judgement. Overall, car handling is consistently less impaired when drivers are under the influence of marijuana than when they are given low to moderate doses of alcohol or any of a

number of legal medications. Because marijuana heightens the impression of speed, stoned drivers tend to slow down and drive with exaggerated care (the only statistically significant finding in these tests), while drunk drivers are inclined to speed up and drive recklessly. Unfortunately, these results are next to impossible to correlate with actual performance on the road, since traces of marijuana in accident victims are almost always accompanied by alcohol. When a post-mortem does show marijuana alone, there's rarely any way of knowing whether the driver smoked an hour or a month before the accident. In the eleven American states that decriminalized marijuana, cannabis replaced alcohol as the drug of choice to some extent, and there was a corresponding drop in highway fatalities.

MYTH: *Marijuana causes criminal and aggressive behaviour.*
FACT: Every serious study and government commission to have investigated the question has concluded that cannabis use does not cause crime—except for the crime of possession. Both human and animal studies have repeatedly shown that marijuana decreases rather than increases aggression.

Many people, particularly young people, in effect convict themselves of marijuana offences because they don't understand Canadian law. What follows is a brief summary of your rights and responsibilities in the event of a bust.

If you are in a public place such as the beach, your car or the street when the police swoop down, they can search you or your car without a warrant only if they have "reasonable and probable" grounds to believe an offence has been committed. If they won't tell you what grounds they have (the smell of smoke, seeing you roll a joint), you can refuse the search. Lodge your objection politely ("I do not consent"), in the presence of a witness if possible, but make no further resistance, especially physical resistance, which could invite a charge of obstruction. The police will probably search you anyway. The evidence they obtain *is* admissible in court, since the Canadian Charter of Rights and Freedoms only excludes illegally obtained evidence if it will "tend to bring the administration of justice into disrepute," a provision vague enough to allow a judge to admit almost anything.

If you are in a vehicle, you are required by law to give your name and address and to produce your driver's licence and registration. (Bicycles are vehicles under the law.) If you don't want to answer any further questions, tell the officer you wish to say nothing more until you have consulted a lawyer. Although you shouldn't remain silent, saying as little as possible is generally the best policy, as you are less likely to blurt out something incriminating or inconsistent that might be used against you in court. Above all, don't volunteer any information that might indicate you were driving while under the influence of marijuana.

Except for cases in which they want to enter private homes or businesses, the police do not need a warrant to search premises if they believe a narcotics offence has been committed there. If they do have a warrant, not only premises and private homes may be searched but also anyone who happens to be within. In circumstances where the police do not have authority to search you, failure to explicitly state your objection to being searched may be taken by them as tacit permission. Police in Canada do not have authority to search premises, persons or vehicles merely on "suspicion" or a "routine check," though according to criminal lawyers this happens frequently, especially to young people.

If you are charged with possession of less than thirty grams of marijuana or one gram of hashish, the police must proceed by summary conviction (as opposed to indictment for more serious charges), which means they have no authority to take your fingerprints or photograph you. But that doesn't mean you will have no record. Even if the court gives you a discharge, the fact that you were charged with a criminal offence will remain on the books for up to three years. The federal government claims that summary conviction records are "untraceable" under the most recent drug legislation. That is untrue. Until your record is purged, any provincial or private employer can turn up your record at the click of a mouse. Since foreign governments recognize no legal obligation to rub out your past, don't be surprised if U.S. Immigration turns you back at the border long after your record has been extinguished in Canada.

If you are busted, you'll get a summons or other type of notice to appear in court. When you show up—if you don't, you'll be arrested—tell the sheriff you are there (this may save you hours of waiting) and approach the judge when your name is called. Address him or her as "Your Honour" and ask for an adjournment so that you can review the details of your case (called the "particulars") and possibly consult a lawyer. The particulars—the history of your case as prepared by the police—will then be given to you by the prosecutor. If there is a search warrant involved, get a copy of the "Information to Obtain" from the federal crown counsel's office or the clerk of the court. These are the facts gathered by the police in support of their application to the court for a warrant. Look it over very carefully to see if they had reasonable and probable grounds to suspect you, and check all facts, including addresses, dates and spellings of names. Even minor errors can get a case thrown out of court.

A lawyer will take care of all these chores for you in court. But even if you get this far on your own, it's a good idea to consult one at this point, especially if you are charged with cultivation or trafficking, or if the inconvenience of a possible criminal record bothers you. Remember, the law doesn't just apply to people in the trade. Technically, merely giving someone a joint at a party is trafficking, which is punishable by a fine or imprisonment or both.

NOTES

CHAPTER 3

Marijuana Myths, Marijuana Facts, by Lynn Zimmer and John Morgan, published in 1997 by the Lindesmith Center, 888 Seventh Avenue, New York, NY 10106, is available at most hemp stores. The center, which promotes harm reduction alternatives to drug criminalization, maintains a web site at www.ndsn.org.

The comparative study of marijuana smoking methods is summarized in *MAPS*, vol. 6, no. 3, published by the Multidisciplinary Association for Psychedelic Studies, 220–2121 Commonwealth Avenue, Charlotte, NC 28205.

CHAPTER 4

There is an extensive literature on psychedelics in other cultures. *Flesh of the Gods,* edited by Peter Furst (New York: Praeger Publishing, 1972), is a useful summary. For a cultural and religious history of marijuana, see *Green Gold, the Tree of Life—Marijuana in Magic and Religion,* by Chris Bennett et al., published in 1995 by Access Unlimited, P.O. Box 1900, Frazier Park, CA 93225. See also Gordon Wasson's *Soma: Divine Mushroom of Immortality* (The Hague: Mouton, 1972).

Andrew Weil's *The Natural Mind: An Investigation of Drugs and the*

Higher Consciousness was published in 1986 by Houghton Mifflin, Boston.

CHAPTER 5

Though a bit dated, the most comprehensive history of Canadian drug policy is still *Panic and Indifference: The Politics of Canada's Drug Laws,* by P. J. Giffen et al. (Ottawa: Canadian Centre for Substance Abuse, 1991).

The Ontario court case referred to is the trial of hemp store owner Chris Clay, which became a constitutional challenge of marijuana laws. Justice J. F. McCart's ground-breaking judgement of August 14, 1997, is reproduced on the web site of the Canadian Foundation for Drug Policy (CFDP) at http://fox.nstn.ca/~eoscapel/cfdp/cfdp.html.

No reliable figure exists for the annual cost of the U.S. drug war, though $30 billion is often cited as a minimum. If this seems inflated, consider that keeping 400,000 inmates (up from 50,000 in 1980) in American jails for drug offences, at a nominal $50 a head per day, costs roughly $20 billion a year.

For an engaging account of marijuana horror stories under U.S. law, see "Reefer Madness," by Eric Schlosser, *Atlantic Monthly,* August and September 1994.

Eric Single's study is summarized in "Economic Costs of Alcohol, Tobacco and Illicit Drugs in Canada, 1992," *Addiction,* July 1998.

See "Three Lies My Government Told Me," *Cannabis Canada,* no. 6, Winter 1996/97, for an account of the documents the magazine obtained. For an analysis of Canada's obligations and options under international drug treaties, I recommend *Drug Prohibition and the International Covenants,* by Glenn A. Gilmour, available through the CFDP in Ottawa.

CHAPTER 7

For a comprehensive work on the genetics and habits of the pot plant, I suggest *Marijuana Botany,* by Robert Connell Clarke, published in 1981 by Ronin Publishing, Box 1035, Berkeley, CA 94701. Readers interested in a technical discussion of pot's buzz will find it in *Marijuana Chemistry: Genetics, Processing and Potency*, by Ernest Small (Berkeley, CA: Ronin, 1977). Both books are widely available at hemp stores.

My favourite source of unusual insights into the lives of hummers and other birds is the *Cambridge Encyclopedia of Anthropology*, published in 1991 and now unfortunately out of print, though widely available at libraries.

The Secret Life of Plants, by Peter Tompkins and Christopher Bird, was published in 1972 by Harper and Row, New York.

CHAPTER 9

The observations on the fourth drive in animals are drawn mainly from *Intoxication*, by Ronald K. Siegel (New York: Pocket Books, 1990).

CHAPTER 10

The pre-eminent expert on medicinal marijuana is Dr. Lester Grinspoon of Harvard University Medical School, author of *Marijuana Reconsidered* (Cambridge, MA: Harvard University Press, 1997), and (with James Bakalar) *Marijuana, the Forbidden Medicine* (New Haven, CT: Yale University Press, 1993). Their web site is www.Rxmarihuana.com.

Shut down by a court injunction in April 1998, the San Francisco Buyers' Club changed its name to the San Francisco Cannabis Healing Center and reopened the next day. The club maintains a web site at http://www.marijuana.org.

On December 10, 1997, an Ontario court ruled in the case of epileptic Terry Parker that the Canadian prohibition on medical marijuana is unconstitutional. Background to the judgement (currently under appeal) can be found on the CFDP web site (see notes to Chapter 5, above).

Bruce Alexander's *Peaceful Measures: Canada's Way Out of the "War on Drugs"* was published in 1990 by the University of Toronto Press, Toronto.

CHAPTER 12

The information here on cybergardens comes from "America's No. 1 Cash Crop," by Michael Pollan, *New York Times Magazine*, February 19, 1995.

CHAPTER 13

For a portrait of a pot courier, see "B.C. Drugs Speed to U.S. via 'Midnight Express,'" by Stewart Bell, *Vancouver Sun*, September 9, 1996, p. 1.

The Office of the Superintendent of Financial Institutions in Ottawa published a guide to money laundering in Canada in 1996 entitled *Deterring and Detecting Money Laundering.*

ACKNOWLEDGEMENTS

Any book written today about marijuana owes an incalculable debt to countless unsung heroes who shaped what has been called the cannabis culture over the past four decades. Whether as growers, dealers, activists or simply consumers of pot, they dedicated themselves to exploring the potential of marijuana and trying to free it from the sanctions of the law. Some of them I have met; others I've corresponded with, including more than two hundred Canadians who responded to ads and letters I placed in newspapers across the country, asking people to tell me about their experiences with marijuana. I salute their courage—nearly all volunteered their names and addresses—and thank them for their many contributions to this book.

Many others, both within and outside the marijuana community, deserve my thanks, among them Barry Beyerstein, Hilary Black, Neil Boyd, Lisette Brouwer, Leeroy Campbell, Della Darwin, Daisy Drake, Brad Dundas, Angus Ellis, Mark Emery, Lindsay Erdman, Kory Haywood, Katy Hughes, Don Jones, Paul Koktan, Dana Larsen, Jean and Ed MacMillan, Darren Morgan, Harry Roberts, Eric Single, Maureen-Ann Sullivan and Kim Woodbeck.

Special thanks are due to Randy Caine, Richard Fears, John Hughes, Debra King, Ralph Osborne, Diane Reichert, Neil Tubb and Andrea

Turton for giving so generously of their time and knowledge. And to my father, Ted Poole, for sharing his experience with psychedelics and the high times of the sixties.

For their many helpful suggestions on all or part of the manuscript, I am indebted to Bruce Alexander, John Conroy, John Mullen, Ted Poole and Kim Poole. Thanks also to Kim for her usual flawless typing of interview transcripts.

My task would have been more difficult without the help of Kay Stockholder and the B.C. Civil Liberties Association; Carl Olsen and Paul Armentano at NORML U.S.A.; Brian Taylor and Lee Wells of the Grandby Hemp Initiative; Patricia Erickson at the Addiction Research Foundation; Eugene Oscapella and the Canadian Foundation on Drug Policy; and the librarians at the Lindesmith Center in New York. As always, the staff at the Vancouver Public Library dealt cheerfully and efficiently with my many niggling requests.

Finally, my heartfelt gratitude to all those who agreed to have their lives dissected under pseudonyms in this book; to editor Barbara Pulling for patiently coaxing me down from my pulpit and turning a tiresome diatribe into a readable narrative; and to my wife, Carole, for her prescient criticism, abiding support and a forbearance of public exposure that is remarkable in someone so private.